The Triad of Solomon

A reconciliation of the
WISDOM LITERATURE
of
The BIBLE
with the
Life-Stage Hypothesis
of
SØREN KIERKEGAARD

"It is said of philosophy that it is the *handmaiden* of theology …
One is not able to see clearly, however, '"whether she bears a
flambeau in front of her lady or carries her train behind her.'"
—Immanuel Kant, *Toward Perpetual Peace*

R.I. Johnston

WESTBOW·
PRESS
A DIVISION OF THOMAS NELSON
& ZONDERVAN

Scripture taken from the King James Version of the Bible.

Scripture taken from Holy Bible: The Revised English Bible with the
Apocrypha © Oxford University Press and Cambridge. 1989

Scripture taken from the Holy Bible, NEW INTERNATIONAL VERSION®.
Copyright © 1973, 1978, 1984 by Biblica, Inc. All rights reserved worldwide.
Used by permission. NEW INTERNATIONAL VERSION® and NIV® are
registered trademarks of Biblica, Inc. Use of either trademark for the offering
of goods or services requires the prior written consent of Biblica US, Inc.

NET Bible® copyright ©1996-2006 by Biblical Studies Press,
L.L.C. http://netbible.com All rights reserved.

WestBow Press books may be ordered through booksellers or by contacting:

WestBow Press
A Division of Thomas Nelson & Zondervan
1663 Liberty Drive
Bloomington, IN 47403
www.westbowpress.com
1 (866) 928-1240

ISBN: 978-1-4908-4893-8 (sc)
ISBN: 978-1-4908-4894-5 (e)

Library of Congress Control Number: 2014922326

Printed in the United States of America.

WestBow Press rev. date: 01/26/2015

Contents

Preface

A brilliant student one would think had everything to live for commits suicide; a respectable family businessman is a foul-mouthed football supporter on Saturday afternoons; a young woman throws up a promising career to study under a guru in a Hindu ashram. But someone you would think likely to makes a complete change and becomes a lifelong, devoted Christian. These are all examples of things of concern to the ordained pastor and the secular counselor alike. It seems, as Paul Tillich indicated, that modern (or postmodern) people are often beset with a sense of meaninglessness that leads to these states of affairs. Perhaps those of the classical world faced death as an intangible, and medieval people were burdened with guilt.

Christians should deal with these problems of meaninglessness today just as the initial preaching of the gospel gave the answer to death, and as the fresh discovery of the doctrine of justification by faith answered people's guilt, this book deals with apparently puzzling yet serious situations like these. Its core argument is that the cumulative ethical outline in the Wisdom Literature of the Old Testament and in the revelation of Christ has correspondences in existential philosophy rooted more in the subjective passion of individuals rather than any objective arguments.

In the Middle Ages, theology was dubbed "queen of the sciences." Some still think of it this way; they may not all be

Roman Catholic; in fact, quite a few of the Reformed persuasion like systematic theology. But this discipline surely cannot and should not be a matter of cold-blooded thinking involving merely rational arguments but rather one for those who have an inward passionate zeal for the Lord of Hosts and love for God, least of all should it lead to the building up of a complete, self-satisfied system. Theology is a passionately human concern, and it is disingenuous to think that those who pursue these matters and seek to engage others for the common good and the greater glory of God are just humanists. Every journey has a starting point, as in *The Pilgrim's Progress*, and all men and women have to start their personal, eternal journeys from themselves, the ground point being the undeniable but apparently absurd fact of their existence.

The aim of this book is to help twenty-first-century people come to terms with their existence and unlock the Wisdom Literature of the Bible in depth to examine how in fact this is congruent with the thinking of Søren Kierkegaard, who was indeed thinking as a biblical Christian albeit in a quirky and unconventional way. The problems of meaning are not merely intellectual but touch the deepest cravings of the soul; they are problems that go down to the most irreducible and elemental fact of anyone's being, his or her existence. Existentialism as a term for a school of philosophy was not introduced until before the Second World War by Karl Jaspers. Although many thinkers to whom the label has been applied, including Heidegger, have rejected it, others, such as Jean-Paul Sartre, whose name has become almost synonymous with it, have embraced it. Unfortunately, his most famous dictum, "Existence precedes essence," is quoted to back up his atheistic idea that life has no ultimate, intrinsic meaning and to think otherwise is "bad faith."

However, if there can be any definition of existentialism that could apply to all in the school, it is that the answer to life is found by *living it* rather than just thinking about it and then confining it to a system. Despite its godless connotations, existentialism has a Christian provenance, first in a latent form in Blaise Pascal, as shown in his *Pensees*, but most significantly in the life and writings of Søren Kierkegaard. Going beyond that, I hope to establish a link between the joined-up wisdom of the old covenant and that of the new to establish a link to salvation through Christ.

Not all biblical scholars would necessarily consider themselves theologians, and although Christian theologians should have at least a good knowledge of the Bible, perhaps neither always has had rigorous training in philosophy, and I do not mean **metaphysics**, but in the more relevant areas of ethics and logic. What also needs to be borne in mind is that there is a dearth of Classical education these days in Latin and Greek at the secondary level and even the finer points of English grammar and linguistics, even for many who enter Christian ministry.

After an initial introduction regarding the basis of the book, I will proceed to a detailed **exegesis** of each of the wisdom books in the regular canon and the Apocrypha, followed by an explanation of Kierkegaard's thinking, an explanation of the processes of logic and grammar as they affect objective and subjective thought (particularly in the area of non-propositional intransitive utterances, demonstrating their importance), leading to a theological conclusion.

This book is not aimed at academics (although I hope academics will read it); it is aimed at those with a pastoral or ministerial outlook who would like an introduction to the Wisdom Literature of the Bible; the history of thought; a biography of the "father" of existentialism, Kierkegaard; an exposition of his thinking; and developments in the fields of neurology and consciousness, along with the general reader, in whom I hope to stimulate a taste for the subjects in the book. I believe these are matters of an urgent, practical, and spiritual concern today for those who wish to consider these things for themselves and for anyone whose business is the care of souls and has a desire to see the kingdom of God grow in terms of individuals in the corporate life of the church.

My thanks go to Rev. Andy Schuman at my church of Christ the Servant, who encouraged me, the staff and library of Trinity College Theological College in Bristol, where I was allowed to borrow books.

Bristol, 2014

Note on the Text

I have followed the usual convention of putting book titles and foreign words in italics, so where I have wanted to emphasize, I have used underlining. Words in bold are technical, theological, and philosophical terms that will be found in the glossary. This also has helped me avoid the use of any footnotes. I am not an academic and may be unaware of every scholar working in the fields covered in my work. However, I have included a bibliography cross referenced with citations using the citation-name system at the end of the relevant texts and paraphrases. Referenced citations to Kierkegaard's own works and a few others are in italics. There is also an index.

For the sake of those unfamiliar with Hebrew or Greek, I will not be using the letters of those alphabets to represent words in those languages but English letters. There are a great many references to such words in the text as well as to other books. Capitals are used for main headings, including noting Kierkegaard's main books.

This book is not a standard Bible commentary; it should be read along with the relevant biblical texts. All scriptural references, including those from the Apocrypha (unless otherwise indicated, usually AV—King James Authorized Version), come from *The Revised English Bible* published by the Oxford and Cambridge University presses in 1989 and ratified by the major churches and Bible societies.

Introduction

Up until the **Enlightenment** in the eighteenth century, it was the generally held opinion of scholars that the older the wisdom, the better it was, and that the most ancient and arcane was the best. This view has been inverted to the extent that we are now led to believe that the latest ideas are the best. Even those who are not enamored of the latest fashion or "flavor of the month" in thought cannot help to have been affected by the earthquake of change that has occurred over the last couple of centuries. European Christianity has undergone decline; why was this?

About a century and a half ago, Denmark was having something of a cultural golden age with storywriters such as H. C. Anderson, artists such as K.A.B. Thorvaldsen, and scientists such as H.C. Ørstead along with the political and social change that came in the wake of the European revolutionary crisis of 1848, all this after loss of territory initially to Sweden, in the Napoleonic wars and later against Prussia. Into this matrix stepped a strange and rather tragic figure, Søren Kierkegaard, a modern Jeremiah, a voice crying out against where he perceived the modern world in Europe was leading. Whereas others sought objective, scientific facts, he looked to inner passions. While some were rejecting classically held axioms of logic, he held to them. While others looked to organized religion or the all-important civil state and what in German is the *menshanman* (clumsily translated into English as the "mass man"), he emphasized the importance of the individual and individual belief. He foresaw in his own way that in a future Europe morally exhausted by two centuries of hectic change and unimaginable war, many might indeed say, "Christianity has been abolished by expansion."

In his *Systematic Theology* (three volumes published between 1951 and 1963), Paul Tillich, a later theologian who thought along the same lines pointed out that whereas in the ancient world, people were afraid of the great unknown of death, which was answered by the resurrection of Christ, and the awful burden of damning guilt that medieval people felt that was answered by the rediscovery of the doctrine of justification by faith by Luther, so many people today are beset and bedeviled by a sense of meaningless in a confusing world. The rediscovery of a divine sense of meaning and purpose though Christ as the incarnation of Holy Wisdom was I believe the subliminal aim of Kierkegaard's life work and is the main objective of this book.

Kierkegaard wrote in an obscure, highly ironical, and pseudonymous style so people would be "caught out" by the truth. This is in line with what Jesus did when he taught in parables. Although one of his aims was to attack the philosophical system of **Hegel** with its attempt to encompass all reality and its dismissal of traditional logic, modern **existentialism** has incorporated these things and twisted much of what Kierkegaard was aiming at to the extent that an existentialist writer such as **Sartre** could get away with using atheism as a starting point and end up with a very grim view of life that denies meaning altogether.

There are several reasons for the misunderstanding of Kierkegaard. First, Kierkegaard wrote in Danish, for his country's people, and his works were not rediscovered until a generation after his death. It took good literary criticism to unwrap what he was saying before it could be translated into other languages. Second, of course, is that not all those reading his works could be expected to be Christians or even theists. Third, the insidious influence of Hegelian logic had by that time infected the intellectual warp and woof of Europe, particularly seen in the writings of Karl Marx.

There have been Christian existentialists and theologians, Catholic and Protestant, although Kierkegaard could be described as a Lutheran par excellence. Although some may use the Bible, they do not use it as their starting point. I intend to start with the Bible.

The **Wisdom Literature** of the Bible is of timeless application, and yet it is a field that is little explored by theologians not least in any joined-up way. It was the objective of Kierkegaard to help people come to life and faith through a wise philosophy that was Christian, since he wanted to upstage Hegel's notion that religion in the form of Christianity was a lesser stage in development and philosophy (that is, Hegelian philosophy) was superior to it, and at the same time perhaps parody the Romantic movement developing in Europe during his lifetime.

Although Kierkegaard thought of himself as a Christian, and many of his writings, especially in his *Journals*, show a deep piety expressed in prayer, it has been remarked that his ideas do not correspond with biblical or historical Christianity. I hope to show in this work that this idea is mistaken and to redeem Kierkegaard's reputation as a truly original Christian thinker. By reference to Holy Writ, I will show his ideas are indeed congruent with the teaching of the Bible and consequently have a bearing on Christ himself and the salvation he offers.

I will be looking particularly closely at the three books in the canon ascribed by rabbinic tradition to **Solomon**: The Song of Songs, or Canticles; Proverbs; and Ecclesiastes, known in Hebrew as *Qoholeth* or the congregational preacher or lecturer. These all bear the seal of his wisdom whether people choose to believe he wrote them or not. Rabbinic tradition says he compiled the former in his youth, collected Proverbs during his maturity, and composed *Qoholeth* toward the end of his life. I contend that this corresponds with the three *Stages along Life's Way* of Kierkegaard—the aesthetic, the ethical, and the religious.

To expand my exegesis, I will be looking at that other canonical wisdom book, Job; taking a judicious look at the non-canonical Wisdom Literature in the Apocrypha; and paying close scrutiny to the marvelous light the New Testament shines on this in the Gospels and the epistles.

I will proceed to a section on philosophy insofar as it is relevant to the main topic: those thinkers who influenced Kierkegaard, those who followed after him; and of course, although it would not be of use to include the whole of Kierkegaard's field of thought, the areas of the stages of life and consciousness pertaining to the Bible he considered.

I will be including an important section on logic and grammar to show how right it is to reject Hegel's attack on classical logic and to demonstrate how Classical logic, which works well enough in the hard sciences, should be used in philosophy and soft sciences and can be used to join up wisdom stages. The section on grammar, "The Tyranny of the **Transitive**," will demonstrate that subjective truth, far from being dismissed as merely irrational, should be viewed as something not subject to the rules of logic but is more fundamental than objective truth.

I will mention how Kierkegaard's thinking has opened up another useful new field of philosophy, **phenomenology**, and how it has helped to throw light on the other very practical areas of **neuroscience, cybernetics,** and **artificial intelligence**.

I include appendices on some pastoral applications, with one on Viktor Frankl, who can truly be called "a knight of faith."

Prologue

From Quidam's Diary[8]

Solomon's judgment is well known. It availed to discriminate between truth and falsehood and to make the judge famous as a wise prince. His dream, however, is not as well known.

If there is any pang of sympathy, it is that of having to be ashamed of one's father, of him whom one loves above all, to whom one is most indebted, to have to approach him backward with face turned away not to behold his dishonor. But what greater bliss can be imagined than to dare to love as the son's wish prompts him and dare to be proud of the father, moreover, because he is the only elect, the singularly distinguished man, a nation's strength, a country's pride, God's friend, a promise for the future extolled in his lifetime and held by memory in the highest esteem! Happy Solomon, this was thy lot! Among the chosen people (how glorious it was even to belong to them!) he was the king's son (an enviable lot!), son of that king who was the elect among kings. Thus, Solomon lived happily with the prophet Nathan. The father's strength and achievements did not inspire him to deeds of valor, for indeed, no opportunity was left for that, but it inspired him with admiration, and admiration made him a poet. But if the poet was almost jealous of his hero, the son was blissful in his devotion to the father.

Then one time, the son made a visit to his royal father. In the night, he awoke at hearing movement where the father slept. Horror seized him. He feared it was a villain who would murder David. He stole nearer, beheld David with a crushed and contrite heart, and heard a cry of despair from the soul of the penitent.

Fainting at the sight, he returned to his couch, fell asleep, but did not rest. He dreamed David was an ungodly man, one rejected by God, that the royal majesty was a sign of God's wrath upon him, that he must wear the purple as punishment, that he was condemned to rule, condemned to hear the blessing of the people, whereas the justice of the Lord secretly and hidden pronounced judgment on the guilty one. The dream suggested that God was not the God of the pious but of the ungodly and that one had to be an ungodly man to be God's elect. The horror of the dream was this contradiction.

While David lay on the ground with contrite heart, Solomon arose, but his understanding was crushed. Horror seized him when he thought of what it was to be God's elect. He surmised that holy intimacy with God, the sincerity of the pure man before the Lord, was not the explanation, but that a private guilt was the secret that explained everything.

Solomon became wise, but he did not became a hero; he became a thinker, but he did not become a man of prayer; he became a preacher, but he did not become a believer; he was able to help many, but he was not able to help himself. He became sensual but not repentant; contrite, downcast but not upstanding; the power of the will had been strained by what surpassed the strength of youth. And he tossed through life, tossed about by life, strong, supernaturally strong (that is, womanishly weak) in the stirring infatuations and marvelous inventions of imagination, ingenious in expounding thoughts. But there was rift in his nature, and Solomon was like the paralytic who was unable to support his own body. In his harem, he sat like a disillusioned, old man until desire for pleasure awoke, and he shouted, "Strike the tumbrels, dance before me, ye women." But when the Queen of the South came to visit him, attracted by his wisdom, then was his soul rich, and the wise answer flowed from his lips like the precious myrrh that flowed from the trees in Arabia.

[*Quidam* means "someone." *Taciturnus*, the silent one, claims to have found the diary in a waterproof container at the bottom of a lake! Perhaps Kierkegaard is exploring the relationship he had with his father.]

SECTION I

Scripture

Overview

The Wisdom Books

During Jewish festivals, it is customary to have readings from the canonical books, which are considered to be part of the *Kethurvim* or "Writings"[26] (**cognate** with the Arabic *kitab*, "book"). The other two sets of scrolls of the Hebrew canon are the Torah or Law and the Prophets. A prime example is the book of Esther, which is acted out almost as a pantomime at the feast of Purim. The Song of Songs is read during the Feast of the Passover, and Ecclesiastes is read during the Feast of Tabernacles, when the building of indwelt, temporary shelters at Jewish homes or in a formal setting in a synagogue remind Jews that we are but temporary strangers and pilgrims on earth.[20] These liturgical appointments are not arbitrary nor accidental and should not be seen as so by the Christian. Just as the Eucharist is an adaptation of the Passover meal and Easter is put in line with Passover as a moveable feast, celebrating the "Christ event" culminating in his redeeming sacrifice at his first coming, so Tabernacles should be seen as looking forward to a correspondence with his second coming and his actions as heavenly high priest in the book of Revelation.[19]

It cannot be said that the bulk of other wisdom writings, that is, the books of Proverbs or Job or the **apocryphal** books of the Wisdom of Solomon or Ecclesiasticus in the **Septuagint** are designated to be read at any particular festival, but the church has recognized the winsome, charming, but mysterious personification of Holy Wisdom as a gracious woman in its calendar as "O Sophia." We will examine later the nature of this apparent heavenly personage or apparent hypostasis.

The bulkier part of the Wisdom Literature cannot be passed over lightly, and even the non-canonical books deserve close analysis because Jesus Christ is the alpha and omega, first focused at his first coming and all creation, and last focused at his second coming, throughout eternity, "even to the end of the world" (Matthew 28:20).

The three main wisdom books are connected in a way that helps us find him through a consideration of our lives. At the bottom of it all is the awful fact of our existence and indeed the question why anything should exist. Until people see into themselves deeply, inwardly, and passionately that there is a personal and sovereign God intimately concerned with them as individuals and their relationships and who is an external being transcending existence, who was seen in the flesh in Jesus Christ, life could indeed be considered meaningless to anyone deeply conscious of his or her existence.

The Provenance of the Wisdom Books

Biblical writings are sometimes dated to as late a date as they can be. A prime example of this is the dating of the book of Daniel, which contains such detailed prophesies of events in the **Hellenistic era** that it is said that it could not have been written centuries before but in the century before Christ, leaving the question why it was not composed in Greek rather than **Aramaic**. There is, however, a gaping hole in this thinking; it is commonly and quite sensibly recognized that the Hebrew canon was not given its final form until after the **Babylonian captivity,** at least to the time of **Ezra**, when the Jews were finally cured of idolatry,[19] but that does not mean inspired Scripture did not exist in the communal context of God's covenant people beforehand.

To preserve ritual purity after the exile, Ezra introduced harsh measures, including divorces for those married to foreign women. Judaism crystallized into the forms apparent at the time of Jesus, and it was probably Ezra who set about collating Scripture. Sadly, just as **Nehemiah** built a wall around Jerusalem to preserve its integrity as the Holy City, some people were building a "hedge" around the law and making it restrictive (with the side effect of the growth of the Pharisee party). Scripture existed in a substantial albeit unpolished and unedited form before this. For example, if we are to believe the Bible, the book of the Law was lost for a while until the high priest Hilkiah found it while repairing the first temple.

Other previous books exist in a state of edited compilation: the book of the generations of Adam (Genesis 5) and the Wars of the Lord (Numbers 21). As public books, they had the authority of Moses and were probably originally compiled by Samuel in the time of Saul.[19] The Hebrew canon was finally fixed in AD 95 by a council of **rabbis** in **Jamina**,[6] after the second temple had been destroyed. There is no reason to believe the editing of the old and new covenants was not inspired by God as much as was their original formats.

However, let us not digress but sum up. It is difficult to believe that the canonical wisdom books, including Job, could have been put in their final form later than the time of Ezra and certainly not after the blitzkrieg of Alexander the Great, when the Septuagint version of the Old Testament was written in Greek along with the apocryphal wisdom books, but that does not mean they did not exist in earlier editions.

Rabbinical and a large body of Christian tradition put the authorship of the books of Solomon in their original unedited form with Solomon himself. His "songs" were written as a young man, Proverbs in middle age, and Ecclesiastes as an old man. There is not too much of a problem with totally agreeing with the notion that the intense relationship of monogamous love is more in keeping with someone in the first flush of youth although tempted by the women of a sensuous harem to promiscuity rather than the polygamous king with many concubines that the Bible says Solomon later became (1 Kings 11:8), and a later writer would surely have borne this in mind.[29]

As we shall see, Proverbs is indeed an edited compilation. Nevertheless, its title in Hebrew is Proverbs (*Mashim*) of Solomon, and a close analysis shows that many were indeed sourced or written by him.[26]

Ecclesiastes is probably an inspired edition of what was recorded of, or written by or of Solomon, as certain negative views about kings (which may be reflective on his part) are in the text and the writer refers to "all in Jerusalem before me" (Ecclesiastes 2:9). In addition, it contains the repetitive phrase "under the sun," which is common in Egyptian texts in the first millennium BC around the time of **Akhenaton**[29] and could hardly have been included in a Jewish text in the Hellenistic era because it would have had immediate allusions to the god **Apollo,** which would have been utterly anathema at that time. *Qoholeth* (the preacher to the assembly) may indeed have been written in its extant form after the exile. However, just as the books of Moses in the **Torah** had the authority of Moses for public reading, they could not have been written in their entirety by him as they describe some things that occurred after his death. We may safely say the books of Solomon have the stamp, seal, and authority of Solomon for public reading and private study.

The story of Job is of a very ancient provenance initially about the story itself but also shown by the language of the Hebrew text, which is different and appears more ancient than other parts of the canon.[26]

I also want to examine that of the wisdom books of the Apocrypha. They are a mixture of divinely inspired and purely human literature, as I shall discuss below. Nevertheless, many people, John Bunyan among them as he testified in his *Grace Abounding*, have found God speaking personally to them in these books. The books are the Wisdom of Solomon and Ecclesiasticus, or the Wisdom of Jesus Son of Sirach. The latter is somewhat unusual in that according to its own prefaced testimony, it was written in Hebrew and translated into Greek over fifty years later. The former is more diverse in nature and may well have been known thoroughly by St. Paul.[29] The ascriptions to Solomon have, of course, nothing to do with him given the fact of the Hellenistic composition but are to give the books a cachet and claim to authority; the latest the final form of both books can be dated to about a century and a half before Christ.[29]

Moving on to the New Testament, in our examination of Wisdom, we have the words of Christ in the Gospels and Paul in the epistles and Revelation.

Wisdom is more pervasive in the Gospels, especially in Matthew and Luke, than a cursory examination may reveal! Jesus constantly made remarks that would not be out of place in the book of Proverbs! The contrast between the man who built his house on the rock and the other who built on sand as the closing words to the Sermon on the Mount (Matthew 7) is a good way of contrasting wise and foolish behavior and incorporating a hidden spiritual message. In Matthew 12:42, Jesus actually compared himself with Solomon and said he was greater than Solomon in the wisdom that he offered; this echoed Proverbs 1, in which wisdom drew attention to herself in self-recommendation: Jesus said he was wiser than even the wisest king; in him, wisdom itself was ever present.[29]

There are many examples of this wisdom in the **Synoptics**; perhaps here we could mention how Jesus overcame moral dilemmas in the same way as when two women came to Solomon to claim the same baby, and he found out the truth by offering to chop the child in half. The woman caught in the act of adultery should have been stoned, but Jesus (perhaps suspecting her accusers had all had her as well) asked those who had no sin to cast the first stone. Another example of when he showed fine fiscal awareness as well was when he was presented with a coin and asked if it was right to pay taxes to the emperor (these coins were issued for just that purpose). He gave a stunningly wise answer here too, even though one of the charges at his trial (which of course did not stick) was that he said taxes should not be paid. It is also interesting that in these cases and many like them, Jesus, unlike Solomon, who drew his sword, never threatened violence.

St. Paul followed Christ in comparing the wisdom of the world, eloquent wisdom, or the wisdom of the wise, with divine wisdom. This occurred specifically in 1 Corinthians and Romans, books no self-respecting scholar would deny were written by him; 1 Corinthians was written probably about AD 55, as Acts 19 helps testify, and Romans about two years later.[26]

The Song of Songs

Jerusalem, Hasefer, 1923

A revolution in biblical exegesis occurred during the Reformation. Up until that time, there was a pick-and-mix approach to the way Scripture was unpackaged. The medieval approach was the fourfold method of the literal, moral, analogical (or mystical), and above all the **allegorical approach**, which was originally fostered by the Egyptian protomonasteries. Although something may be said for the other approaches, the Reformation largely swept away three of the four and promoted the literal understanding of Scripture wherever possible.[14]

When today one says that one takes the Bible literally, this can often be misunderstood, but to do so is only to say that one should read the Bible in the literary form it was written in; straight narrative such as in the historical books of the Old Testament and the Synoptic Gospels should be taken as straight narrative; poetry should be taken as poetry. As in "The Lord rides on the storm clouds". Prophesy should be read in the same spirit as the prophet who wrote it, and so on. The Bible contains many literary genres, including one not present today, the **apocalyptic** (which makes it wide open to misinterpretation by the uncritical). But what concerns us directly here is the way the Song of Songs should be interpreted.

Surprisingly, the accepted interpretation of this book among conservative Jews and Christians is allegorical! The plain, literal meaning of the text as an erotic love poem is abandoned; instead, it is seen as an expression of God's love for his people, either Israel or the church.[20] The reformers retained this way of interpreting this text while encouraging literal meaning elsewhere.

Although there is be an element of truth in this tradition, as I shall show below, it stifles a more literal interpretation and **heuristic** expansion that lead to broader truths in an existential context. Let us proceed then to an interpretation of the book. In following chapters, the other Wisdom Literature will be expounded and linked and then the overall existential corollaries given.

Solomon is said to have written over a thousand songs (1 Kings 4:32), and the Hebrew title Song of Songs (*Shir Hashirim*) may well be taken as the "best of songs" or perhaps an edition of the best. Indeed, the way the book divides into solos between the bridegroom or male-peace (*shelomah*) and the female-peace (*shulamith*)[26] interspersed with chorus-like responses by the "companions" may indicate something of a compilation of the best. The chorus of companions resonates with the Egyptian custom of the companions of the bride sitting around her feet at her betrothal or marriage and ministering to her. We know that soon after Solomon secured his throne after the death of his father, he married an Egyptian princess (1 Kings 3:1). Psalm 45 probably relates to this, and the canticle may well do too, as just as in Saxon times here in England, the queen from another royal line was seen as a "peace weaver," so here, peace was woven by the royal lovers. The book divides into roughly thirty songs and responses that may be reduced to two sections of seven each. [28] Some of these shorter sections (2:7, 3:5, and 8.4) may well be taken as a harmonious duet by the lovers. The longer sections are solos and are particularly present in the middle of the book. The whole then presents us with a carefully crafted and inspired choral work that may or may not be accompanied. The language of course is highly sensuous and would fit better in the lyrics of an Omar Khayyam or Hafez poem or that of an Arab poet such as Abu Nahas or even some Chinese literature (which also hides sensuality under a discreet veil of nature) than a Western poet. But even given that there may be some comparisons, that seems odd. Who in the West today would compare his sweetheart to a race horse (1:9)? Who would compare her teeth to a flock of sheep (4:2) and her hair to that of goats (4:1)?[29] Arab horses are of course among the best and most appreciated, but there may be something of a subtle allusion here as the Hebrew for horse is *sus*, and puns nicely with "Susannah," the lilies, and the rose of Sharon.

The sheep and the goats speak of sacrifice, and their wool was used to make temple and tabernacle curtains. The girl has a natural beauty and is not "pale and interesting" (1:6), but she and the companions make allusions to things used in temple worship and for feasting: wine, spices and oil; myrrh—a purifying spice; perfumed spikenard; frankincense; and henna, used as a cosmetic and to this day as body art before marriage (the Middle Eastern honeymoon is sometimes known as "henna nights"). The fruits mentioned are symbolic of sweetness and fertility: the small Palestinian apple, raisins, ripening figs (the tree of which fruits up to four times a year in Palestine), blossoming vines, pomegranates (which were simulated on the robes of the priests) and are not just a fruit on their own but are used to flavor and color food (as in the Arab cheese *gibnah roman*), cinnamon, saffron, and sugar cane.[26] Many of these things are precious and expensive; all are delicious.

Other plants mentioned with religious overtones are cedar and pine, used in the building of the temple and palm fronds for the hosanna. The roses, lilies, and meadow flowers point to a natural beauty, a chaste, closed garden with a fountain (4:12) in spring refreshed by rain. Animals are alluded to; the dove and its cooing can be taken as a symbol of monogamy, as **Tertullian** noted.[26] The gazelle (in itself a Semitic word) indicates speed and agility; the sheep and the goats mentioned above together with the offspring of twin lambs and fawns (7:3) are indications of nurture.

A curious passage in 2:15 refers to jackals despoiling a vineyard, and again, unfortunately, this has been taken allegorically in the past to mean the bad habits that inhibit spiritual life and growth together with suggested remedies on how this may be overcome. However, in the clear, allusory, erotic language of the text, it is probably better to say that they may be the unclean forces that would attack a virginal or monogamous chastity. The text at 2:2 also refers to a lily among thorns, as this plant indeed grew so.

11

The Rose of Sharon is red and produces a fragrant gum—the beloved is the most desirable of women.[29]

There are references to precious metals and jewelry both for the *shelomah* and the *shulamith*,(the bride) in the former case to a richly decorated litter (Hebrew *aperion*) that may have been based on Egyptian models.[26]

There are references to crafts and buildings, especially tents (1:6), huts and towers (7:4, 4:4, 8:10), walled cities (Tizrah, Damascus, and Jerusalem), and mountains (4:1). These are possibly symbols of carefully guarded chastity or virginity.

Toward the end of the canticle, *shulamith* appears described in full readiness for love from head to toe (6:14–7:9), and full consummation is reached.[29]

To many commentators, the key text in the book is 6.3: "I am my beloved's and my beloved is mine," but this ignores the parts of the book where *shulamith* experiences the existential angst of parting (3:1–4) occurring after the jackals (2:16–18), showing a strong desire for heterosexual union and then her song in (5:2–8). In both passages, the lover is lost. Later in chapter 3, the lover is found and clung to, but in chapter 5, *shulamith* does not find him and cries out that she is faint for love.

Chapter 5 is particularly interesting: *shulamith* has prepared for sleep; she did not want to put on her clothes, dirty her washed feet, or disturb her freshly anointed hair. Her lover came to the sort-of door found at the time with a kind of lattice that could be seen through but not easily opened from the outside. When she opened it, her fumbling lover had gone. Dashing out into the street in a state of despair in her perfumed undress, she was taken for a lady of the night by the night watchmen and beaten up.

The key verses here are indeed a contrast to 6:3; the beating heart sank and was replaced by panic, desolation, and turning bowels. "I opened to my love but my love had turned away and was gone, my heart sank when he turned his back; I sought him but could not find him; I called but there was no answer" (5:4–6). This is the state of the soul reaching out from a purely aesthetic life, as we shall see, but is equally like the church of Ephesus in the Apocalypse that was concerned chiefly with its own activism and had forgotten its "first love" or the half-naked church of Laodicea, which could not be bothered to admit the outsider Christ who knocked on its door, perhaps leaving it to the lowliest of its officers, the doorkeeper.

In summary, the book covers all the pleasures of the senses: sight, sound, smell, taste, and touch covered by plants, animals, materials, artifices, music, song, and voices. All these things may be legitimately enjoyed. Perhaps the greatest aesthetic pleasure is found in the monogamous, heterosexual bonding between man and woman.

However, there is a dark side in the text I have hinted at above: aesthetic pleasure on its own is ultimately unfulfilling, especially in the face of separation of the beloved. All created things are subject to demise, no more so than the absence or death of pleasure or a partner. Solomon himself moved from his monogamous love to polygamy and many concubines. These women led him astray into idolatry and the worship of false gods, and his love life and experience of the aesthetic lost their edge.

In many ways perhaps, the Canticle can be seen as a cryptic *mashal* or proverb on the sensual life we all experience to a greater or lesser extent; it not only promotes the sensual joys of monogamy but also exposes the ultimately unfulfilling nature of the aesthetic life. It is the first aesthetic part of the triad of Solomon that will lead to the other wisdom books and the sober reflection of Ecclesiastes.

The book makes another point about the sensual worship of the divine; this too is ultimately unfulfilling. There are many allusions in the book to worship: doves, sheep, and goats are sacrificial animals, and the spices and smoke of incense, the precious materials used in the building of a temple, the references to temple architecture, and some of the fruits and flowers mentioned, particularly the pomegranates and the lilies used as decorative motifs in the temple of Solomon. Perhaps the *mashal* of this book is to say that even an aesthetic approach to worship, legitimate enough as it may be, can disappear down a black hole if it is not centered on the beloved. Aesthetic religion is often accompanied by aesthetic worship. Indeed, some are so preoccupied with religious ritual that they do not have time to think what life is really all about; I think the rituals of Bali are a prime case in point.

In the end, a purely aesthetic approach to worship leads to the spiritual equivalent of polygamy and adultery—idolatry. There is Old Testament allusion to this, especially Ezekiel's almost-pornographic description of Israel and Judah as a couple of sisters weaned into the most immoral behavior from an early age. This passage (Ezekiel 23) about Oholah and Oholibah is so explicit that it was considered unsuitable by the rabbis for public reading in synagogues and by extension forms no part of any Christian liturgy. There is also the sad story of the prophet Hosea, who was commanded to marry a prostitute and take her back again after her adultery as a sign that God kept His covenant even if his people did not. Surely, if there is to be any allegory in the book, it is not so much that it shows God's love for his people but rather that his people, collectively and individually, be faithful to him. This way, they avoid the poison of idolatry whether in its cruder forms or as in the fascination with material things, celebrity, and mammon that is so prevalent today.

A further point to be made here is particularly germane in our day: the book is unashamedly and blatantly heterosexual. In passing, it makes a good point in favor of monogamy, something about which the law was never laid down explicitly in Holy Writ, although there are cases of people who, just like Solomon in his later life, had problems with more than one wife! It is interesting that no one these days is pushing for the legal right to polygamy.

Just as the early joys of romantic love in a wedding lead to the real business of building a family and home in a community, so the insights of the Canticle can lead to the world of general wisdom in Proverbs and the non-canonical wisdom books where *shulamith* transforms into the dignified and industrious figure of Lady Wisdom, where the pursuit and enjoyment of pleasure turns into the pursuit and pride in sober duty. I will now give a progressive analysis of the text of the Canticle here rather relegating it to an appendix.

The best exposition of the text in my opinion is Songs 1-13 and is given in paraphrase below. This saw it as a single love song in a long sequence rather than separate love songs that were cobbled together containing unrelated lyrics. It splits into a semi-continuous progression of two sets of seven scenes each, from the arrival of the princess at Solomon's court to her acknowledgement of her as queen. The young princess is from Nadia (6:12), and the chorus comprises the ladies of the harem. According to Goulder[28] then.

<u>Part 1</u>: Prenuptials and the wedding

<u>Song 1</u> (1:1–8). The princess arrives. She expresses her love for her fiancé and asks to be guided to the audience chamber.

<u>Song 2</u> (1:9–27): In the audience chamber, the king gladly greets her, and they start their intimacy.

<u>Song 3</u> (2:8–17): The king continues his courtship and invites her to a love nest in the country.

Song 4 (3:1–5): The princess awakes to find the king gone (on official business perhaps), and she goes looking for him. She eventually finds him and enjoys some intimacy again.

Song 5 (3:6–11): The wedding procession as recited by the chorus of the harem. The princess arrives in a magnificent litter escorted by the pick of Solomon's guards to the king with the crown that his mother, Bathsheba, gave him.

Song 6 (3:11–4:8): The wedding itself: the king takes in the beauty of his bride from head to toe, including her face behind its tantalizing wedding veil. He can't wait to enjoy in full the spotless perfection of his lady friend.

Song 7 (4:9–5:1): An erotic conversation between the king and his new wife as they consummate their union. However, the chorus is not very far away and has the last word, telling them to make love until they are satiated.

Part 2: Consolidation of relationship.

Song 8 (5:2–8): The princess is now queen. King Solomon goes to her apartment, but she does not open to him in time, and he goes. Following him, the queen can't find him and gets beaten up.

Song 9 (5:10–6:3): The ladies of the night are given a description of the king (with whom they are presumably not acquainted) so the queen can find him. The harem chorus joins in, and she finally finds him in his garden.

Song 10 (6:4–7:1): The reunion. The king is reunited with the queen and makes the classic remark, "I am my beloved's and my beloved is mine."

Song 11 (7:1–10): The dance. The harem suggests that the king enjoys Abishag the Shulamite for a bit of a change, but the queen will brook no competition. She dances before the king. Apart from her sandals, all that is mentioned in between of the queen's anatomy up to her beautiful face seems to be bare flesh, so it appears that she is dancing naked before the king to arouse him. He certainly appreciates her beauty and does get turned on.

Song 12 (7:11–8:4): Privacy. The queen takes the king into the countryside on a "henna night" for a bit of *al fresco* love away from the pesky harem. She regrets that public displays of affection such as that shown between brother and sister are denied them.

Song 13 (8:5–10): The king's only true love. The appeal is made by the queen, "Wear me as a seal over your heart, for love is as strong as death, passion cruel as the grave; it blazes up like a blazing fire, fiercer than any flame." Only a permanent relationship where he is as committed to her as she is to him will do.

Song 14 (8:11–14): The queen's final test. The king is willing to come to the queen whenever she asks from his vineyard.

The Book of Proverbs

Solomon and a council of wise men planning a building
A Bible card published by the Providence Lithograph Company 1896

Wisdom sayings have a long pedigree in the Middle East and are appreciated as much as pithy remarks, irony, and puns. However, the wisdom found in the Hebrew canon and Apocrypha is not the abstract philosophy of the Greeks but the intensely practical *hokma* and matters of *bina*, that is, understanding, *tebuna*, insight, and *sekel*, prudence. It is the art of success in this world, from humble craft skills to advice given to kings.[26]

In scripture, we have the straight sayings of the book of Proverbs designed to keep us in healthy welfare or on the pathway of God. Then there are the dialogues of Job, which delve deeper into the mysteries of existence, as does the monologue of Ecclesiastes, but even here, discussion is based solidly on concrete examples and never flies off into metaphysical speculation. The writing down of memorable wisdom sayings is probably very ancient, dating to well before the Davidic dynasties in the civilizations of Egypt and Mesopotamia. In Israel, a class of sages, the *hakim* (cognate with the Arabic *haq,* "truth"), who were equal in status to the prophets and priests, would compile and edit sayings under royal patronage, particularly under Solomon (1 Kings 4:29–34) and Hezekiah (Proverbs 25:1). There are important technical rhetorical devices the *hakim* used that should be noted; again, they are practical and not mere sophistry or flourishes; they are aids to memory or means of avoiding error or paradox.[29]

For example, the English proverbs "One man's meat is another man's poison" and "What's sauce for the goose is sauce for the gander" are paradoxical, so which one is true? Looking to another language, Machiavelli noted in his own democratic insights, "Let no one quote to me the [aristocratic] proverb that "He who builds on the people builds on sand.""

Scripture itself trumps these examples when Ezekiel came out against the proverb, "Parents eat sour grapes and their children's teeth are put on edge" (Ezekiel 18:2), meaning you will pay for the sins of your forbears. No! says Ezekiel; every individual is responsible to God for his or her own sins. I mention the above to show that there is a worldly wisdom that runs counter to and may adulterate the wisdom of God. As Job 28 insists, true wisdom comes from God. St. Paul was keen to point this out in 1 Corinthians.

What then were the literary devices used by the *hakim*? They were the use of poetic parallelism, synthesis (Proverbs 13:10), comparisons (17:1), and antithesis (10:1); these avoid the traps of paradox. Then there are devices that are aids to memory that may not survive translations from Hebrew, like the use of alliteration and acrostic pattern (31:10–31). There are also numerical sequences (30:15). Not restricted to the wisdom books, riddles, fables, and allegories may be used. Parables are an extension of comparison and of course much used by Jesus. For example, Proverbs 17:1 echoes the parable of the prodigal son.[29]

We now need to analyze these books starting with Proverbs itself. It should be noted that the word *mashal* in Hebrew has a much wider connotation than the word proverb in English and includes parables, riddles, allegories, fables, and even jibes or what have been termed "**taunt songs**." Let us first look at how the text divides up and second at its main characteristics.

The title of the book is *M'ishle Shlomoh*, the sayings or proverbs of Solomon. The didactic tone of Proverbs 1:1–7 is sensitive and deuteronomic and reminds one of a teacher of the law (like Kierkegaard's pseudonym Judge Wilhelm). It may bear the mark of a final editor who polished it up under divine inspiration.

The main proverbs attributed to Solomon himself split into two sections (1:8–9:18).[26]

Although it is possible many of the sayings are very ancient and could be said to predate the time of Solomon, the main proverbs attributed to Solomon himself split into two sections: first the ancient ones, from 1:8 to 9:18,[j] and those from 10:1 to 22:16, which he may have written or gathered from international contacts, particularly Egypt (**Amenemope**).

The other sections in the compilation are the anonymous ones (22:17–24:22) and those of the otherwise unknown Augur (30:1–33) and King Lemuel (31:1–9). The "Massa" mentioned may be in Northwest Arabia. Finally, the editor wrote an inspired epilogue about the virtuous woman (31:10–31). The nature of the text indicates there were probably two editions made: one during the reign of **King Hezekiah** (25.1) in the seventh century BC and another after the Babylonian exile.[26]

Characterizations

The first thing to note about the characters in the text is that the recipient of the proverb is often "my son." Proverbs as such may have been used as dictation exercises in ancient Egypt, and the paternal tone is no different here[29]: 2:2 refers to the (writing) tablet of memory and alludes to the postexilic Greek theory that the memory worked a bit like a reusable wax tablet. The idea being, I think, was to keep on studying wisdom and not erase it. I will be discussing the personification of Wisdom as a woman, but an important caveat is that the word *wisdom*, unlike many Hebrew words, is feminine in gender.

A suitable analysis of the text gives a breakdown into a numerically significant seven sections (with perhaps some subsections[26]).

1. Chapters 1–9

This is an introductory section in which Wisdom recommended herself in a set of concise versifications longer in tone than the rest of the book and in the style of a wisdom school or that of a father instructing his son. The key verse is perhaps 1:7, the well-known "The fear of the Lord is the foundation of knowledge; it is fools who scorn wisdom and instruction."

2. Chapters 10–22:16

The bulk of the book is devoted to "the proverbs of Solomon." These are really one-liners in Hebrew joined up as a parallel in three ways rhetorically.

1. resemblance, for example, "There is a rod in pickle for the arrogant, and blows ready for the fool's back" (19:21).
2. difference, for example, "False scales are an abomination to the Lord but accurate weights win his favor" (11:1).
3. synthetic parallelism, e.g., "A gold ring in a pig's snout is a beautiful woman without good sense"(11:22).

King Solomon presented the proverbs as axiomatic statements he found on reflection to be subject to challenge and that were to be listened to and obeyed to the glory of God.

3. Chapters 22:17–24:34

"The words of the wise and also the sayings of the wise," in other words, a series of godly sayings compiled from anonymous sources. This section has close parallels to an Egyptian text, "The Instruction of Amenemope." It deals in detail with a range of issues too varied to go into here except to make the point it was designed to educate someone in God-fearing dignity and success in the world and also to point out that divine wisdom was not restricted to any specific ethnic group, a point about inclusivity and of the **universal** St. Paul realized when he quoted a Greek poet.

4. Chapters 25–29

"The proverbs of Solomon which the men of King Hezekiah copied" were the "B" side of chapters 10 through 22. However, they do contain a striking proverb quoted by Christ: "If your enemy is hungry, give him food, if thirsty, give him a drink of water" (25:21). This is followed by "and the Lord will reward you," indicating that Christ's teaching was more practical than that of some of his contemporaries.

5. Chapter 30

"The words of Agar son of Jakeh of Mossa [in northwest Arabia?]." These proverbs reflect in part Isaiah, Job, and Psalms. But a curious fact is verses 15–33, the numerical proverbs, e.g., 30:15: "Three things there are which will never be satisfied, four which will never say. Enough!" These may have been keys to didactic riddles. Again, the reference to Massa in Arabia indicates the divine bestowal of wisdom to all humanity.

6. Chapter 31:1–9

"The words of Lemuel King of Massa." The teacher of the king was his mother—again the feminine influence.

7. Chapter 31:10–end

This is **acrostic** poem in order of the Hebrew alphabet, again with didactic intentions no doubt. Here is a young ladies' marriage guide to being wise, prudent, and virtuous wives, an example of wisdom any good man would desire.

The above seven sections could be said to be the "Seven Pillars of Wisdom"[26] in her house (9:1), with a call to all to "come and eat the food that [she] has prepared and taste the wine that [she] has spiced" (9.5).

   a.   A recommendation of wisdom
   b.   An exposition of the wisdom of Israel's king.
   c.   An exposition of the wisdom of Israel's people.
   d.   An exposition reflected prophetic wisdom painted by numbers(!) and by a foreigner.
   e.   An exposition of universal, godly wisdom by a Gentile king's mother.
   f.   A poem in praise of feminine virtue from A to Z (*aleph* to *tau*) in the Hebrew alphabet).

Dramatis Personae of Proverbs in Order of Appearance

It is useful to extract from Proverbs the typology found there in more than one place to give extra force and order to any exegesis. What follows is a personal list of my impressions of these types. A good exercise for the reader is to read Proverbs with this list and find the references for themselves.

The Simple are shrewd, but they will come to grief if they do not listen to wisdom's words.

The Poor do not have enough money to be happy, but they are better than greedy liars. They should be helped. Their oppressors will become poor. It is better to be poor and honest than rich and dishonest. Though they are helpless against wicked rulers, good people know they have rights. Those who despise the poor despise the God who made them.

The Young need knowledge and discretion.

Borrowers are the slaves of lenders.

Drunkards pay for their behavior in state of health and mind.

Fools scorn knowledge and instruction; they do not listen to the reproof of wisdom, so any education or praise of them is wasted; they get a portion of disgrace and scorn. They spread gossip, talk too much, cannot keep secrets, can't deliver messages or apply proverbs, repeat mistakes, and are unemployable. They are subject to anger and lack sensibility, and any projects they have are utterly in vain.

Mother offers teachings that are like a garment or chain or tablet of memory about the neck.

Evil Sinners are bloodthirsty slayers and plunderers of the innocent. Devious and subversive talkers, they are sleepless unless planning evil. They will be cut off from the land and cursed by God.

Wisdom was bestowed by the Lord and linked with discretion. She calls at the place of counsel (the city gates) and wants to fill *the simple* with her spirit; she laughs at the fate (terror, storm, and anguish) of *fools* who don't listen to her. Paying attention to her is like silver, gold, jewels, or coral. She saves from adulteries, she gives longevity, prosperity, and honor, and she crowns with a garland those who love cherish and embrace her. She is the tree of life and laid the world's foundations.

The Insolent love being rude and have no fear of God and no wisdom.

The Stupid hate knowledge and spend money fast; they have no fear of God or any wisdom, and think they know best.

The Upright have ability.

The Blameless are shielded by God and are watched on their way. They will dwell in the land.

The Adultress has loose, smooth, honeyed words and forgets her original partner and the covenant; unconcerned with her twisted nature, she leads to the no-return of death.

The Son is trusting, loyal, faithful, not too self-reliant, honorable, and pious. God rewards a son but can chasten him. He walks straight, sleeps well, and does not fear traps.

The Wise spread wisdom and knowledge, walk in the way of life, think before acting or talking, and are known for their understanding. They do not tell lies.

The Scornful are met with scorn by God.

Your Wife should be surrounded with your continual love. Be content with her, and drink water from your own cistern.

The Wicked have no mercy; they are slanderous, hurtful deceivers who spread gossip and rumors and are cruel to their animals. They are caught in a shroud of sin and will perish in their folly. They run when they are stood up to. Hated by God, they are destined for destruction; disaster will come upon them like a storm.

The Ant is an example of a hard worker who avoids slumber.

The Scoundrel or Knave is a mischief maker who needs the remedy of being broken.

The Lazy are subject to poverty or slavery; they are always caught unprepared because they never harvest; they are difficult and unreliable.

The Conceited give insults when corrected, do not ask for advice, and are wise in only their own eyes. They never become wise; they are arrogant, proud, and inconsiderate.

The Shameless Woman is wise in her own ways but stupid. She is a time waster who tells the foolish that fraud and theft are better than honesty. She leads to death.

The Miser is cursed.

The Honest are safe; they treat others fairly and rescue them by standing firm. They lead happy lives.

The Proud are disgraces.

A Nagging Wife is like a dripping tap. It is better to be away from her in solitude.

A Capable Wife has her husband's confidence; she does good, weaves cloth, brings food, rises early, grows food on her own land, and works hard and late. She is generous to the poor and needy.

Her husband is respected by others. She is strong, respected, and mild in counsel.

Hypocrites hide hatred behind masks of flattering words, but the evil they do can be seen.

The Humble are respected.

Friends are not to be forgotten; a close neighbor is better than a distant relative. A hurtful rebuke from a friend is better than an enemy pretending to be friendly.

The Selfish are in a hurry to get rich; because they are unfaithful to God, they will become poor.

Rulers who are righteous have strong, happy subjects; wicked rulers have a miserable people who are happy to see their downfall.

Strong Drink is to cheer those who really need it, not drunkards.

The Apocrypha

The Apocrypha tends to contain true inspiration and clearly some fiction as in the case of the stirring book of Judith, which contradicts itself over a matter of kings; however much many evangelical Christians have found it has spoken to them as John Bunyan[26] did, it behooves anyone who reads it to do so cautiously and critically in light of accepted canonical Scripture in the Judeo-Christian tradition.

Ecclesiasticus

The first of the apocryphal books we shall examine was originally written by a Jew in Hebrew. It was translated, as its preface indicates, into Greek by his grandson. Despite its Hebrew provenance, it was never accepted in the canon because of the clear **Sadducee** sentiments of the author; it is clear he did not believe in a life to come but only that a good name would live on (for example, 39:11).

Like the Sadducees, he was a temple rather than a synagogue man; he had an interest and knowledge of the temple, its priesthood and rituals, and also Israel's history (Chronicles 44). But his major interest lay in Wisdom and the Law. In fact, he came close to identifying Wisdom with the Law (Chronicles 24:23). That did not mean, however, that Wisdom was restricted to Israel more clearly than the earlier literature, which would not have been aimed at a wider Mediterranean world (1:9–10): Wisdom is gifted to all godly people with true worship as its outward expression (14:10). The wise were predestined and were heirs to her overflowing generosity (Chronicles 1:14–17). Wisdom was given a more sensuous slant with those who desire her, wish to look in her window, want to listen at her keyhole and pitch their tents in her cooling shade that is there for her children (Chronicles 14). Also in 24:13–22, Wisdom recommended herself by her sweet, spicy fragrance. These verses are certainly more redolent of the Canticle than Proverbs.[29]

In an expression of self-recommendation that is like Proverbs 8, Wisdom stated her place in creation before time. She was the Word, the Logos, and her establishment was Zion. Unlike Proverbs, the book really divides into only three parts: the preface; the series of moral statements with recommendations of Wisdom; and from 44 onward, "the praise of famous men,"[29] which is well known and need not concern us.

Some of the advice given, such as confining unmarried daughters, beating sons and servants, a certain amount of contempt for the poor, and being unwelcoming to strangers adds weight to its not being in the canon. In addition, some sayings of Jesus that were echoed in the text may be discerned. For example, the young man in 6:23–30 was advised to "put your feet in Wisdom's fetters and your neck into her collar. Stoop to carry her on your shoulders and do not chafe at her bonds" (6:24–25). The writer seemed to be portraying Sophia as something of a dominatrix! Jesus surely knew this passage, and his response to this was in Matthew 11: 28–30, where he advised those who were weary to take up his yoke, the ironic difference being that his yoke was easy and light! It is clear from this and similar sayings that he identified himself with Holy Wisdom but not the whole of the ideas of the Apocrypha.

The Wisdom of Solomon

The other apocryphal wisdom book to note was originally written in Greek by a single author, which means it could not have been included in the Hebrew canon. Of course, nobody has ever thought that it has any connection with Solomon despite its desire to identify with him. This does not, however, detract from its value.

The book divides into four sections: chapters 1–5, the role of Wisdom in destiny, individual and corporate; chapters 6–9, the sources of Wisdom; chapters 10–13 Wisdom in Israel's history; chapters 13–15, the evils of idolatry; and 16–19, the deliverance from Egypt.[29]

The writer seemed to have a clear aim: to contrast the true, godly Wisdom who took her seat in Zion from the godless, worldly, Greek wisdom of the age that even he seemed to have been affected by. What is particularly interesting is that right from the start, he stated that God revealed himself to the simple in heart (such are the kingdom of heaven), that Holy Wisdom is a Spirit of discipline, and that the "Spirit of the Lord fills the whole earth, and that which holds all things together knows well everything that is said" (1:7–8). Here is a clear statement of the universal omnipresence of the Holy Spirit and one that stamped the Holy Spirit with the nature of Holy Wisdom.

There is also a clear contrast with Ecclesiasticus in 2 in that unlike the wicked, who say that no man has ever returned from the grave saying, "Let us crown ourselves with rosebuds before they wither" (2:8) and know that the servants of the Lord are a living condemnation of what they stand for, the writer knew "God created man imperishable and made him the image of his own eternal self" (2:23). He wrote that the Devil's spite brought death into the world and that the experience of death was reserved for those who took sides with him: this judgment would be messianic (3:7–9) and spirit-driven like fire. The day of judgment theme is carried on in chapter 5.

The nature of Wisdom was given in 7:22–30 (the writer balked at stating her origins). She was a holy, intelligent Spirit, subtle, lucid, clear, and invulnerable; loving, good, generous, carefree, omnipotent, all seeing, and spiritually and materially omnipresent. She arose from the power of God. Putting himself in the shoes of Solomon, the author described how he longed to win Wisdom as his lovely princess bride with virtue as his object. Wisdom brought her fruits (of the Spirit), temperance, and prudence, solved problems, puzzles, and portents, and made him a great and respected king. The section ends in chapter 9 with a prayer empathizing with Solomon for Wisdom from God.

The book traced the history of humanity since the fall and how Wisdom had guided the thinking and craft of the righteous— Noah, Abraham, Lot, Jacob, Joseph, and Moses. From there, the writer moved on to describe the Exodus and the fundamental evil of idolatry.[29]

There are a few caveats that need to be noted in the application of this book in that it shows traces of contemporary Platonic and Stoic thinking. In particular, the writer hinted at the preexistence of the soul in 8:19: "A good soul fell to my lot … I entered an undefiled body." Also, he fell into the trap of stating the contemporary notion that instead of the universe being created

ex nihilo, out of nothing, there was a *material prima* or original, formless matter: "For thy almighty hand which created the world out of formless matter" (11:17). Also, he showed the influence of the **Stoics** by adapting their four cardinal virtues of self-control, prudence, courage, and justice, not that this was wrong in itself; St. John was not afraid to adapt to **Stoic** terminology by calling the incarnate one the word or *logos*.

Ecclesiastes

Melancholia I, 1514
Albrecht Dürer (1471–1528)

Before examining Kierkegaard's stages along life's way in relation to the Bible, we need to examine the third set of Scriptures relating to his last or religious stage of life secured by a leap of faith. We should bear in mind that he sometimes referred to the last two stages as blending into one another as the "ethico-religious" stage; first Ecclesiastes, and then Job.

Let us set the scene. The autumn leaves are falling. Propped up against their house, a Jewish family has erected a temporary shelter with a flimsy roof that is not much protection against the elements. It is here that they will live and eat for the next week. It is the Feast of Tabernacles or *Sukkoth*. The autumn weather reminds them (as Christians might with their "harvest festivals") of the joy of the final harvest of the year and the transience of time and the seasons. The festival will include the liturgical reading of the book of Ecclesiastes.[6]

The Hebrew name for the book is *Qoheleth*; this can be approximately translated as "preacher to the congregation." Its inclusion in the Hebrew canon at first seems strange due to its apparently incoherent style that verges on the paradoxical and even the self-contradictory, its attack on the conventional portrayal of the kind of Wisdom in the books discussed above, and its unorthodox lack of dialogue markers.[29] Despite this, rabbinical opinion (Rabbi Akiba at Jamina) held, "At the beginning and the end are the words of the Law." It may be induced that it contains the Law.[6] Of course, it claims to have as its source the thoughts of Solomon as an old man reflecting on his experiences. Perhaps in a strangely prophetic way, it shows up as a voice crying in the wilderness, the crisis in Wisdom teaching being experienced at the time the book was finally edited along with the editorial remarks at the beginning and end of the book giving it credence. By tradition, Ecclesiastes reflects Solomon's religious reflections on life in old age.[26] There is ironical humor here in the switch to the religious stage in that the testimony he offered contrasts with the pompous stone monuments testifying to other ancient kings' achievements.

Ecclesiastes has a rambling style, but two expressions that keep recurring are *hevel*, a puff of smoke or wind translated as "meaninglessness" or "vanity," and "under the sun," meaning the warmth of life outside the grave.[29] The writer described how he tried to find life in the aesthetic stage of wine, women, song, and much else but found it worthless and then sought wisdom in the ethical stage, which indeed has its benefits and is better than folly, but found death inscrutable. He was not unduly pessimistic knowing that the spirit returned to God. Death, however, remained a mystery.

Those who want to pin down a date for the book have little to go on. Even the statements that the writer was "king in Jerusalem" (Ecclesiastes 1:1) and "all my predecessors" (1:16) do not necessarily mean Solomon abdicated or was referring to previous kings.[26] What this does indicate is that the book is written as a royal testament,[13] a type of document common at the time in which a king described the achievements of his life, often chiseled in walls of stone for modern archaeologists to discover. In a sense, the book is an ironical parody of these grandiose inscriptions because it says it was all *hevel*.

As I have indicated above, the strongest evidence that the book originated from about 1000 BC comes from the continued use of the phrase "under the sun" in the text; this expression was common in Middle Eastern writings of that era[13] but would not have fit in well with a Jew writing in the Hellenistic era as it may have had overtones of reference to the god **Apollo**.

The greatest thing about the book is its anti-agnostic and anti-atheistic stance. In spite of all the random absurdity of life and the uncertainty of things to come that *Qoheleth* mercilessly exposed, he clung to faith in God and his covenant like a limpet to a rock.

The book was a favorite of **Martin Luther**, who wrote, "This book ... deserves to be in everyone's hands and to be familiar to them" and "The benefit that the book can give has been neglected" (*Luther's Works* Vol. 15).

The themes and applications of this complex book may now be analyzed and Christ found in it. The book starts by stating it is the words of the king who was Son of David—if not Solomon, then at least an allusion to him. The next words are the constant background theme to the book translated in the English of the King James Version as "vanity" and in the New International Version as "meaninglessness." As mentioned above, the original Hebrew word is *hevel*, with "vanity of vanities" rendered as *hevel hevellim*. *Hevel* is used elsewhere in the Old Testament to signify the brevity of human life as in Job 7:7 and Psalm 39:5. So a "vanity of vanities" (AV) is something that is transitory and insubstantial. Interestingly, the original Hebrew of Adam and Eve's son Abel is also *Hevel*.

Other Wisdom teachers, who were more pragmatic, did not make such wide-ranging inductions or abstractions, but *Qoheleth* did right from the start, and the thrust of the book is an expansion of this basic theme.

Chapters 1 and 2

Qoheleth tried to find meaning in a life, which seemed to be a series of impersonal cycles of nature (1:4–11); here, he tried to find meaning in work, learning, or pleasure, in other words, the aesthetic stage of life. A subsidiary theme of the book appears in 1:9, "things done under the sun,"[26] that is, under heaven—the things of earth and the earthly life. The writer sensibly concluded it was best to enjoy these things while they lasted as "a gift of God," something to thank him for, which the ungodly would not. In 2:12–16, *Qoheleth* compared Wisdom with folly and concluded that the wise and the fool would end up dead and forgotten. Nevertheless, Wisdom was better than folly because in itself it has its own reward. This is the *ethical* stage of life

Chapters 3 and 4: The Uncertainty of Life "Under the Sun"

Here, *Qoheleth* turned to life's problems. God had determined the "times and seasons" of things and called the shots, so like a soldier under a general, we cannot work out exactly what God is doing or why (3:11). Again, it is better to live for the moment and make the most of it. Fortunately for the Christian, death has lost its sting. But like the animals (Latin *anima*, "soul"), we die and again can't take our possessions with us. It is sensible to accept friendship (3:12–13), joy in our useful work (3:13, 22) and community (4:7–12) as gifts from God with thanksgiving, but *for* them as we do, as we do not know when life will end.

Chapter 5: The Theology of Wise Imperative[29]

It is not unusual for Middle Eastern people today to indicate what they *must* do in a given situation almost as a matter of ritual: the young bride must go to the hairdresser's; she must have all her body hair removed before marriage, and she must have an appropriate dowry. Here, things are more to do with the sanctuary of God, which would be in keeping with the priestly concern of a Solomon. In particular, it is better to say nothing before God (who knows our concerns anyway as Christ said in his introduction to the Lord's Prayer) than to make vows or say things before God that are not meant.

Here we have a firm anchor of the book in the Ten Commandments, as such foolishness is "taking the Lord's name in vain" (Exodus 20:7; Deuteronomy 5:11). The Lord's name is not *Hevel*. It is my contention that those who put this book into the canon must have noticed this. As Christ also said, "Do not go babbling on like the heathen who imagine the more they say the more they will be heard" (Matthew 6:7). The word of Christ about the fall always being with us and the love of riches are also echoed in 5:8–11. On the other hand, honest, hard work is rewarded with a good night's sleep,[26] the nearest thing in this life to a quiet state of death, whereas "the abundance of a rich man permits no sleep."

Chapters 6:1–9

In the **Masoretic text** of the Hebrew Bible is an indication that the first half of the book stops at verse 9.[29] The concert of eternity is being squeezed into temporal time in that even if a man lived two thousand years and had hundreds of children, it would mean nothing if he had not enjoyed what he had for the moment, that is, existentially.

It mentions a proper burial, another priestly concern with correct ritual, but here also it hints at resurrection, which is what burial as opposed to cremation, say, signifies. The stillborn are said to be better off than those who lack the gift of contentment, which is a direct corollary of the Tenth Commandment.

Chapters 9 and 10

The theme of mortality is reiterated. Death comes to all, both the good and the bad, so life even as a "dog" is better than a "noble" death as a lion. The dead know nothing of life that goes on under the sun,[26] although that does not mean the souls of the dead are not in God's hands. The themes of time and chance in life that occur in chapter 3 are brought out again in 9:1 (*O fortuna velut luna!*), but wisdom is again praised as better than weapons. As Sun Tzu put it, the supreme excellence is to obtain victory without fighting, but the trouble is no one remembers generals who win that way: "A great king came to attack ... There was in it [the town] a poor wise man, and he saved the town by his wisdom. But nobody remembered that poor wise man" (9:14, 15).

Chapter 10

The theme of meaninglessness, *hevel*, dies away, although the theme of us mortals under the sun does not. The destructive, erosive nature of folly against Wisdom is pointed out, as are the topsy-turvy nature of human affairs and accidents, although sage advice is given about overcoming the vicissitudes of fate through the use of sharp tools, diligent maintenance, activity, prudent speech, and spending money. Thus, *Fortuna* can be overcome by the exercise of *virtu*. Throughout, the advice of enjoying the good things of life while they last is reiterated.

Chapter 11:1–7

Again, repetition of the themes of time and chance found in chapter 3 occurs, with specific application and allusion to agriculture. In other words, some risks must be taken in life if there is to be any kind of harvest or success.[26] This is the quality of *virtu*. Though in the inscrutable providence and will of God, we cannot know the result, if we don't try, we don't get; nothing ventured nothing gained.

Chapters 11:7–12:8

This is the well-known passage that enjoins remembrance and consciousness of the Creator, who gives life to us and in the end takes it back. It is not entirely pessimistic about death, though, as it says that although the body of dust goes down to the grave, the spirit returns to the God who gave it. This echoes *Qoheleth*'s ritual concern with the burial that prefigures resurrection as a seed is planted in the ground (12:8). The days of darkness (in **sheol)** will be many (11:8), but that does not mean they will be eternal. The advice to the young is to "let their heart and eyes show you the way" (11:9; Hebrew *kalb*, "heart") with joy (the aesthetic stage of life), but to remember God will judge if you behave like a dog perhaps (Hebrew *kaleb*), or perhaps as the **Talmud** notes, "for the good things we refused to enjoy"; then anxiety (*angst*) can be cast off.[6]

The reiteration of "remembering our Creator in the days of our youth" (12:1) is followed by an allegorical or parable-like description of old age and the fragility and loss of pleasure that it brings: the "strong men" may refer to the limbs losing their muscle tone; "the women grinding the mill are few"—we lose teeth; "those looking through the windows see no longer"—the eyes grow dim; "the sound of the mill fades" could refer to incapacity for work; faint birdsong to the loss of hearing; fear of heights with the associated fear of breaking brittle bones; and the almond tree in blossom with white hair and loss of mobility with dragging yourself along like a defunct grasshopper. Old age, of course, ends in death: a silver cord, golden bowl, wheel, and pitcher broken, possibly suggesting the complete breakdown of bodily functions preceding it. The passage then concludes with the *hevel hevellim* that started the book.[26]

Chapter 12:9–13: Final Editorial Comment

Qoholeth may well have been a priest[29]: in addition to his concern for the house of God, he acted in the priestly role of "imparting knowledge to the [assembly] people." These are words inspired by the one true shepherd; the "sharp goads" and "nails driven home" of 12:11 may well remind us of the crucifixion, and the warning not to add to the Word of God is echoed in the Torah and at the end of the book of Revelation. Too many "me" books and much study are bad; it is better to live by the light of wise experience existentially, by the "university of life," as we say.

Finally, in 12:13, 14, the end of it all, the *aleph* and *tau*, the alpha and omega, is the only sensible stage of living: the religious stage to fear God and obey him, knowing he knows all and will judge all.[20]

Stylistic Interpretation

It is difficult to summarize Ecclesiastes, but some features make it seem like a tone poem or symphony in a minor key, carefully crafted by a good composer. Firstly, there are two expressions that occur like counterpointed leitmotifs in the book scattered many times throughout the text: the word *hevel* discussed above, but also the expression "under the sun" (which is an exact translation of the Hebrew). The latter of these two expressions draws a distinction not so much between this earth and heaven as between the land of the living and that of the dead, sheol. To be alive is to see the sun and experience its warmth and light in the world of human time compared with whatever kind of life (if any) exists beyond the grave, beyond temporal experience.

Qoheleth's inquiries and observations were skeptically restricted in this sense; it is not so much that he did not believe in existence beyond the grave, but he refused, unlike other nations, to speculate on it. His observations were about this life. Second, on top of the background boogie beat of "vanity under the sun,"

43

Qoheleth superimposed several "movements" to his tone poem of life split into two main sections. Beginning at 6:9, a movement deals with cycles and times: Wisdom, folly and pleasure, work and toil, fate and fortune, human relationships, vows and death coming to all.

Another movement reiterates many of these themes but much more in the style of an orthodox Wisdom teacher and concluding with a "coda" of an allegory of old age and death.

Third, as a skilled composer can be recognized by the chord shapes in his work, so *Qoheleth* repeats many of his themes in a chain on the enjoyment of this transient life and Wisdom and folly to make a varied but well-rounded and thoroughly memorable work. If we take the view that the editor of the remarks at the beginning and end of the book was not the original author, it may well have been memorized verbally or even sung as some kind of choral piece even to musical accompaniment before it was written down.

A modern composer, Samuel Barber, wrote a one-movement extended cantata with four subdivisions for a large orchestra with a choir and incidental soprano, alto, and tenor solos based on the personal devotions of Kierkegaard, which he records in his *Journals*, called *Prayers of Kierkegaard* (*Opus 30*, 1954).

Martin Luther had his own summary of the book in his commentary on it.

> The summary and aim of this book then is as follows: Solomon wants to put us at peace and to give us a quiet mind in the everyday affairs and business of this life, so that we live contentedly in the present without care and yearning about the future and are, as St. Paul says, without care and anxiety (Phil 4:6). It is useless to plague oneself with anxiety about the future. Or as Christ Himself put it "sufficient unto

the day is the evil thereof." (Matthew 6:34 AV; *Luther's Works* Vol. 15)

The Relationship of *Qoholeth* to God's Law and the Gospel

I hope I can indicate that *Qoheleth* is the most God centered and indeed messianic of the Wisdom Literature. It is not a book for moralists or Pharisees, but its most sublime statements regarding the requirements of God's Law and the promise of a redeeming Christ are understated and entwined in the text. It encourages those who are willing to embrace the religious stage of life and make a leap of faith, and yet it indicates that life should indeed be enjoyed for its aesthetic value with no need for unnecessary asceticism.

There is also value in wise morality and ethics. The abandonment of pleasure (2:1–11) and Wisdom (2:12–16) leads to an almost epicurean view of simple, honest enjoyment of life with the acknowledgement that times and seasons unknown to us lie in the hands of the Almighty, incidentally strongly condemning any futuristic prediction or interpretation of prophesy, which nevertheless has ethical lessons. Above faulty human justice (3:16)—most brutally seen in the trial and passion of Christ—is the knowledge that God is the ultimate righteous judge (3:17).

The commandment not to take the Lord's name in vain is seen strongly in 5:1 and contrasted with the hypocritical prayers and vows of fools (as in Jesus' parable of the tax-collector and the Pharisee). False vows lead to the wrath of a righteous God. The love of money, with the covetousness implicitly forbidden by the tenth commandment, is stressed in 5:10–17; again, Christ's words "it is easier for a camel to pass through the eye of a needle than for a rich man to get into the Kingdom of Heaven," the uselessness of storing "riches on earth," and the parable of the man who built himself new barns only to find he was called to die spring to mind. The commandments against theft (extortion and bribery) and murder (anger) are strongly hinted at in 7:7, 8 as is warmongering. Adultery (the ensnaring woman) is condemned in 7:26.

Qoheleth concluded after all this that only God was righteous, but he had found only one righteous man (7:28). Who can this be, if it does not prefigure Jesus Christ? The righteous get what the wicked deserve, and of course, all must die anyway (8:14). Was this not true of Christ? It was all very unfair, wasn't it? So in addition to taking the sins of the wicked in atonement, he was also taking on the crazy unfairness of life upon himself and took it to sheol before his resurrection to new and meaningful life.

In addition to all the above, two other points can perhaps be induced by their absence in the text.[29] First, as I have mentioned above, in spite of his down-to-earth observations, *Qoholeth* was making it absolutely clear that he was dedicated to the God of the covenant in alignment with the first commandment rather than an agnostic, atheistic, or even non-theistic view. Second, by studiously avoiding any picture of God or even a description of what he was like, by metaphor, *Qoholeth* was free of any hint of imagery and was in line with the second commandment against idolatry.

The man or woman who has finally given up on an aesthetic way of life and the pursuit of duty through wisdom and ethics is ready to make the leap of faith into the religious, theistic stage of life that *Qoholeth* said was the foundation of existence. When this occurs, the person in "losing their life will find it," and the wholesome pleasures of life and wisdom and ethics in duty fold back on it and will take their place in life. Of course, it makes sense only to those who have accepted Christ and have been born again, or to give a more word-for-word and I believe better translation of the Greek *ex ouranou,* born of heaven.

To anyone else, like many a Jew and indeed *Qoheleth* himself, the future, especially after death, remained unknown. So I would like to add one final aside in exegesis of the text: *Qoheleth* was not a prophet but an inspired wisdom teacher; he knew that to those of us under the sun, the future was unknowable. It was only to those prophets inspired by the Holy Spirit or angelic revelation prior to Christ that God made the future known, and if their predictions were proven false, according to the Law of the covenant, they were liable for the death penalty. An obvious ramification of this is that all fortune-telling is condemned as useless or worse. It is also the height of folly to give future and definite predictions of unfulfilled prophesy as for example with the book of Revelation. We may be able to see that a prophesy has been fulfilled in the past, as indeed many of those relating to Jesus were, but if one gives an interpretive prediction just because one fancies oneself a prophet, one has become "a fly in the ointment" of the church as well as a fool.

The Book of Job

On the rear gates to the Bristol Zoo is a quote from the book of Job: "Ask of the beasts and they shall tell thee" (Job 12:7 AV). As one strolls around these gardens considering all the strange fauna collected from every corner of the globe, one is indeed faced with many of the questions concerning the nature of creation, life, and existence.

Although somewhat apart from the other Wisdom Literature, the book of Job shares many of the themes of Ecclesiastes. It discusses why the righteous suffer and die unjustly. In short, its main highlight is **theodicy**. But my main interest here is not so much the unfairness of life—life isn't fair—but on our response to life as it is.

The book, or at least its story, is of ancient provenance and may have its origins in the southwest part of the Arabian Peninsula. In Hebrew, it has a peculiar archaic style that backs this up.[26] For this reason, I have included the more well-known quotes from the AV parallel to the word-for-word REV translation I am using.

A cursory reading makes the book seem like three or four men chewing the fat on the town rubbish heap as to what life is all about, but the book divides fairly straightforwardly: the tragic prologue (chapters 1 and 2), speeches containing the battle of wits (actually a kind of series of dialectics) between Job and his friends (3–31), Elihu's speeches (32-37), then Job's submission to God through the divine monologue, and the final epilogue in which Job is restored. (38–42:6); [26] On reflection, in terms of Aristotle's *Poetics*, the story is a kind of comedy because it begins badly but ends well; a tragedy would begin well and end badly.

Chapter 28:1–11 is of interest in that it describes humanity's technical ability, especially in mining operations, but what follows is a description of the kind of wisdom that can be associated only with God in creation; even Job's unorthodox take that being wise should not shield him from affliction that cannot be counted as judgment from God does not prevent him from thinking he may have an answer to it all. In the divine speech in chapter 28, the primary question asked by God is not to suggest that his creation is not open to objective, scientific enquiry; it is an existential one: "Where were *you* when I laid the Earth's foundations" (38:4). It is a question that we can all ask ourselves. The encyclopedic list of the marvels of nature of meteorological, biological, and other things culminates in a stunning description of reptilian, almost dinosaur-like power as seen in Leviathan (crocodile?) all fitting into this category. So the questions become, Why do we exist as individuals? Why is there such strange diversity in nature instead of a kind of lumpen uniformity? Why does anything exist at all? All this in the end is held only by the Wisdom of God, which covers suffering in history and the individual.

Finally, Job realized this and submitted in a leap of faith and wonder. Job certainly took the attitude of the infinite resignation, in Kierkegaard's religious phase discussed below, in terms of the suffering that God has allowed to be inflicted upon him, but his attitude of faith in the end brings, in true Old Testament style, only temporal restoration of health and possessions rather than eternal reward beyond the grave. Like *Qoheleth* though, Job is not afraid to believe in resurrection when he stated, "I shall discern my witness standing at my side and see my defending counsel even God himself whom I shall see with my own eyes, I myself and no other" (19:26, 27) or "though worms destroy this body, yet in my flesh shall I see God" (19:26 AV)

In addition to the technological skills of humanity, which are in a way spin offs of the fall, when humanity became aware of knowledge for good and evil (as I shall discus below in my chapter about the fall) and the contrast with the marvelous creative power of God, Job can be subject to other analyses, perhaps one of the most penetrating of these by the existentialist writer Martin Buber.[17] In addition to treating Job as an individual, Buber, as a Jew, saw his sufferings as relating to the whole of Israel. The critical question for him was not so much why God permitted the suffering but why as an omnipotent being he made Job suffer. Buber discerned four views of God's relationship to man's suffering in the text. According to Buber, there are four views.

The first is in the prologue. God had gratuitously allowed a creature, who was ultimately under his control (Satan, the hinderer or adversary) to wander the earth and to entice a God-fearing man to find if he could break his faith. The non-breakage proved man was true as man and still blessed God. The same "blessed" word as we might put as an adjective in colloquial English is *barekh* in Hebrew and used when Job's wife told him to curse God and die.

A second view is shown by Job's friends; theirs was a simplistic, dogmatic view of causality of suffering caused by sin. What is particularly hurtful to the individual is that this is often the sanctimonious view. Yet as Jesus pointed out to those who wanted to know which sin a man was being punished for because of his disability, he remarked that his suffering was to show the glory of God in his healing. Like the good physician he was, he never passed judgment on those he healed. The God of a man's soul often defies commonsense and any reasonable and rational system, as Job found, and may even appear to be cruel, but it is not a commonsense universe.

A third view is that of a complaining Job. It is that of a God who goes back on his revelation by "hiding his face and treating him as an enemy" (13:24). Justice to him is a God-approved human activity, but God seemed to oppose it by his acts. So although he realized he could not be free from sin, his sufferings far outweighed it. He found he could not have a simple, single faith in God and his justice; there was an incompatibility between human concepts of justice and God's way of working Job could not fathom. Nevertheless, he still experienced God, but it was in the realms of suffering and contradiction. Oh, if he could find God and hear him and directly reason with the deity! God is remote; he seems to rage and yet is silent.

The duality of a truth known to man and a reality sent by God must be reconciled somewhere in the nature of God's unity. There is an eclipse of the divine light. God is indeed the Lord who "makes the light creates darkness" (Isaiah 45:7). Without being unduly smug, the Trinitarian Christian should find it easier to answer this cry of Job. We know God has a part of himself that shares in our suffering and that he is not an irreconcilable lump. As the old hymn K in Rippon's collection put it, "When darkness hides his shining face I rest on his unchanging grace" Furthermore, there is weight given to divine command theory discussed below.

The fourth and final view is that given in the speech of God himself, who finally broke through the stormy darkness and *did* confront Job. God was not just giving a demonstration of his mysterious nature here; God knew Job would not understand the secrets of nature in full, which our science now has revealed only in part; powerful examples from the world of nature were given and contrasted with the skills of humanity. But what was really revealed to Job was not the hidden, ultimate justice of God, which may recompense and compensate, but a justice that was manifest in the created order, one that graciously gave and distributed. In vain, Job had tried to penetrate to God through the human confusion of divine remoteness, but God had drawn near to him instead without losing any of his sublimity.[17]

As we will later find, we must not subject the passionate God to the rules of logic; they are far less commonsense. God justified Job finally because, unlike his friends, he spoke rightly (42:7), and his friends were forgiven for their attitude when he prayed for them.[26]

Job fits in with the Wisdom books. Job 28:1–11 describes humanity's technical ability, especially in mining operations, but what follows is a description of the kind of wisdom that can be associated with God only in creation. Even Job's understanding that being wise should not shield him from an affliction not counting as judgment from God did not prevent him from thinking he may have had an answer to it all.[29] But in the divine speech in 28, the primary question asked by God was again an existential one: "Where were *you* when I laid the Earth's foundations?" followed by a list of the strange diversity of nature. All this was held together only by the Wisdom of God, covering suffering in history and the individual. Finally, Job submitted in a leap of faith and wonder. Job took the attitude of "infinite resignation" in terms of the suffering God had allowed to be inflicted upon him, but his faith eventually brought, in Old Testament style, only temporal restoration of health and possessions rather than eternal reward beyond the grave. But like *Qoholeth*, Job was not afraid to believe in resurrection when he stated "though worms destroy this body, yet in my flesh shall I see God" (19:26 AV).

The secret Wisdom of God, which was under his control and was the key to Job's suffering, showed the great gap that existed between God and humanity and was summed up in Ecclesiastes 5:2: "God is in heaven and you are on earth, so let your words be few." Ecclesiastes and Job knew that wisdom did not lead to an easy life and that everything ended in death, but they still preferred wisdom to folly.[17]

Three Aspects of Wisdom in Job

1. Simply as a literary category, as good advice, and instruction. This can cover everything from behavior at court to mining operations. Although it is latent in all flesh, it has to be developed and cultivated to bear fruit. If not, it results in folly.

2. More to the point, regarding Kierkegaard's ethical stage, is to see wisdom as a lifestyle as with Socrates, say, or as someone fluent in German would put it, *weltanschauung*: the world outlook of the man of duty who lives out his wisdom in his life rather than one who just pays lip service to it. Even so, the secret wisdom known only by God, which was under his control and was the key to Job's suffering, shows the great gap that exists between God and man and is summed up in Ecclesiastes 5:2: "God is in heaven and you are on earth." Wisdom followed assiduously in a life of duty can lead only to despair that can be resolved only by a leap of faith.[29]

The third aspect of wisdom lies in the personalized, divine, Holy Wisdom as discussed above.[26]

53

New Testament Wisdom Presentation

Before moving on to a theology of the person and agency of wisdom, we must examine how it is presented in the wisdom Christology of the New Testament, in which it is clear that it crystallizes in the being of Christ.

In the **Synoptic Gospels,** Jesus' teaching, particularly in the Sermon on the Mount, followed the wisdom format but with much more power. Many of his sayings (Matthew 7:7; Luke 14:11; Mark 9:43) have much in common with the poetic meter in Proverbs.[26] More to the point, there are at least five passages in the Synoptic Gospels that indicate Jesus identified himself with the person of Wisdom.

1. Matthew 11:16–19 and Luke 7:31–35. Jesus was reacting to the criticism that unlike John the Baptist, he was no ascetic. "God's wisdom is proved right by its results" (Matthew 11:19). "Yet Wisdom is proved right by all who are her children" (Luke 7:35). By far, the best explanation is that Jesus was saying that his wise teaching and that of the Baptist would be justified in their fulfillment despite current rejection. Eating and drinking had nothing to do with it.

    Matthew 11:25–30 and Luke 10:21. After a heartrending cry of doom over the cities that rejected him, both gospels have "I thank you Father for hiding these things from the learned and wise and revealing them to the simple." Jesus cried this in the Spirit after hinting at his divine preexistence by saying "I saw Satan fall from heaven" (at the angelic rebellion). As mentioned above, the sayings in Matthew echo Ecclesiasticus (6:28, 6:30, 24:19, 51:23, 51:26, 51:27). Jesus had no problems eulogizing his own merits and qualities as did Wisdom herself in the Old Testament and Apocrypha. This is humility, not egotism, as he was acting as the wisdom teacher getting attention.

2. Matthew 12:42 and Luke 11:31. "The Queen of the South [Sheba] will appear in court when this generation is on trial; for she came from the ends of the earth to listen to the wisdom of Solomon and what is here is greater than Solomon." So Jesus was wiser than the wisest of men; he was Wisdom incarnate. There should be no doubt that this is what Jesus meant.

3. Matthew 23:34–36 and Luke 11:49:51. Jesus had just finished giving the Pharisees a tongue lashing: "This is why the wisdom of God said 'I will send them prophets and messengers'" [Luke 11:49]. The Wisdom of God will send prophets and wise men: I [Jesus] am sending you prophets and wise men and teachers of the law" (Matthew 23:34). Therefore, Jesus was the Wisdom of God.

4. Matthew 23:37–39 and Luke 13:34. These passages of doom against Jerusalem do not mention wisdom specifically, but they clearly echo the threat uttered by wisdom in Proverbs 1:24–30. Also in Ecclesiasticus 24:7–12, Wisdom said her dwelling place should be in Zion or Jerusalem; because her city had rejected him, its doom was certain, and he grieved over it.[29] (i-v)

In contrast to the Scribes and Pharisees, Jesus was closer in his earthy, shrewd, and ironic way to the wisdom teachers, getting to the heart and minds of the common man. But he was more than just using wisdom as a literary device or recommending a sage and righteous lifestyle; he was Wisdom itself, as we will find St. Paul explained.

Wisdom in the Epistles

A highly educated Pharisee, St. Paul was aware that there was a divine Wisdom and a worldly wisdom. A good place to start is in 1 Corinthians 2:3; this distinguishes between divine Wisdom, which is seen as foolishness by the world, and that of the wisdom of the world, which is seen as foolishness by God. At the end of Paul's parentheses in Romans in which he declared that despite their rejection of the gospel, God still had a plan for the Jews, in Romans 11:33–36, he ended with an exalted doxology that extolled the inscrutable depths of God's Wisdom that echoed the final chapters of Job.

Paul was in line with the wisdom teachers of the past, but in 1 Corinthians, he referred to a *secret* wisdom and used it as a descriptive category of Christ himself.[26] Christ was more than Wisdom; the agent of creation had become part of creation, and humanity itself was seen as the main reason for creation: a kind of pre-**anthropic principle** in creation.

Spiritually mature, Christian wisdom of the new age and covenant was seen as not really available to the newly born again but only to those growing spiritually who responded to it as a gift of the sanctifying Holy Spirit. In 1 Corinthians 1:30, Paul stated that Christ was God's and our wisdom prefigured in Proverbs and Ecclesiasticus: "God has made him our wisdom and in him we have our righteousness, our holiness, our liberation." Christ was the Wisdom of God. This messianic conclusion was forced on Paul by the Christ event itself, whereas before, it would have not been clear at all[29]; creation and salvation were held together in the person of Jesus Christ through the Holy Spirit and having their origin in the Father. What is particularly interesting is that Paul was not thinking of it in a detached, objective way but in the subjective terms of his own experience of salvation through Christ as mediator between humanity and God.

In addition to creation and salvation being seen in Christ as an expression of divine wisdom, it may also be seen that Christ displaced the Torah as an expression of the divine wisdom: "The law was given through Moses, but Grace and Truth came through Jesus Christ" (John 1:17). So instead of following the Torah for salvation, all that became was to have faith in Jesus Christ. "I will not nullify the Grace of God; if righteousness comes by Law then Christ died for nothing" (Galatians 2:21).

A wisdom Christology may be inferred in three other major passages.[29]

1. Colossians 1:15–22. Here, Paul indicated Christ's primacy, preexistence, creative sovereignty, and source of salvation in the church.
2. In Hebrews 11:4, the preeminence of Christ the Word, in terms of wisdom categories, without stating the word itself is noted; the incompleteness of the previous revelation is also noted.
3. Most important, the prologue to John's gospel in John 1:1–18 clearly stated Christ's preexistence as "word" and "light" and activity in creation. In doing so, John was appealing to two types: the Jew knowing Ecclesiasticus

(3:5; 7:10, 22, 25, 27; 9:12; 14:12 and 29) but also to the Greek Stoic in terms of the *logos.*

It is not too difficult to see how the essence of wisdom relates hypostatically to the whole of the Godhead. **Hypostasis** is cognate with *sophia*, Greek for "wisdom" or its Hebrew equivalent *hokmah*[26]; they are all feminine in gender. As I have noted above, feminine nouns are in the minority in Hebrew, so it is not surprising that personalization should take place. But Wisdom in the Old Testament is not God though she is close to him.

I have also noted that Holy Wisdom is shown incarnate in Christ and that in both the New Testament and Apocrypha (especially the Wisdom of Solomon), Holy Wisdom is seen as an attribute of the Holy Spirit. Both the Son and the Spirit come from the source and fountain, the Father, or as Calvin was unafraid to say in his *Institutes,* "the divine parent." A good, broad Wisdom theology for the Christian then is to consider that it is an attribute and energy shared by all three persons of the Trinity and seen in its most immediate form in the incarnate Christ of the Gospels. At the same time, it should strip away all notions of a wholly "macho" God, as Wisdom has the womanly qualities of beauty, dignity, desirability, mild counsel, and generosity. A good analogy might be that of the solid figure of the tetrahedron, which has four faces of equilateral triangles, each representing a trinity.

Before we finish with the topic of Wisdom, it may be profitable to consider how it impacts on two deviations from orthodox Christianity. The older is **Arianism**, which states that Christ was not one with the Father from all eternity as part of the Godhead but was the "firstborn" of God's creation and therefore a creature. The creed, however, clearly states that Christ was "begotten, not created." A close examination of the Hebrew text of Proverbs 8 (often quoted by Arians) is needed to make this clear: Proverbs 8.22: "He created me the first of his works." The word translated as "created" is the Hebrew *ganah*, which can also mean "beget" as in human procreation, and it is clear from 22–25 that it means a royal birth in the very nature of the Godhead. The firstborn had the right of primogeniture as firstfruits, inheriting the father's attributes, and had the right to priesthood in the family.[4] "He is the image of the invisible God, his is the primacy over all creation" Colossians 1:15 has this Old Testament implication in mind. In fact, one may tentatively say that Christ offered himself as a firstfruit in sacrifice back to the Father.

The second, more-recent deviation is the worship of Sophia as a separate divine person. There was a fairly recent, short-lived heresy in the Orthodox Church that saw Wisdom as the "fourth" member of the Godhead, but it had little impact and died out. In addition, there have been attempts by some feminists to conduct acts of worship of Sophia. It has to be admitted that this has been precipitated by the idea of an all-male teaching clergy and by extension an all-male God. But God of course is Spirit, and those who worship should do so in spirit and truth. Spirit and the Godhead are fully integrative of gender.

Philosophy

Background and Chronology

It is not my intention to give a long history of philosophy as Bertrand Russell did in *The History of Western Philosophy* or as Richard Tarnas did more recently in *Passion of the Western Mind*. Philosophy deals with "second order" subjects, that is, rather than just thinking about things like cooking or medicine in a practical sense, it deals with the shape, number or the structure of languages.

Philosophy can be roughly said to deal with thinking about thinking! Philosophy is a wide field in which the main areas are aesthetics (what is beauty), **metaphysics** (the study of what can be said to be seen or unseen, concrete or abstract), logic (the study of verbal reasoning—from the Greek *logos*, "word"), ethics (what is morally right or wrong) and **epistemology** (the study of what can be truly known with confidence—from the Greek *pistis*, "faith").

We will be concerned mainly with the last three of these fields, those relevant to our concern. What is now called "science" (from the Latin *scientia*, "knowledge") was originally called "natural philosophy," which Aristotle started to cover in his book *Physics*, Greek for "nature."

In our chronology, we will look at those thinkers who came before Kierkegaard and influenced him, focus on the man himself and those of his contemporaries he reacted against, and examine the thinkers who followed in his footsteps. It is only right that we start with **Socrates** (470–399 BC) since like Kierkegaard, he was deeply concerned with morality, and he considered philosophy to be not so much what we thought but what we did and the way we lived our lives. He also used a lot of devastating irony to undermine any pretension in opponents not so much to teach them anything concrete or objective but to teach them something about themselves. He himself did not write anything, but it is clear from what Plato wrote of him that he used obscure language as much as Kierkegaard did and rarely said exactly what he meant. A good example of this is when the oracle at Delphi called him the wisest man in Athens. He replied that he really knew nothing. However, what he meant was that maybe the oracle was right because although he may indeed have been ignorant of many things, he *knew* he knew nothing.[24]

This use of irony and indirect communication was not restricted to Socrates. Jesus used it as his main method of teaching in parables such as describing the kingdom of heaven as like a mustard seed. Jesus' sense of humor was dry, ironic, and even sarcastic as when he accused the Pharisees of "straining off a midge but gulping down a camel" (Matthew 23:24) or with another similar remark, "It is easier for a camel to pass through the eye of a needle [*sic*] than for a rich man to enter the kingdom of heaven" (Matthew 19:24). Kierkegaard's master's dissertation, "The Concept of Irony,". Kierkegaard sometimes thought of himself as the master of irony.[12]

Another technique Socrates used that has been in philosophy ever since, including that of Kierkegaard and his *bête noir* Hegel, is **dialectic.** Dialectic is simply a discussion of enquiry between two people or points of view. A simple form of this is the common questions and answers you might find in a newspaper or government information sheet. This method reached its zenith in the Middle Ages, when to save precious parchment, students were examined by verbal dialectic argument using strictly laid-down rules of logic. When you mention dialect these days, people often think of dialectic materialism. This is a Marxist term; Marx took much of his thinking from Hegel's work on history and the way he tried to change logic, but as I have indicated above, this is not the only use or meaning of dialectic.

We need to mention **Aristotle** (384–322 BC); he laid down the basic laws of logic, which we will discuss later. Another point about him is that whereas Plato believed the gods had imprinted all knowledge in the human mind and facts about the world could be discovered just by reasoning about them (**innatism**[27]), Aristotle believed that facts could be determined by the use of observation with reason (**empiricism**[22]). Aristotle was of course a giant in the history of thinking, but there is no reason to discuss all his work here.

Jumping forward in time, we perhaps need to mention two French philosophers who were not so much instrumental in Kierkegaard's ideas on life stages but that of ideas of consciousness—René Descartes (1596–1660) and Blaise Pascal (1623–1662). The former is important not just because of the way he reintroduced the concept of innatism as **rationalism,**[22] the notion that everything can be figured out just by thinking about it, into Western philosophy. He is important also because he thought that the only thing one could be completely sure about was one's own thinking as a doubting being, summed up in the well-known saying, "I think therefore I am."

René Descartes by Franz Hals (1582–1666)

Actually, the more I think about this remark, the more I think it could apply to any bodily function other than using your brain, but propriety forbids me to state examples. It does, however, raise the profile of the ramifications of **consciousness**; Kierkegaard would examine consciousness while at the same time reject the idea that it was the only thing we could be sure of and also critically examine rationalism itself.

Blaise Pascal —unknown artist

Pascal was both a genuine Christian and someone who was much closer to Kierkegaard's way of thinking. His best-known work is *Thoughts on Religion and other Subjects*, which is usually shortened to *Thoughts* or *Pensees*. Prefiguring existential thinking and accepting at the same time Descartes' spirit of doubt, he saw the human condition as painfully ambiguous: we are certain only of our own uncertainty. "Man is a reed, the frailest in nature, but he is a <u>thinking</u> reed"[14] superior to the rest of nature and to the beasts who do not know they will die.

Pascal divided human reason into roughly two parts: the first, comparable to Cartesian rationalism, he called "the spirit of geometry," where abstract analytical judgments could be made;

and second, what he called "the spirit of finesse,"[22] which by the experience of bumping around the world, reason grasps intuitively. Pure reason for him could never bring meaning to life or overcome sin; only **God's grace** could do that. One of his famed quotes relates to inward passion is, "The heart has its reasons, of which reason knows nothing."[14]

The intellectual world of the eighteenth century following was largely dominated by the largely English philosophy of empiricism, the central idea of which was to state that our knowledge of the world derived from our direct experience of it through our five senses and our introspective thinking about them.[22] This is not without its problems, because as any stage magician knows, our senses and perception can or can be made to deceive us at times. Nevertheless, our experience of the world directly or through less-deceivable instrumentation is the basis of the scientific method.

Immanuel Kant —unknown artist

Now we need to come to Immanuel Kant (1724–1804). His major effect on philosophy was to try to weave together the two approaches to knowledge of **empiricism** and rationalism. Perhaps his major contribution in the field of the theory of knowledge (epistemology) was to distinguish between the world of things that can be experienced by us, which he called "phenomena," and things in themselves (German: *sich in ding*), which he called **noumena**. Although the latter may be speculatively thought about, they were unavailable to us.[22] We shall examine the ideas of **phenomenology** later.

He made the distinction that others had made that some things can be appropriated only by faith, not reason. Perhaps more pertinent was his distinction between analytic logic, which as in the case of Pascal worked on the data of the sensed, natural world, and his introduction of dialectic reasoning, which operated independently of experience, giving an apparent knowledge of noumena[22]; Hegel was later to expand dialectic reasoning to suit himself.

Also important is Kant's contribution to the field of ethics in his *Critique of Practical Reason* (1788). Here he divorced ethics from divine or any other kind of authoritative demand and placed ethical decisions purely in the hands of the individual: according to his **categorical imperative**, you should "act as if the principle of your action were to become by your will a universal law of nature."[27]

This contrasts with his "hypothetical imperative," in which behavior is governed by a desired outcome, which unlike the former may be governed by self-interest. What he is saying is that everyone should have an individual, altruistic moral code approximating the Golden Rule of doing as you would be done by. This is very interesting because it forms part of the argument that St. Paul built up in the book of Romans as to why we were all under the judgment of God: the Jews had a moral code built on the Law of Moses that was impossible to keep. But everyone no matter what else they believed had their own systems of what was right and wrong and yet they were guilty and liable for judgment because all broke their moral codes. It is interesting that if we take the notion of the categorical imperative rigorously, it would be wrong, as Kant realized, to also tell the whitest of lies, and who has not lied?

Kant also had a theory of aesthetics he published under the title *Critique of Judgment* in which he denied the existence of an idealized existence of beauty, or more significantly, a designer of beautiful objects (which could be God), although he wrote that each of us had a "disinterested pleasure" in discerning beauty we might share with others because of our common or **universal** humanity.[27] Kierkegaard commented on Kant's ethics in his *Journal* in 1847.

> There is only one mistake in Kant's theory of Radical evil. He does not make it clear that the inexplicable, the paradox, is a category of its own. Everything depends upon that. Until now, people have always expressed themselves in the following way: the knowledge that one cannot understand in this or the other does not satisfy science, the aim of which is to understand. Here is the mistake; people ought to say the very opposite: if <u>human</u> science refuses to understand that there is something which it cannot understand, or better still, that there is something about which it clearly understands that it cannot understand it—then all is confusion. For it is the duty of the human understanding to understand that there are things which it cannot understand and what those things are.

Kant was arguably the last of the great Enlightenment thinkers; afterward, things took a turn. For a start, there was the beginning of the Romantic movement. We could start with **Fichte** (1762–1814). Denying the possibility of "things in themselves," he started to argue that the first subject, the ego, was the proper subject of enquiry, in fact, that the world was just one universal superego or "absolute ego."[27] However, he hung on to Kant's notion of dialectic, applying it to this.

Johannes Gottliebe Fichte and Friedrich Wilhelm Joseph Schelling

Engraved by Johann Friedrich Jugel after a painting by Heinrich Anton Dähling (1808).

Schelling (1775–1854), who followed him, was initially influenced by Fichte but later rejected many of his ideas. His initial, seminal idea was in the relationship between conscious and unconscious thought. According to him, the theoretical side of our personalities was governed by our unconscious self, and the practical self then consciously acted it out. This he thought particularly true in creative activities such as art. Like Fichte, though, but more individualistically, he saw this as working itself out subjectively.

Where Schelling showed himself a precursor of Kierkegaard was in papers of 1804. Here he posited three important ideas: first, that although the world through science could be shown to be rational and cohesive in its content, no rational or rationalistic account could be given of its existence. (This was the old chestnut of why anything exists rather than nothing at all.) Second, that the finite world must exist from God, not by a comprehensible process but by a *leap* whereby God's creative ideas fall in a timeless process into actuality. Third, although the content of reality is rational, embodying God's creative ideas, its actual being (the natural world) is one of a state of turning away from God: that is sin and unreason.

History represents the struggle to return to God by humanity and nature; its goal is to reunite with him.[27] This is like what St. Paul said.

> Up to the present as we know, the whole created universe in all its parts groans as if in the pangs of childbirth. What is more, we also, to whom the Spirit is given as the first fruits of the harvest to come, are groaning inwardly while we look forward eagerly to our adoption, our liberation from mortality. (Romans 8:22–23)

Enlightening as Shelling's ideas were, he sought truth in all religions, not just Christianity; his ideas were also more conducive to a will to power rather than a will to meaning.

It may have escaped the attention of others, but a cursory inspection of Schelling's terms seems to reveal that he must have influenced Kierkegaard; except in Schelling's case, there is a leap from God into creation, whereas for Kierkegaard, men and women needed to leap back to him! Kierkegaard made disparaging remarks about Schelling in a letter to his brother Peter on February 27, 1842, while he attended some lectures given by him while he was in Berlin.

> Dear Peter. Schelling drivels on intolerably. If you want to form some idea of what it is like then I will ask you to submit yourself to the following [thought] experiment as a sort of self-inflicted punishment. Imagine Parson R'.s meandering philosophizing, his entirely aimless haphazard knowledge, and Parson Hornsyld's untiring efforts to display his learning, imagine the two combined and in addition an impudence hitherto unequalled by any philosopher; and with that picture

vividly before your poor mind go to the workroom of a prison and you will have some idea of Schelling's philosophy and the temperature one has to hear it in [Kierkegaard did not enjoy hot interiors]. Moreover, in order to intensify it he has conceived the idea of lecturing for longer than usual, and so I have decided not to attend his lectures for as long as I meant to. The question is, which is the better idea … Consequently I have nothing more to do in Berlin. My time is too precious to allow me to take in drop by drop what I should really have to open my mouth to swallow all at once. I am too old to attend lectures and Schelling is too old to give them. His whole doctrine of potency betrays the greatest impotence.

Poor Schelling! I am inclined to think he was having more of a struggle trying to present Hegel's ideas than his own.

Georg Wilhelm Friedrich Hegel

Steel engraving by Lazarus Sichling (1812–1863)
After a lithograph by Julius L. Sebbers (1804–1843)

We now come to Georg Wilhelm Hegel (1770–1831). He held some fruitful ideas, particularly in his consideration of consciousness, although if you look at the portrait of him, you will be left with the indelible impression from his expression that here was a man who was haunted by the thought that he had unleashed an intellectual monster on the world, was afraid to go back on what he had started, and knew it.

Hegel had a magpie mind in his youth and a particular taste for the classics and Greek tragedy. Like Kierkegaard, he had university training in theology. After leading a fairly undistinguished career as a private tutor, schoolmaster, fee-salaried lecturer, editor of a Catholic newspaper, and finally headmaster of a secondary school, he decided he could encompass all philosophy in his *Phenomenology of Spirit* and in *The Science of Logic*, a three-volume work published in 1812, 1813, and 1816.[27] This caused a sensation in Germany and brought him the fame he craved and offers of university professorships. The married Hegel eventually settled into a secure post as professor of philosophy at Heidelberg in his latter year and semiofficial philosopher for the Prussian state.[11]

Many of his ideas on the nature of consciousness; the philosophies of history, nature, and art; social ethics; and civil society have inspired other thinkers. But to get his overall philosophy to work, he had to divorce it from the rules of classical logic. This along with his attempt to encompass all of philosophy within his own "system" provoked Kierkegaard more than anyone else to attacking him.

The development of Hegel's ideas on Christianity is important. He considered himself a Lutheran, so perhaps his Erastian idea that church and state should not be separated any more than it was in the ancient Greek *polis* is understandable. His take on Kant's "categorical imperative" (Kant's version of the Golden Rule) was, "What you can will to be a universal law among men valid also against yourselves according to that maxim act." Furthermore, his *Life of Jesus* stripped him of all supernatural and miraculous acts. Hegel compounded this in two more books, *The Positivity of Christianity* (1795) and *The Spirit of Christianity and its Fate* (1799). In them, Jesus was seen as almost a figure from Greek tragedy wishing to infuse the "mere letter" of the Jewish law with the "beauty" of Hellenistic morals. His term *positivity* represented those laws of freedom and dignity in the Judeo-Christian tradition he thought were no longer infused with a spirit of human dynamism and becoming fetters. Hegel even hinted in these works that Jesus may have been partly, unwittingly, responsible for this.[11]

There is no transcendence or "otherness" in Hegel's god: he is totally immanent. Hegel's **panentheistic** god or "absolute spirit" contains not just the world but also its contradictions and sin as part of its essence. He viewed history as the gradual elimination of those contradictions leading to ultimate unity with the Absolute. He dreamed of a mass *volkreligion* and saw his philosophy transcending religion An initial work, *The Philosophy of History*, was introduced by the remark, "The history of the world is none other than the progress of the consciousness of freedom." He expounded on this idea by examining the progress of world history.[11] This interest in history influenced a later "left wing" Hegelian, Karl Marx.

My main interest in Hegel is in two areas: first, how he tried to systematize all knowledge, and second, how (worst of all) he tried to change the rules of logic. The second point I will deal with in my section on logic; suffice it to say at this stage that he took up Kant's and Fiche's ideas of dialectic reasoning, and rather than seeing it involved only with the non-phenomenal world, he decided it should apply to reality as a whole, everything.

However, we first need to his look at his "system." This is rather complex, even for philosophy students, but it basically sees everything in a state of change or flux, an upward spiral rather than an endless cycle that leads to a final condition of absolute knowledge. His philosophy of absolute idealism saw human progress leading to a state in which all subjectivity would be extinguished and only the pure world of objective knowledge of the absolute spirit (Hegel's idea of "God") would be left.

Hegel was a rationalist who believed the absolute could be conceived through pure reason and the ultimate attainment of humanity in perceiving it was philosophy. Religion, specifically Christianity, took a subsidiary place, as here, God was conceived of only symbolically.[11] He also saw the nation state as the absolute in human affairs; everyone in it should submit to it. This laid the foundation for the later absolutism in Germany and Russia. There is much more that could be commented on, but even Hegel felt that his complex system was not quite finished and that perhaps one of his followers could write a conclusion or "postscript."[12] This led Kierkegaard to write *Concluding Unscientific Statement,* a deliberately long-winded parody of this.

It would be profitable at this point to introduce some technical terms. First, because of his belief in absolute spirit, Hegel is what is termed a **monist**; he was saying that only one basic substance existed, not a variety. Second, he was a **panentheist**, that is, he held that God's creation and God's essence are one and the same. Hegel was also fundamentally an **idealist**[18] (not to be confused with the common usage of the term as of someone who has, perhaps, unrealistic ideals); he was the sort of philosopher who thinks that ideas, not concrete things, are the basis of reality. Both the natural world and human consciousness were to him but manifestations of his absolute spirit. All forms of idealism posit the union of the knower and the known; the object of perception and the one who perceives it are not separate.[11]

Hegel's system goes a step further: subjects and objects are dependent parts of the same thing, "universal absolute spirit." Hegel achieved this trick by changing the rules of logic to suit his thinking; it is a bit like a creative accountant adding two and two to make five. It works like this: one gets two ideas that may be contradictory. One is the **thesis** and the other is the **antithesis**. They are combined to make what he called the **synthesis**. The counterplay of two contradictions was how Hegel redefined the term "dialectic,"[18] and dialectic continues to be thought of in this way by many people. Probably the best known, most basic, and blatant example of this is how he combined the idea of being with the contradictory notion of nonbeing. Hegel ended up not with the sensible thought that these two cancel each other out but with the synthesis of becoming so that when a thing changes, it is what it was not a moment before and it will be what it is not now.[22]

Everything becomes a process without discernible end. Apart from Marx's take on Hegel, it is not too difficult to see where else this system led; it gave epistemological respectability to the hypothesis of biological evolution, the system also meant that because Hegel's god was not apart from his creation but bound up as an extension of essence with it, he, she, or it is in a continual state of change. We may add that some organizations nowadays, if they are not involved in the nitty-gritty business of day-to-day living, are more obsessed with following a process than they are with the result. One thinks of the Circumlocution Office in Charles Dickens *Bleak House*; much time and money is wasted in the public sector and civic affairs such as this.

In a way, Kierkegaard was a prophet of this state of affairs when he wrote in his *Journal* of 1846, "The time will come when it will be considered just as bad taste to give results (now so much in demand and so popular) as it was at one time to point out a moral." In regard to the point of process, perhaps we should also mention the twentieth-century idea of process theology, which while giving the appearance of being biblical and theistic, is obviously related to Hegelianism.

We will discuss Hegel's attack on classical logic he set down in his book *System of Logic* in further detail in the section on logic. There is no transcendence or "otherness" in Hegel's god; he is totally immanent. Hegel's god or absolute spirit contains not just the world but also its contradictions and sin as part of its essence. As mentioned above, he viewed history as the gradual elimination of those contradictions leading to ultimate unity with the Absolute. No doubt the Marxists who followed him saw history in these terms, but also perhaps social Darwinists and Nazis did as well.

Kierkegaard was not alone in being critical of Hegel, but perhaps he was much more scathing. He wrote in his *Journal*,

> If Hegel had written the whole of his logic and then said, in the preface, that it was merely an experiment in thought in which he had even begged the question in many places, then he would certainly have been the greatest thinker who had ever lived. As it is he is merely comic. [And in 1848 after "the year of revolution"]: How often have I shown that fundamentally Hegel makes men into heathens, into a race of animals gifted with reason: For in the animal world, "the individual" is always less important than the race. But it is the peculiarity of the human race, that because the individual is created in the image of God [emphasis added] the "individual "is above the race. This can be wrongly understood and terribly misused: *concedo* [I concede]. But that is Christianity, and *that* is where the battle must be fought.

What a condemnation of the idea of the "mass man" of eugenics and the idea that humanity was just a "naked ape" this is! But those who hide behind the bulwarks of any perceived systematic theology or ecclesiology and fail to internalize their Christianity fare no better.

> In relation to their systems most systemizers are like a man who builds an enormous castle and lives in a shack close by; they do not live in their own enormous systematic buildings. But spiritually that is a decisive objection. Spiritually speaking a man's thought must be the building in which he lives— otherwise everything is topsy-turvy. (*Sickness unto Death.* Taken from *A Kierkegaard Anthology* [1])

It is often remarked that Hegel influenced Kierkegaard. Where he did it was in reaction, but one reaction is particularly interesting. It is that of the use of dialectic: whereas Hegel used the idea in his system to try to modify normal logic, Kierkegaard used the concept of "dialectic tension" in the psychological and spiritual realms in which normal reasoning does not work and the irrational or non-rational holds sway.

It is possible here to summarize the history of thought up to the time of Kierkegaard thus.

1. Initially, everyone believed in just rational thought but accepted, as did Pascal, that some things had to be accepted by faith.
2. Descartes introduced the idea of rationalism whereby it was possible to prove everything (including the necessary existence of God) by the use of pure reason.
3. The empiricists put forward the idea that we can really know things only by our direct observation of them and reflection on them.

4. Kant attempted to reconcile the notions of the empiricists and rationalists with his own system.

5. Hegel finally decided that the best way forward was to keep idealism and rationalism—the notions that pure thought and "spirit" on their own can be the answer to everything—by discarding rationality and the proven rules of logic altogether by his own system.

Kierkegaard's Biography

(Abstracted from a Kierkegaard
Anthology[1] with added comments)

**Sketch of Søren
Kierkegaard**

**Søren's father Michael
Pederson Kierkegaard**

**The Stock Exchange, Copenhagen, 1842, with quays both sides.
(Danish Museum of National History, Fredericksburg Castle)**

Søren Aabye Kierkegaard (1813–1855) was born in Copenhagen, a fair-sized capital city with all the amenities one would expect, including quaint, Baroque architecture. It was the center of cultural life in the Northern world. His was a large house near the city hall at Nytorv. Apart from his study trips to Berlin and a trip to his father's birthplace at Saeding in Danish Jutland, he spent his life in its environs in the main Danish island of Zeeland. His family's origins were on the cold, windswept, sandy heaths of the peninsula of Jutland. His father, Michael Peterson Kierkegaard, described Saeding as "not a village, not even a hamlet, but a scattered parish in the heath country where only shepherds [which he was] and peat-diggers could make out a scanty existence."[7] It was a desolate place where perhaps one felt naked before the all-seeing eye of God as much as one was exposed to the elements, a place where there was nowhere to hide, where the small, stone Lutheran church, even with its brightly painted, predominating pulpit, suggested the utmost poverty and desolation. Søren Kierkegaard remarked on a visit there.

> Here everything lies naked and unveiled before God; and there is no place for the many distractions, the many nooks and crannies where consciousness can hide and from which seriousness so often has trouble in recovering the dispersed thoughts. Here consciousness must definitely and precisely hedge itself in. Truly here upon the heath one may well say. "Where can I escape from your Spirit, where flee your presence." (Psalm 139:7)

Most houses were built of clay blocks, but when Michael made good, he built a thatched house of bricks and timber for his mother and two sisters, the Red House. It was in his downtrodden poverty in this desolate landscape at age twelve that Michael had climbed to the top of a knoll while he was herding sheep and had cursed God, an event that would haunt the family. But poverty was not to be Michael's lot in life. When he was sixteen, his uncle, Niels Saeding, took him to Copenhagen and got him working with a cousin as a "hosier" or cloth merchant. As a shepherd, Michael knew about wool, of course, and additionally was astute and intelligent and soon took over management. He went into trading foodstuffs as well, and in 1788, he was licensed by royal patent to deal in Chinese and East Indian wares as well as merchandise from the Danish West Indies (now the American Virgin Islands) and became very wealthy. However, in 1796, at age forty, he retired and left the business to his nephew. He had been married but two years, and just before his retirement, his wife died. He soon married again to Anne Lund, who had been a servant in his house and who was a distant cousin.

Søren was the last of the children born when Michael was fifty-six and Anne was forty-five. Michael did not lose the **pietism** of his youth and brought up all his children in what he considered the fear of God. There is opinion that Michael not only thought of Søren as his Benjamin—the youngest of his tribe—but also as his Isaac, who could be sacrificed for his guilt about cursing God.

Søren found his father's pressure in this regard intolerable. He later wrote, "To cram Christianity into a child is something which cannot be done." Regarding his role in his father's eyes, Søren later wrote,

> There are two thoughts which arose in my soul so early that I cannot indicate in any way their origin. The first is that there are men whose destiny it is to be sacrificed in one way or another for others in order to bring the idea out (and I wish my peculiar cross was one of them). The other thought is that I

should never be tried by having to work for a living partly because I thought that I should die very young, and partly because I thought in consideration of my peculiar cross that God would spare me this suffering and problem.[7]

Søren believed his family was under a curse. Indeed, before he was twenty-one, his mother and five of his siblings died, leaving himself, the youngest, and the eldest, his brother Peter.

In 1821, when he was eight, Søren started school. After grammar school (Danish *Latinskol*), Kierkegaard went to the University of Copenhagen in 1830 and spent ten years there with a year out, from 1837 to 1838, teaching Latin at his old school. As many students do, he let his hair down somewhat in his early years there in what could be described as the most abandoned and aesthetic part of his life. Although his father wanted him to study theology, Kierkegaard felt his first love was philosophy. After studying this, he spent two years on theology and completed a master's degree in 1841 with "On the Concept of Irony with Constant References to Socrates." After finishing a theology degree in 1840 and his spell as a Latin teacher from 1837 to 1838, he had the official right to preach.

In 1840, he went on a holiday down memory lane to Jutland and soon got engaged to Regine Olsen, whom he had met at the house of the Rørdams, friends of his family, in 1837, when she was only fourteen. Along with the relationship he had had with his father, who had died in 1838, this relationship was to play an important part in his life and thought. He broke off the relationship in 1841 after only four months not because he did not love her but for emotional and philosophical reasons. He wrote in his *Journal*, "If I had faith I would have remained with Regine." Toward the end of her life, after the man she was to marry later (Fritz Schegel) was dead, Regine declared she had loved Kierkegaard all along.

Regine Olsen age 18   and age about 50   Søren's brother
Emil Bærentzen   Bishop Peter
(1799–1868)

A week after breaking his engagement, Kierkegaard traveled to Berlin and enrolled in a course in Hegelian philosophy under Professor Schelling, one of his classmates being Engels! After four months, he had worked out what Hegel was about and returned to Copenhagen to begin what he considered his calling and vocation as a celibate writer. Unfortunately, while he was there in 1843, he bumped into his old flame, Regine, in a church. She nodded to him. To avoid her, he fled to Berlin and wrote what is arguably his greatest work, *Fear and Trembling*. He returned to write with only a few trips away from Copenhagen until his death.

Kierkegaard's writings fall into two clear parts. From 1841 to 1845, he lived comfortably in a large flat in the Nørgaard, writing his pseudonymous works; they form a complete series and involve about half a dozen pseudonyms, some of which appeared in his final works and provided the substance of his outlook on the human condition.

After this period and a gap of over a year, Kierkegaard, exasperated by the complacency of established Christianity, began his "attack on Christendom." Realizing that perhaps his method of indirect communication had not worked, he published polemical works in his own name largely in pamphlet form until his death.

Attacking the state church alienated him from all but his closest friends and family. He had a particular relationship with a satirical daily, *The Corsair*. The editor, Goldschmidt (who had spent a week in prison for satirizing the king) was initially in favor of Kierkegaard's attitude in his work and gave a favorable review to *Either/Or* in his publication. Kierkegaard in response wrote a sarcastic letter to him to the effect that to be praised thus was an insult and that he would rather have had the book attacked as an offense. Naturally slighted, this gave Goldschmidt the opportunity to make personal satirical attacks on him in his paper rather than attacking his ideas.[14] *The Corsair* was sold off in the same year, 1846, and Goldschmidt went on to other journals and books, later feeling ashamed at the hurt he had caused Kierkegaard. Along with his broken engagement, this attack probably hurt Søren more than anything, though he did not admit it.

In 1848, Denmark suffered attack by Prussia over a claim to Schleswig-Holstein following the death of King Christian VIII. Help had been expected from Sweden-Norway, but apart from some volunteers from Denmark's previous province of Skåne, there was none. The upshot was that any hope for Nordic unity such as had been first mooted at the treaty of Kalmar in the fourteenth century, was lost, and only a cultural unity could be hoped for, although considerable Nordic economic and geopolitical unity was achieved after World War II.

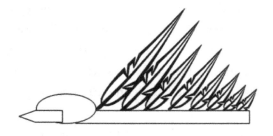

**Author's representation of the logo of the Nordic Council,
an inter-governmental forum for co-operation between the Nordic countries**

It is a stylised swan.The eight quills represent the five Nordic countries of
Denmark (HQ) Sweden, Norway, Finland and Iceland, and the three
autonomous territories of Danish Greenland, The Faeroes and the
Finno/Swedish Åland islands.

In addition, in 1848, the rest of Europe was shaken by revolutions, and the Communist Manifesto came out. It was a time of crisis. Kierkegaard saw a sea change in moral and social outlook that he expressed in his 1846 *The Present Age*. Nothing, he wrote, least of all humanism, "the dregs of Christianity," could halt "the leveling process," and the godless world would exalt the "mass-man." The pseudo-religious culture of Christendom with which real Christianity had been confused would be extinguished, and the individual would be free to choose God rather than humanism. True Christianity would be free of the traditional and cultural rubbish that had surrounded it and be an offense to worldliness.

Kierkegaard spent the remains of his not-inconsiderable inheritance through publications in this attack. It was perhaps a mercy then that in October 1855, just before the last of his pamphlets was due to be printed, he collapsed, exhausted, in the street and was taken to the Frederik's Hospital. He knew he was dying as so many of his siblings had. He refused to see anyone ordained in the state church on principle, and this included his brother, Peter, who was connected with the romanticist Bishop Gruntvig.

Those who did visit him on his deathbed, including his niece and his brother-in-law, were struck by his demeanor. It can be fairly said that a man reveals his true character on his deathbed, and he was said to have a radiance of spirit, gentleness, humor, a sense of proportion, and above all a calm and peaceful faith at his end. He was only forty-two. His birthday, May 5, was the day Danes remember as the day they were liberated after World War II. He died on November 11, Armistice Day after World War I. Many Danes remember these dates in connection with him.

Denmark has had an ambivalent relationship with one of its more famous sons. If you look hard in Copenhagen, you will find an out-of-the-way bronze statue of him copied from a smaller, arguably better, one. But there is no doubt about the impact he made.

Kierkegaard's Works and Pseudonyms

(According to a Kierkegaard anthology[1]
with added comments)

At this stage, it will be profitable to take a parenthetic look at the chronological sequence of Kierkegaard's works together with the **pseudonyms** he used before we examine the seminal work related to the stages of life, together with my interspersed comments. Kierkegaard is hardly concise in his writings; they tend to be verbose, somewhat toffee-nosed, stuck-up, deliberately obscure, and full of classical allusions that those without a thorough grounding in the ancient classics are probably unaware of, and just as full of direct Latin quotations (though somewhat thankfully, as he admits, he was unfamiliar with Hebrew). He did, however write in grammatically correct Danish and was a literary contributor to this somewhat idiomatic language. For those who are bothered to wade through his work, his flashes of prophetic insight shine through.

Like many Danes, he had a liking for the quirky and had a quirky sense of humor; in writing indirectly in pseudonyms, he was having fun devising them as much as he was being serious in hiding behind them. Kierkegaard was a voluminous writer who covered many genres, some within the same book. First, he kept a diary combined with what rhetoricians and writers call a "commonplace book," in which seminal thoughts and feelings (and in his case occasional prayers) that one has on the spur of the moment are noted. It covers all his active life as a writer over twenty years from 1834 to 1842 and up until his death and is published as his *Journals*.

After his master's dissertation on Socrates, his second work was *Either/Or* (1834–1842). In it, he discussed the aesthetic and ethical stages of life under the pseudonym "Victor Eremita," that is, the winner or victor in loneliness. In the "banquet," he was described as a ladies' tailor, and it is difficult not to surmise that this was an allusion to Shakespeare's stalwart woman's tailor, one of Falstaff's conscripts. He is the fictional compiler and editor of the texts Kierkegaard claimed to have found in an antique bookshop.

But there were other pseudonyms in the text: "A" is the moniker given to the fictional author of the first text (*Either*) by Victor Eremita, whose real name he claimed not to have known; "Judge Wilhelm," the fictional author of the second text (*Or*); and "Johannes," the fictional author of a section of *Either* titled *The Diary of a Seducer*. He then gave his pseudonyms a rest and wrote *Two Edifying Discourses* (1843) under his real name. *The Concept of Dread* was written in 1841. *Fear and Trembling* (1843) followed under the pseudonym "Johannes De Silento," Silent John. This pseudonym is an allusion to the Grimm's fairy tale "The Faithful Servant"; it makes sense when we consider the events of the story. The faithful servant Johannes was turned to stone because he warned the king of three dangers. The king felt terrible about what had happened to Johannes and vowed he would do anything to return him to normal. Afterward, the king had two sons, and Johannes—as a stone figure—told the king that if he would cut off the heads of his sons and sprinkle their blood on the stone, Johannes would return to normal. The king did this. After

Johannes became normal, he brought the king's sons back to life. The story ends with the queen exclaiming, "God be praised, he is delivered, and we have our little sons again." In the context of Kierkegaard's book, in which he analyzed the Old Testament story of Abraham and Isaac, Abraham was the one compelled to be silent in the face of God's will when he was told to sacrifice his only, long-awaited son. This book dealt with the movement of faith from the ethical to the religious stage of life.

Repetition was also written in 1843 under the pseudonym "Constantine Constantius." Here, the pseudonym is an allusion to Zeno's paradox that "proved" motion was impossible. Constantine was constant or immovable. This book carried on the theme of *Either/Or* in that it examined the ethical stage of life.

Philosophical Fragments (1844) was written under the name "Johannes Climacus." Kierkegaard's *Concluding Unscientific Postscript* (1846) was his main attack on Hegel written under the same pseudonym. The work has the subtitle *De omnibus dubitandum est*, "Doubt Everything," parodying Descartes. The book is deliberately long winded; it is five times longer than *Philosophical Fragments* because it satirized Hegel's idea that his "system" needed just a short postscript to tie up its loose ends.[12]

> "Hegelian philosophy culminates in the thesis that the outer is the inner and the inner is the outer." [Or to put it in pithier English, "Hegelian philosophy turns everything inside-out."] Instead: "Revelation is signalized by mystery; happiness by suffering; certainty of faith by uncertainty; the ease of a paradoxical religious life by its difficulty and truth by its uncertainty" (*Concluding Unscientific Postscript*).
>
> As Pascal put it "suffering is the natural state of the Christian."[14]

Difficult as this may seem at times it is but the outworking of God's infinite love.

Kierkegaard took this name of Johannes Climacus from a Greek monk (c. 570–649) who was the abbot of Saint Catherine's of Alexandria on Mount Sinai. He was the author of the work *Ladder of Paradise* (532; *klimax* being the Greek for "ladder"). Climacus's work was written for a monastic audience; he wrote that no one should attempt the contemplative life without first warring against and subduing the passions. The ladder is thus a series of thirty steps that led to impassibility and imperturbability; Climacus strove for the heavenly vision. It is read every Lent in Orthodox monasteries, and is appointed to be read aloud in church or in the refectory. Actually, for Danes, the theme of Jacob's ladder was a common one. One is reminded of the Nina and Fredrick song, "We are climbing Jacob's ladder, soldiers of the cross." But for Kierkegaard, the pseudonym Johannes Climacus represented the subjective approach to knowledge.

In Climacus, Kierkegaard put himself in the shoes of a nonbeliever. The ladder was not then the ascent to God but was meant to call to mind an ascending series of logical plateaus on which the logician, represented particularly by Descartes and Hegel, proceeded from one premise to the next. Johannes rejects this method in spiritual matters, thinking it ridiculous to approach the "Absolute" in any way except through faith. He was concerned with subjective knowledge and with the leap. Though Johannes was "no Christian," he led the reader up to the point at which he could make a decision. Subjective creatures could not appropriate objective knowledge, the avowed goal of rationalistic philosophers.[3] Thus, Kierkegaard was concerned with knowledge that would encourage the soul to turn to God.

But again, Johannes claimed not to be a Christian since he had not reached that knowledge of God. The rigorous ascent to God toward impassibility had been replaced by the very passionate and subjective approach to truth whereby the believer, by virtue of the absurd, finds himself before Christ.

A Stage on Life's Way (1846) was written under the name "Hilarius Bookbinder," the editor-compiler-discoverer of this work. *Hilarius* is Latin for joyful or merry. This joyful bookbinder introduced himself, acknowledging the strangeness of a mere bookbinder becoming a publisher. Kierkegaard seems to have been trying to blur the definition of authorship. What was a bookbinder or for that matter Kierkegaard doing publishing?

Let us not forget that Kierkegaard, true to the name Hilarius, was seeking to have fun as well. The pseudo-editor claimed that the work, which comprised three sections corresponding to Kierkegaard's three stages, had been written by different authors. Kierkegaard's little joke was that these separate entities were "left in a bureau, forgotten until their fortuitous discovery years later." Bookbinder claimed to have discovered them only after "realizing that he had inadvertently failed to return them to their rightful owner." He added, "It may be strange for a bookbinder to publish, but ... his sense of duty overrides any reticence he might have."

"William Afham" was the author of the first of the three parts of the stages entitled *In vino veritas* ("in wine, truth"). *Afham* is Danish for "by himself." Since this work was the companion piece to *Either/Or*, it may seem surprising that we encounter a new pseudonym. However, since the religious stage was presented for the first time, the new pseudonym may be justified. Just as in *Sickness unto Death*, Kierkegaard was to write on "despair of willing not to be oneself"; here, as in most of the works up to 1846, he was not willing to reveal himself.

The "Married Man," also known as Judge William, was the author of the second portion of the stages, *Reflections on Marriage*. He was also the author of the second (ethical) portion, or part two of *Either/Or*, otherwise known as author B. He symbolized the ethical stage in his advocacy of marriage, which concept, as we have said elsewhere, was a forward-looking commitment known as repetition, contrasted with the backward-looking (aesthetic) concept of recollection.

"Frater Taciturnus" was the author of the third section, the religious stage. Frater Taciturnus is Latin for the "brother who remains silent." Again, Kierkegaard played with the theme of writing without attributing the work to his own name. Moreover, his work *Guilty?/Not Guilty?* contains "Quidam's" diary. *Quidam* is Latin for "someone." Taciturnus claimed that he "retrieved this diary from the bottom of a lake while he was relaxing with a naturalist, who was doing research." Thus, Taciturnus's find of the book "wrapped in a watertight container" was similar to Bookbinder's find, which is again similar to Eremita's find of the documents comprising *Either/Or*. Note further that a naturalist and, if you will, a supernaturalist were together on the lake, each with his find, another quirky little joke! It is as if Kierkegaard gave us a new either/or, a choice between the findings of the rational scientist and the artifacts of the religious heart.

In sum, the stages had been compiled by a bookbinder who had never published before; the work was by Afham (that is, "by himself"); the next stage was by a Married Man (Kierkegaard had broken off his engagement and thus could not adhere to the repetition of the ethical stage—keeping himself in the aesthetic stage); finally, the last stage was written by someone who remained silent and quoted from Someone.

The use of pseudonym authorship was used afterward only in *Sickness unto Death* (1849) and *Training in Christianity* (1850), when "Anti-climacus" was used. Actually, in the latter book, Kierkegaard pretended merely to be the editor. The prefix *anti* does not mean "against." An old form of *ante*, "before," as in "anticipate," the prefix denotes a relation of rank, as in "before me" in the First Commandment. In his *Journals*, Kierkegaard wrote, "Climacus is lower, denies he is a Christian. Anti-Climacus is higher, a Christian on an extraordinarily high level." Kierkegaard considered this work and *Training in Christianity* to be among his most important. They certainly display great psychological insight.

In all his other works from that point, in his largely second period of authorship, Kierkegaard wrote under his own name. The use of indirect communication and irony was largely abandoned, and in his last publications, freely distributed pamphlets in the last years of his life, he was polemical. In chronological order, they are *The Present Age* (1846), in which Kierkegaard argued that the present age drained the meaning out of ethical concepts through passionless indolence. The concepts are still used but are drained of all meaning by virtue of their detachment from a life view that is passion generated and produces consistent action.

In *Edifying Discourses in Various Spirits* (1847), Kierkegaard discussed different aspects of living in three long essays. In the first, Kierkegaard talked about double mindedness and ethical integrity and left the reader to work out the clues to the nature of the good. In the second, he discussed how if we focused on the birds and the lilies in silence, we would come to realize the joy of being human. In the third part, Kierkegaard argued that suffering was an integral part of true Christianity.

Works of Love (1847) dealt primarily with the Christian conception of *agape* love in contrast with erotic love (*eros*) and the preferential love (*phileo*) given to friends and family.

The Point of View for My Work as an Author (1848) explained his pseudonymous writings and his personal attachment to them. Kierkegaardian translator and scholar Walter Lowrie called this an autobiography "so unique that it has no parallel in the whole literature of the world." It has been compared favorably with Augustine's *Confessions*. Kierkegaard left this work unpublished because it seemed to be self-glorifying. His brother, Peter, published it posthumously.

Two Discourses at the Communion on Fridays (1851) bears the dedication, "To One Unnamed, whose name shall one day be named, is dedicated along with this little work the whole of the authorship from the very beginning." This refers evidently to his former fiancée, Regine Olsen, and is an intensely devotional work viewing God as love and lover.

Kierkegaard's polemical pamphlets against organized religion are compiled as *The Attack upon "Christendom."* (1854–1855). This frenetic, exhausting attack no doubt contributed to his death. They consist of about two dozen separate pamphlets each no more than a paragraph or two.

He preached a sermon in 1851 on the subject of *The Unchangeableness of God*, in which this classic dogma which dominated Catholic, Protestant, and even Jewish expressions of theology from the first century AD until the advent of process theology in the twentieth century is reiterated. The dogma was that as a perfect being, God must be totally unchanging in every conceivable respect. The text is taken from the epistle of James (1:17–21).

> Every good and generous action and every perfect
> gift comes from above, from the Father who created
> the lights of heaven. In him there is no variation, no
> play of passing shadows. Of his own choice he bought
> us to birth by the word of truth to be a kind of first
> fruits of creation.

The sermon was dedicated to Søren's father. It is obviously a snub to Hegel's god, who was in a state of flux and who would later be taken up by the process theologians. The sermon was published in 1855, shortly after his death. The polemic would not have the last word; an unchangeable God of agape love would.

The Lived Philosophy

In giving something of an overview of Kierkegaard's "lived philosophy," it does not pay too much to examine his position in Western philosophy. For one thing, this writer thinks too much philosophical history has been set on tram lines by books such as Bertram Russell's *History of Western Philosophy* and for another that he does not fit neatly into any of its categories. Of course, he was the enemy of systems and dogmatism, particularly that of the idealist Hegel, and was an admirer of Socrates. But he should be examined as a unique Christian writer who tried to give passionate personal faith a philosophical basis.[14]

Kierkegaard never said there was no such thing as objective and scientific knowledge or truth; in fact, he had considered taking up physics as a field of study under the physicist Øersted at Copenhagen University, but for him, the really important truths were those relating to subjects rather than objects as in Jesus' remark, "I am the truth"(John 14:6)(emphasis added). The bottom line is our own existence; anyone who has reflected on it deeply can find it absurd, and indeed, existence as a category for humans can be found[3] only in the individual despite our being social animals with no man being an island, as the poet put it. We do not have to go through a Robinson Crusoe experience to know we all have to choose our way through life, but our liberty to choose is often driven by

95

necessity. Passionate "fear and trembling" forces one to make the right choice and gain liberty.

What makes Kierkegaard different from other thinkers such as Socrates is the way he viewed **sin**: "Christianity marks a cross before speculation; it begins with the doctrine of sin and therefore of the individual" (*Concluding Unscientific Postscript*). In addition, as God is the source of all being, everything about humanity and the individual must stand in existence before God. Overall, existence is moreover a mass of tensions: eternal and the instant of time; transcendent and immanent, finite and infinite together with a range of contrary emotions. Existence is paradoxical. Kierkegaard admired Socrates and to some extent Aristotle among other thinkers because Socrates used the **mimetic method** to lead men to see the truth about themselves: Socrates did not pretend to be wiser than others when he said, "I know nothing." He would ask questions until the subject, for example Alcibiades, would be left with nothing but his own being. The questions had no objective content but would confront learners with the negative condition with which they learned something about themselves.

Aristotle too paid tribute to prudent silence,[12] but Kierkegaard attacked Socrates and Aristotle for their love of definition. "The man who really loves cannot find peace in defining it" (*Works of Love*). The idea of a theology, which is all definitions in which objective statements about God are more important than subjective I-thou worship of him is abhorrent to Kierkegaard.

Of course, Kierkegaard recognized that Jesus, particularly as seen in the **Synoptic Gospels**, used methods similar to those of Socrates: mimetic, irony, and the indirect communication of parables to force the listeners to confront themselves; the teachings of Jesus are concerned with subjects, not objects.

Kierkegaard's personal approach was to write and publish under pseudonyms, often Latinized, such as Johannes Climacus, John the Ladder. In this way, Kierkegaard tried to give each "writer" a different personality and trick the reader into the truth. As with Socrates, and to some extent Jesus, no objective truths were conveyed, avoiding cognitively perceived knowledge and bringing home to the reader the subjective and concrete truth of existence.[12] Another point about Kierkegaard's writing was his idea of "reduplication" or the self-possession by reflection and affirming liberty, leading the true self being attracted to another similar self in an I-thou relationship. Soulless, non-self-aware things such as magnetic materials being attracted to each other have no choice in the matter.[3]

The Stages or Spheres of Life

Kierkegaard's works can be analyzed only by treating them as theater and not as dry, abstract text. What is clear, however, is that he saw life as having three separate spheres of existence. One may move from one sphere to another usually in progression, but everyone exists in one sphere or another. He attempted in his writings by indirect communication to lead the individual to see at which stage he or she was.[14] The movement from one stage to another can be made only by the individual making a "leap," a denial of the basic meaningfulness of the stage at which one is and an absolute choice for the next one. The value of the lower stages will however be restored in the upper ones.

As was the case for another nineteenth-century thinker, Nietzsche, for Kierkegaard, passion rather than cognition was what marked humanity: "Passion is the real measure of man's power, and the age in which we live is wretched because it is without passion."[24] Passion was what subjectivity and existence were all about. However, this passion must be spiritualized by interior self-examination and eventually by Christian faith if it is to be positive. This passion, as will be explained below, started with the self-indulgent aesthetic stage and ended properly in a spiritual stage, which involved both suffering and self-forgetting love. In between was the ethical stage in some way related to the last stage, the religious stage. Each stage has its own pathos: the aesthetic stage has pathos; the ethical stage has pathos of action, and the final transforming pathos of existence is religiosity or the "paradoxical religiosity" of Christianity. To Kierkegaard, truth was something that was held passionately, inwardly, and subjectively.[14]

Before analyzing Kierkegaard's thinking on life stages and his views on consciousness, it would pay us to give an outline of the thinking he gives in his ironical attack on Hegel in *Concluding Unscientific Postscript*.

> There are three existence spheres: the aesthetic, the ethical, and the religious. To these, there is receptively corresponding border territory: irony is the border territory between the aesthetic and the ethical; humor is the border territory between the ethical and the religious. Irony emerges by continually joining the particulars of the finite with the ethical infinite requirement and allowing the contradiction to come into existence. Irony is the unity of ethical passion, which in inwardness infinitely accentuates one's own I in relation to the ethical requirement and culture, which in externality infinitely abstracts from the personal I as a finitude included among all other finitudes and particulars.
>
> An effect of this abstraction is that no one notices the first, and this is precisely the art, and through it, the true infantilizing of the first is conditioned. The desperate attempt of the miscarried Hegelian ethics to make the state into the court of last resort of ethics is a highly unethical attempt to finitize individuals, an unethical flight from the category of individuality to the category of the race. [The ethicist in *Either/Or* had already protested against this directly and indirectly, indirectly at the end of the essay on the balance between the esthetic and the ethical

in the personality, where he himself had to make a concession with regard to the religious, and again at the end of the article on marriage in *Stages along Life's Way*, where even on the basis of the ethics he championed, which was diametrically opposite to Hegelian ethics, certainly jacked up the price of the religious as high as possible but still made room for it.]

Most people live in the opposite way; they are busy with being something when someone is watching them. If possible, they are something in their own eyes as soon as others are watching them, but inwardly, where the Absolute requirement is watching them, they have no taste for accentuating the personal I. Irony is the cultivation of the spirit and therefore follows immediacy; then comes the ethicist, then the humorist, then the religious person."[1]

Kierkegaard is not always an easy read! His work has a baroque elaboration rather like the architecture and ecclesiastical interiors of the churches of Copenhagen. This is deliberate, though, and unlike Kant, who is unwittingly dry and prolix. But the basic ideas of the three stages of life are there together with the junctions or crossover points from one to the other: irony from aesthetical to ethical and humor from ethical to religious. If the latter seems odd at first, remember that people in extremes of stress, including soldiers in battle, will sometimes burst into laughter at the absurdity of it all, and Sarah laughed at the birth of Isaac.

The three spheres of life are, however, best seen as complete human worlds, not just stages, with their own outlooks, motivations, and ways of behaving as frames of reference.[12] Anyone can live in one of these spheres at any one time. And although everyone lives at the most basic default aesthetic sphere some of the time, not everyone progresses beyond it. Some people consciously choose it.

The first two spheres of life are examined mainly in the works *Either/Or* and *Stages along Life's Way*. The religious sphere is examined in *Fear and Trembling*. This latter slimmer but more-powerful work majored on the dilemma Abraham faced when required to sacrifice Isaac.

It is possible to see these spheres as a kind of Venn diagram of three circles in line of contact with the crossover points where the circles touch.

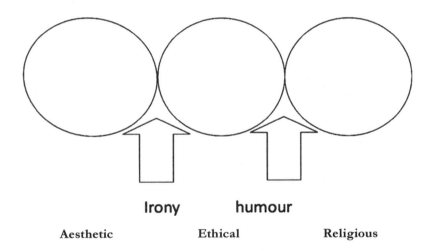

Irony   **humour**

Aesthetic   Ethical   Religious

It is also possible to imagine the three spheres as concentric—one inside the other—with the aesthetic stage the innermost, the religious the outermost, and the ethical in the middle.

In his theory of human motivation, the humanist psychologist Abraham Maslow gave a "hierarchy of needs" for the individual based on reasonably stable and intelligent people. It is often displayed in diagrammatic form as a triangle, with the basic needs at the base and the highest needs at the apex. The basic need at the bottom is physiological, for basic bodily functions; the next, second need is for safety not only of oneself but for one's property, family, and lifestyle; third comes love and belonging, including sexuality, family, and friends; fourth, something in contradistinction to the former comes esteem, which includes not only self-esteem and confidence but the respect and regard you are held in by others. Finally comes self-actualization, in which people fulfill the need to be creative and transcend themselves. This theory is not without its critics.

The Aesthetic Sphere

The Young Solomon

Perhaps Kierkegaard would have seen what Maslow was getting at when he described the aesthetic sphere of life; he examined this in a very witty passage in *Either/Or*: "All men are bores, the word itself suggest the possibility of sub-division." To him, there were different hierarchies in the aesthetic sphere; at the lowest rung were those who lived just for their bodily functions and lusts, the totally uncouth and bestial, "Those who bore others are the mob, the crowd" who like to keep themselves extremely busy. In a characteristic flourish of aristocratic, snobbish individualism, Kierkegaard wrote of them,

> This species of animal life is surely not the fruit of
> man's desire and woman's lust. Like all lower forms
> of life, it is marked by a high degree of fecundity and
> multiplies endlessly. It is hardly conceivable that nature
> should require nine months to produce such beings;
> they ought rather to be turned out by the score.[8]

Further up the hierarchy comes the elect, the aristocracy, those who "bore themselves" but "entertain others" and seek esteem in the world of social success—the successful businessperson, homeowner of possessions. Such are the people, like the man in the gospel who decided to build a bigger barn on the day before he was called to die, perhaps have forgotten "they can't take it with them." Kierkegaard dismissed them with hardly any less contempt.

> Of all ridiculous things, it seems to me the most ridiculous is to be a busy man of business, prompt to meals and prompt to work. Hence when I see a fly settle down in the critical moment on the nose of a business man, or see him spattered by a carriage which passes him in even greater haste, or a drawbridge opens before him, or a tile falls from a roof above him and strikes him dead, then I laugh heartily.[8]

At the top of the aesthetic hierarchy are those who might be termed aesthetes in common usage of the word, that is, aristocratic hedonists who like Solomon of old or Oscar Wilde, cultivate a kind of refined hedonism. Nevertheless, the sophisticated pursuit of refined sensation and beauty in art, music, or sexuality is still governed by a desire for the "pleasure principle." The result of being governed by this from the crudest to the most refined person is that consciously or unconsciously one is never in control of oneself.[12]

Insects, which are not sentient beings, are controlled entirely by instinct and are a bit like minirobots. They are most like this; even an intelligent, sentient cat or dog, say, that may love its owner, is still centered on the outside world of objects. Of course, being dumb animals, they cannot communicate verbally. It is the outside world of objects that matters to the aesthete.

Perhaps one could include in this sphere those who have passionate interests and hobbies, some of which may seem geeky to anyone else, but they are driven to be top of their chosen fields and held in the highest regard. The trouble is when you reach the top and are the unbeatable world tiddlywinks champion, say, you cannot go any higher and are left with nowhere to go.

This is also true in the world of academic success; many intelligent young people who you would think have everything to live for have committed suicide. Often, they have done extremely well at school and are set maybe for a first at Oxbridge. It can be puzzling to some, but if it can be discerned that they have reached the peak of the aesthetic stage and are living in the state of unresolved despair (discussed later), it makes sense. Let us not forget there are those for whom their religion is not so much a matter of faith or even ethics but a matter of ritual and beauty. They are living in an aesthetic state and are in great danger of falling into idolatry.

Those wrapped up in the world of work and business, with or without a family, and who have no heartfelt faith or purpose in life, often exhibit what Viktor Frankl called the **Sunday neurosis**—not having anything to do and being left with a spiritual vacuum on what should be their day of rest and reflection.[16] Which leads me to an anecdote. A curate freshly arrived at a new parish asked the vicar what sort of religion was prevalent in the neighborhood. "They're autobaptists" the vicar replied. "They spend Sundays washing their cars." As something of an elitist, Kierkegaard was aware that he could have fit into the top notch of hedonists,[12] and due to his own philosophical self-analysis, he tended to concentrate on them. Surely Solomon/ *Qoholeth* in describing their earlier experiences of pleasure fit into the peak of aesthetes themselves!

We will examine the implications of human consciousness later, but at this stage, it should be noted that even the sophisticated hedonist or aesthete is governed by what Freud later called "the pleasure principal," which is fundamentally animal in nature and not fully human. When St. Paul declared, "the carnal man knows not the things of God," he had this in mind. In fact, the word *carnal*, as we have it in the King James Version (AV), is a translation of the Greek *psyche*, which would be better translated as "soul, soulish"; the Latin equivalent of this is *anima*, stick a Norman-French "l" on the end and we have *animal*, a creature that has life but is governed by its outwardly directed desires. Nevertheless, carnal or soulish people become consciously aware of a creeping boredom in their lives. The following passage in *Either/Or*[8] examined this aspect of the human condition and used *boredom* as repetitively as *Qoholeth* used *hevel*.

> It is usual to say that idleness is a root of evil ... to prevent this one is advised to work ... a beautiful woman who neither sews nor bakes, nor reads nor plays the piano, is happy in her idleness, for she is not bored. So far from idleness being the root of all evil it is good. [Just like the lilies of the field?[7]] Boredom is the root of all evil ... indeed one may say that every human who lacks a sense of restful idleness proves that their consciousness has not yet been elevated to the level of the humane. There is a restless activity which excludes them from the world of spirit and puts them with the brutes ... whose instincts always compel them to be on the move ...
>
> In the case of children, the ruinous character of boredom is universally acknowledged. Children are always well-behaved as long as they are enjoying themselves ... they are already learning to be bored. In choosing a governess one should take into account mainly her aesthetic qualifications for amusing children [prospective teachers take note!] ... but so pervasive the influence of habit and boredom that this is practically the only case where the science of aesthetics receives its just dues. If one were to divorce a wife because she were tiresome, or demand the abdication of a king because he were

boring to look at, the banishment of a preacher or a prime minister because he were tiresome, or even the execution of a journalist because she were terribly tiresome, one would find it impossible to force through. What wonder that the world goes from bad to worse and its evils increase more and more, as boredom increases.

Boredom (emphasis added) is the root of all evil. The history of this can be traced to the beginning of the world: Adam was bored so Eve was created. Adam and Eve were bored together; then they and Cain and Abel were bored together as a family. Thus, boredom entered the world and increased in proportion to population. The peoples of the world were bored en masse so to divert themselves they conceived the idea of constructing a tower high enough to reach the heavens. This idea is itself as boring as the tower was high [What about some modern structures or even the space race?]. This constitutes a terrible proof of how boredom gained the upper hand ... It is proposed to form a constitutional assembly [The king set up a parliament to avoid the revolutionary mood in the 1840's] these days. Can anything more tiresome be imagined, both for the participants and for those who have to hear and read about it? It is proposed to improve the financial condition of the state by practicing economy. What could be more tiresome [and so what does one read about in the newspapers and hear on the news today, when it is not gruesome sensation: boring finance] ... Instead of paying off its national debt ... it would be easy for Denmark to negotiate a massive loan. [Does this sound familiar?] Why not consider this? Every once in a while we hear of a man who is a genius and who therefore neglects to pay his debts. Why should a nation not do the same, not to pay its debts but for merriment? ... Everything would become free:

theatres free, women of easy virtue free, drives to the
park free, funerals would be free together with their
eulogies. But [of course] no one should be allowed to
own any property. Except in my [Kierkegaard's] case,
because it was my idea …and I may not be able to hit
on a better idea when all the money has gone.

Kierkegaard was probably at his most witty, fluent, and satirical in
the above passage but then got to what he observed as the crucial
point about boredom.

Now since boredom, as shown is the root of all evil,
what can be more natural than the effort to overcome
it? Here, as everywhere, however, it is necessary to
give the problem calm consideration: <u>otherwise one
may be driven by the demoniac spirit of boredom
deeper and deeper into the mire, in the very effort
to escape</u>. [A kind of spiritual quicksand] (emphasis
added). Everyone who feels bored cries out for
change … it is necessary to act in accordance with
some settled principle …

Boredom is a pantheism that has a conscious fear
or hatred of distinguishing between good and evil.
If we remain in it, it becomes evil … one annuls it
only by amusement … Saying *work* annuls it is to
betray confusion for through idleness certainly can be
annulled by industry, seeing that this has its opposite,
boredom cannot, as one sees that the busiest workers
of all, those who in their officious buzzing about most
resemble humming insects, are the most boring of all;
and if they do not bore themselves, that is because
they have no idea what boredom is; but in that case
boredom is not annulled.

The principle Kierkegaard suggested being used was what
he called **crop rotation**, an analogy with farming to keep things

growing. The aesthete needs to "rotate" from one pleasure to another, for example, one tires of one's own country and goes on endless tours abroad, or one tires of eating off fine china and moves to silver or gold plates. Like Mr. Toad in *Wind in the Willows*, the pleasure seeker always tires of one form of excitement or sensation and has to move on to another. If pleasure seekers do not follow this palliative and at least forget a previous pleasure so they can go back to it, they are forced to become more inventive in their pleasure seeking to the point of perversion. "One who has perfected himself in the twin arts of remembering and forgetting is in a position to play battledore and shuttlecock with the whole of existence." By filling one's life with little empty surprises, one can avoid thinking what life is all about. In the area of personal relationships, the pleasure seeker always avoids commitment, which lies in the ethical sphere. This applies to friendships and marriage. Like Dante, one falls in love with the idea of the woman (his Beatrice) or man rather than the real person. In the end, the result of even the most extreme pleasure (like the *petit mort* some say they experience in sexual intercourse) is *death*.

Boredom leads to bitter world-weariness, cynicism, and above all, despair. This state of despair is further explored in *The Concept of Anxiety* and *Sickness unto Death*, a precursor to the later idea of "existential angst." The danger then for the sensitive, eternal soul is to move closer and closer to suicide. Some shoot themselves; others may jump off bridges. Perhaps the more boorish types are luckier and are given more chance of salvation when they are found merely trying to drink themselves to death, get into drugs, or are found in tears, dying of boredom.

I have discussed how this gut-wrenching despair is explored in the Canticle, where in chapter 5, *Shualimith* had prepared for sleep; she did not want to put on her clothes, dirty her washed feet, or disturb her freshly anointed hair. Her lover came to a door not easy to open from the outside. When she opened, her fumbling lover had gone. Dashing out into the street in a state of despair in her perfumed undress, she was taken as a lady of the night by the night watchmen and beaten up. The key verses here are indeed a contrast to 6.3: the beating heart sinks and was replaced by panic, desolation, and turning bowels. "I opened to my love but he had turned away and was gone; my heart sank when he turned his back. I sought him but could not find him; I called but there was no answer" (Canticle 5:6). This is the state of the soul reaching out from a purely aesthetic life. The Canticle, however, concluded in the ethical sphere of marriage.

To sum up then, Kierkegaard's aesthete was someone seeking fulfillment from objective activity in everything from eating and drinking to romance (which was examined in "Diary of a Seducer" in *Either/Or*) or even intellectual pursuits. In this sphere of existence, life is engaged in sensually, and for short term, pleasure, commitment, and responsibility are avoided and life is lived for immediate satisfaction. Reflection on the use of everything, like women and friends, say, as mere objects of one's pleasure is not considered, and there is a lack of genuine moral principle in the behavior because life is not seen as a contrast between good and evil but only between satisfaction and dissatisfaction, fulfillment and frustration. Any apparent ethical behavior does not spring from within but is entirely contingent on legal or social sanctions; any religion beyond social custom is sheer hypocrisy.

There is a lack of consideration of the consequences of one's actions. These things are ultimately unsatisfying, and boredom results, which turns into despair. In the worst cases, this can result in suicide. In other cases, it can lead to a cynical apathy in which "the world is round but everything on it is flat," as the seducer Gaston in *Gigi* exclaimed, can be gauged this way, especially among the young who have not advanced beyond this sphere from drunkenness and vandalism. While these mischievous activities are not utterly wicked, they are misdemeanors. One cannot be bothered to do anything, and if one does, one regrets it. We see many problems in society on our city streets on weekends, promiscuity, and perverted sex to the apparently brilliant student who commits suicide. In any case, those who choose to live entirely in this sphere are unethical, unspiritual, lost, and in need of salvation.

Summary of the Aesthetic Sphere

The aesthetic stage is not exactly hedonism, which prescribes a laid-back attitude to life. Kierkegaard's aesthetes are absorbed in enjoying themselves to the extent that they are always moving from one pleasure or sensation to another. This change is necessary, as boredom would otherwise set in, which would be fatal. The central focus is on material things, not on that which is right or spiritual. It varies from the downright bestial to refined activity in the arts, romantic love, and even science or adventure, but these pursuits eventually become sterile and futile. In the end, despair in self-satisfaction of living restlessly from moment to moment leads to a boredom and self-disgust in which death is longed for. The aesthete is tired of living and scared of dying. The only hope of salvation from this state is if despair sets in, but it has to be the right sort; if it is "weakness despair," it is buried in the self-conscious and not awakened.

Despair

Before looking at the other two spheres of human existence, let us examine the psychological state that drives people from a lower to a higher one. That is a specific kind of despair over one's own human condition; this is not the despair one might feel about one's terrible garden, say, or the chances of one's football club, but a definite aggravated despair over moral standing, especially before a holy God.[1] This is chiefly done in *Sickness unto Death* and in *The Concept of Dread* (the Danish word may also be translated as "anxiety" or *angest*, a vague fear unlike the Danish word *bang*, which has a direct object) and in *Fear and Trembling*.

It is in fact an examination of self-despair, which is also known as a consciousness of or conviction of sin. It is not until one has been pushed to the very edge of existence that one has a perspective that provides a deeper insight into human reality.[1] In *Sickness unto Death*, Anti-Climacus introduced the book with a reference to John 11.4: "This illness is not to end in death." This quotation came from the story of Lazarus, in which Jesus raised him from the dead. However, Anti-Climacus raised the question, would not this statement still be true even if Jesus had *not* raised Lazarus from the dead?

While the human conception of death is the end, the Christian concept of death is merely another stop along the way of the eternal life. In this way, for the Christian, death is nothing to fear. The true

Sickness unto Death that does not describe physical but spiritual death is something to fear, according to Anti-Climacus. *Sickness unto Death* was a companion piece to the *The Concept of Anxiety*, which is also a "psychological" work and moves beyond the earlier preliminary psychological considerations of anxiety in the face of freedom or anxiety derived from and leading to sin. Like its companion, this work is short but dense. In it, Kierkegaard considered the spiritual aspects of despair. As anxiety was related to the ethical, despair was related to the religious, that is, to the eternal.

Some Christian thinkers often remark that the terminology Kierkegaard used takes on a different meaning from its normal usage. For example, it is as if Kierkegaard used the word *self* as a verb rather than as a noun, "to self." Much of this is a misunderstanding because what he was out to do was to offer an ironical take on Hegel and parody his language. This is especially true in the complicated paragraph at the beginning of *Sickness unto Death* truncated below.

> Man is **spirit**. But what is spirit? Spirit is the self. But what is the self? The self is a relation which relates itself to its own self … Man is a synthesis of the infinite and the finite, of the temporal and the eternal, of possibility and necessity. In short, it is a synthesis. A synthesis is a relation between two factors. So regarded, man is not yet a self.

What Kierkegaard was saying was that the spiritual self lay between the psychical and the physical. The physical records the senses of the event, and in Kierkegaardian psychology, the psychical is the identifying and the interpretative element that processes the memory. There is no Hegelian synthesis of the two; the self is found in the activity of the relation; the noun becomes a verb—one selves to be saved.[12]

Kierkegaard was playing with Hegel's notion of the synthesis of ideas. Manipulating the jargon, tongue in cheek with ease, he was saying that the definitions of spirit and self were justifiable, but he added that so-regarded people are not really their *true* selves. He was standing against Hegel and other idealists by saying that people were not what they were supposed to be in principle, that their very existence lay poles apart from their ideal nature. People were not unities; they were fragmented disunities.[3] They were not their true selves; in fact, they were not selves at all. This corruption that can be viewed from a psychological standpoint as despair is not just any old individual sin but **sin** itself.

The sickness unto death, which Kierkegaard recognized as a "death instinct" long before Freud, was a mortal disease existing consciously and unconsciously and requiring the radical cure of faith. In addition, he was saying that people were indeed a "synthesis" of body, soul, and spirit. Indeed, holiness could not be achieved until they were integrated. There had to be a dynamic, ongoing relationship, a tension or "dialectic" between these parts of someone's personality. In fact, with regard to the ethical and the sensual, this can be found in many of the Proverbs: the answer to living life in the world lies not in self-indulgence or in a false asceticism but in a balance between the two. Once this has been achieved, it is possible to look outside oneself in spirit for the "other," which is God.[3]

This sickness unto death is what Kierkegaard called despair. According to Kierkegaard, people are "in despair" if they do not align themselves with God or God's plan for the self. In this way, they lose their selves and their eternal selves, which in *Sickness unto Death,* Kierkegaard defined as the "relation's relating itself to itself in the relation." Kierkegaard defined humanity as the tension between the "finite and infinite," the "possible and the necessary," and was identifiable with the dialectical balancing act between these opposing features, the relation. While one is an inherently reflective, conscious being, to become a true self, one must be conscious not only of the self but also of being aligned with a higher purpose that is God's plan for the self. When one denies this true self or the power that created and sustains this true self, one is in despair.[1]

There are three kinds of unconscious and conscious despair presented in the book: being unconscious in despair of having a self, consciously not wanting in despair to be oneself, and consciously wanting in despair to be oneself. The first of these is described as "inauthentic despair," because this despair is born out of ignorance. In this state, one is unaware that one has a self separate from its finite reality[12]; you are just one of the crowd, a **mass man** who may or may not be happy to go along with everyone else and behave like them. One does not realize that there is an eternity and accepts a finite existence because one is unaware of the possibility of there being a life beyond it.

The second type of despair is consciously refusing to accept the self outside immediacy, defining the self by only immediate, finite terms. There is no sense of the transcendent. This is the state in which one realizes that one has a temporal self but wishes to lose this painful awareness by arranging one's finite life to make the realization unnecessary.[12] One tries to blot out the pain by concentrating on outside objects and pleasures. Pascal wrote in his *Pensees* that people have "a God-sized hole in them"[14] they try to fill with things like the excitement of gambling or sport, but it remains an empty hole nothing can fill.

The third type is conscious despair that combines an awareness of the self with a refusal to submit to the will of God. In this stage, one accepts the eternal and may or may not acknowledge the creator but refuses to accept an aspect of the self that one in reality is, that is to say, the self one has been created to be.[12] In this state, a number of mentally unhygienic conditions may emerge. First, you may become extremely introverted, believing you are the only one who feels this way (and being upset by that as well); second, it can lead to a **catatonic** feeling of helplessness and inactivity. Third, the despair may lead to a schizophrenic fragmentation of the personality. Fourth, the subject may commit suicide in despair as a means of destroying his or her true selfhood. Finally, the despair becomes passionate and leads to a state of rage. One becomes offended by the despair one feels. Paradoxically, in this state, there is cause for hope because the subjects see their true selves they are alienated from, either temporal or eternal, crystallize around them, and an active, willful fight is made to resist that.[12] Unpleasant as this may be for the subjects in their states of "conviction of sin" and for many around them, it is a fight the subjects cannot afford to win. If they are not to be left in a permanent state of mania, they have to make a step of faith to find themselves.

"To not be in despair is to have reconciled the finite with the infinite, to exist in awareness of one's own self and of God."[1] Specifically, Kierkegaard defined the opposite of despair as faith, which he described by the following: "In relating itself to itself, and in willing to be itself, the self rests transparently in the power that established it" (*Sickness unto Death*). However, the self gets its determination to break away from despair from the grace of God. Kierkegaard did not labor the point; his concern is to define the nature of despair. To be in despair is not only misfortune and misery—no, it is ruination.[1] Tragically, it is often the human condition and it is something that we are all subject to before we become reconciled to God.

Sentient animals do not despair; despair is an indication of a superior being's spiritual existence. However, despair was not originally and does not have to be a necessary part of human condition; it was *not* imparted to us by God. God could foresee it in the human condition, but he did not cause it; that was a result of the fall in the garden of Eden. Despair, it must be emphasized, is not the same as depression, that is, a mental illness that may be suffered by the most godly people. No, no, despairing lies in unregenerate humanity itself.

The self, that is, the dynamic, selving, saved self, can ultimately rest only in its creator. Fortunately, human beings do not just have sentient bodies as do animals, nor are they purely spirit beings; it is the combination that gives hope in a state of despair, for just as the dying Christ cried out on the cross, "My God my God, why have you forsaken me" (Matthew 27:26), so the man or woman in a state of final despair can cry out to God when dying to his or her old self and being reborn from heaven in their true selves.

There is also "defiance despair" in which people realize they are eternal beings but are offended by that; they would rather hang on to their misery and selfhood than have it taken from them. But if this battle is won, the eternal soul is lost, and it is a triumph of the will resulting in total negation and the torment of hell.[3] The alternative is to proceed on the road to true selfhood. Lucifer declares this in Milton's *Paradise Lost*, the demonical despair that shows itself in ethical perversion, the root of which is the lie.

> The Devil's despair is the most intensive despair, for the Devil is sheer spirit without a body that is his own and hence unqualified consciousness and transparency; there is no obscurity in the Devil that could serve as a mitigating excuse. Therefore, his despair is the most absolute defiance.[1]

Despair then is the sickness unto death, except this death is never ending. The road to salvation starts with a despair that is perceived and is given up rather than hung on to. But it cannot be ignored. The aesthete needs to despair in truth to step into the ethico-religious spheres; as Jesus said, "Whoever loves himself is lost, but he who hates himself in this world will be kept safe for eternal life." (John 12:25).

Kierkegaard believed God accorded the individual with the highest importance (after all, the words he wanted inscribed on his gravestone were not his name but "the individual"), and he never suggested the self's merging into God as you get in Hinduism, say, nor any belief that borders on **pantheism**. God is ultimately so interested in us personally that he sent his Son to die for individual men and women. It is social and ecclesial organization that seeks to herd men; it is God who calls each person individually. The offence of absurdity and paradox is Christianity's greatest weapon of apologetic against speculation (as discussed in *Fear and Trembling* in the section on the religious sphere below).

The possibility of offense lies in this; individual, sinful human beings are directly before a holy God and as a corollary, that an individual person's sin should be of concern to God. The gospel is an offense not because it focuses on individual sins but because it is against selfish, non-selving, human nature itself in the face of a holy God.

> It would be best of all to explain for once that the real reason that men are offended by Christianity is that it is too high, because its goal is not man's goal, because it wants to make man into something so extraordinary that he cannot grasp the thought.

Kierkegaard may have had a deep interest in both psychology and the state of society, but his main interest was in the human condition caused by sin with a big "S": The voluntary act of remaining in unrepentant sin especially if it is combined with the kind of despair that will not accept forgiveness: there can be no Hegelian syntheses between faith and despair, nor there any double-minded Cartesian tension between faith and doubt.

The Ethical Sphere

The Mature Solomon

Those who live for themselves and the pleasure they can wring out of life are faced with a problem: they have to live in a society in which certain roles are forced upon them that restrict the amount of liberty they have just to have fun if they have not gotten too jaded. Many have to work to live, so they take on that role. But that is not the only one; for example, someone may be chair of a sports club as well as a member. So there are professional roles, familial roles, character roles, and roles within roles.

Most roles are socially useful and hold society together; the trouble is that putting on a role puts a strain on someone, if for example one is expected to be a foul-mouthed supporter of his football club but polite when dealing with business clients. Roles empty people of their true selves. Aesthetes seek libertarian freedom with its lack of predictability, but they are fleeing the true freedom they seek in the ethical sphere. There is an additional danger for these people: the roles they put on and the emptying of their true self this entails means that in fact they become nobodies who can be defined only in terms of their social relationship to others.

It is a bit like having a wardrobe full of masks you put on for your roles. When Jesus called the Pharisees hypocrites, he was in fact saying they were play actors because the word *hypocrite* means the kind of big mask actors of his day wore; they were the two comedy/tragedy masks we recognize as symbols of theater. (It is quite possible Jesus may have seen a play or two at the Greco-Roman theater near Nazareth.)

The terrible danger in psychological masks is that instead of protecting the self, they can lead to a fragmentation of the personality—schizophrenia. If life is a masquerade, there will come a time when masks have to come off,[12] and it did not fool Jesus anyway as he could see right through people; his verbal assaults on the Pharisees were meant to shake their masks off. Judge Wilhelm in *Either/Or* put it like this.

> Can you think of anything more frightful than it might end with your nature being resolved into a multiplicity? That you might become many like those unhappy demoniacs, a legion, and thus you would have lost the inmost and holiest thing of all in a man, the unifying power of personality.[8]

This is a reference to the man possessed by a legion of demons in Luke 8:32–37 whom Jesus healed. He was possibly the worst case of multiple demonic possession that resulted in additional schizophrenic behavior, you can imagine, but when he returned home, people were amazed at his soundness of mind. The central point is this choosing an ethical code to live by people become *whole and integrated* personalities. This is the first step toward true holiness that is appropriated by faith in the religious sphere. In fact, many people are driven to this choice by the very despair they have felt. It is a question of either remaining in their state of misery *or* choosing to admit one has been selfish and develop a moral code.[12] One recognizes that there is good *and* evil, whereas before, it was a neutral category.

The word **universal** has a few meanings in philosophy in the sense that is used in the areas we are concerned about; it means that which is common to all humanity, or as some anthropologists say, "the psychic unity of mankind." In our analysis of Proverbs, we have seen that not only did Solomon collect proverbs, many of which showed an Egyptian influence,[26] but there are also proverbs directly edited into the book from outside sources, from King Lemuel say, or Agar the Arabian.

The point is that ethical wisdom is not restricted to those who are within the covenant of God but is an aspect of **common grace**. So actually, the ethical code does not have to be Christian or even religious at this stage; it could be that of *Qoholeth*'s wise imperative, where wisdom is seen as better than folly, a strict observance of the Torah, codes of chivalry as with the samurai or medieval knights, or even Kant's "categorical imperative"; the moral code of Confucius would be another example.

But it is interesting that the more pantheistic a religion or society is, the less ethical it is. The Romans had a whole expanding pantheon of gods, but they invented the arena in which people and animals were killed just for fun. Any roles that you previously had that are incompatible with your ethical standards will now be abandoned. In fact, those moving into the ethical sphere from the aesthetic have to lose themselves to find themselves; they need to make the moral leap, choose themselves, and find freedom. The biggest ethical leap in most people's lives, religious or not, is to get married and take responsibility for a family, and that is what the proponent of the ethical sphere in *Either/Or*, Judge Wilhelm, proposes. Here, rather than commitment to a particular moral code, it is possible to see the ethical sphere of life as commitment to a human.[12] This is what happens at the end of the Canticle. This loss of apparent freedom results in happiness rather than being footloose and fancy free.

Unfortunately, not everyone who marries has considered it a serious ethical commitment;: there has been, at least in the past, too much of an emphasis on romance, which is purely aesthetic. Those who marry for this reason only, seeing the other person merely as an object of their desires, are far more likely to find their relationship crashing on the rocks. We all know what damage a high divorce rate has meant to individuals and their children as well as the fiscal cost. Louis Dupré put the change from the aesthetic to the ethical like this.

> In the choice of oneself as an absolute, one leaves the aesthetic stage into the freedom of the ethical. As soon as a person takes possession of themselves and becomes free there arises an absolute distinction between good and evil. For the speculative attitude (which is included in the aesthetic, because of its lack of commitment), this distinction is only relative: good and evil can be integrated in a single system. The distinction becomes absolute when we make it so by a personal commitment. This means that good and evil are absolute only insofar as we will them. Such a statement does not reduce them to mere subjective determinations—they are objective and universal in themselves—but they become themselves only in the free decision of absolute choice. Nothing but a conscious, personal acceptance can make objective standard into absolute values. Even in their subjective acceptance, however, the objective ethical standards are a limitation of the spirit ... The absolute of the ethical man is expressed as an existence which is extremely limited and, as such, relative. (*Kierkegaard as Theologian*, Yale 1963)

In other words, those who come out of the aesthetic into the ethical sphere are more balanced and self-assured. Many of the practical ethical attitudes expressed in this sphere can be found in the descriptions of decent people found in Proverbs and to some extent in the Apocrypha, particularly in the description of the worthy wife, who has now moved beyond the heady, romantic honeymoon found in the Canticle, and the hardworking, honest, and wise man. These people often follow and find it of profit to study the wise sayings in the biblical Wisdom Literature.

There is possibly, however, a dark side. First, one's ethical code may to some extent be in conflict with others. What, for example, of the Japanese soldiers in World War II who saw any surrender by allied soldiers incompatible with their code of fighting to the death? Or of the Nazi youngster who saw nothing wrong in slaughtering Jews? What about the member of a criminal gang or family who has his own commitments in it but none outside?

Second, it may indeed be possible for people to retain their psychological integrity, but in the ethical sphere, where good is distinguished from evil, to deliberately choose an evil path as Satan has.

Proverbs recognizes these as evil sinners and the wicked, and adulterous and shameless women. It is interesting to see how the symbols of the faithful and faithless woman are developed in scripture until they cumulate in the book of Revelation in the picture in chapter 12, and also that of the faithless whore of Babylon in chapters 17 and 18, in which the word incidentally has strong metaphorical overtones of idolatrous worship. The New Testament describes such as having their "consciences seared by a red-hot iron" (1 Timothy 4:2 AV). Utter perdition awaits them unless the mighty power of the Holy Spirit chooses to break them: there are the mad, the mad and the bad, and then the just plain bad.

The remedy for aesthetic despair then is commitment. It does not have to be a Christian commitment according to Kierkegaard's scheme of things, but it brings about true, integrated selfhood through ordering one's life around it. The choice whether one is driven to it or not is internally passionate and emotional; it is genuinely subjective. Many people find it in a committed marriage, and if they can find the ideal woman described in Proverbs, so much the better, but in any case, it is found that ethical duty brings freedom. The person of duty's ethical urge is described by Viktor Frankl as the "will to meaning" in his *Introduction to Logo therapy*.

> Man's search for meaning is a primary force in his life and not a "secondary rationalization" of instinctual desires. This meaning is unique and specific in that it must be fulfilled by him alone; only then does it achieve a significance that will satisfy his own will to meaning.
>
> There are some authors who contend that meanings and values are nothing but "defense mechanisms reactions formulations and sublimations," but I for myself would not be live merely for the sake of my "defense mechanisms," nor would I be willing to die for my "reaction formulations" [like an animal]. Man however is willing to live and die for the sake of his ideals and values.[16]

One is reminded of St. Paul: "For me to live is Christ; death is gain" (1 Philippians 1:21). But it should be remember no matter how noble it may seem to lay down one's life for one's family country or beliefs, those things may not necessarily be Christian. An integrated personality may be achieved at the cost of committing oneself to an arbitrary absolute that has only temporal value and no bearing on eternal life.

Summary of the Ethical Sphere

The ethical stage: the leap of passion aesthetes make to take themselves out of their default sphere is one of self-judgment and examination. Two parallel paths now need to be followed: the first is to live altruistically with a code of ethics and wisdom; the second is to treat life vocationally, living in self-awareness, responsibility, and duty. Sometimes, this involves a change of lifestyle but more often a self-conscious commitment to good, social behavior. Unlike the aesthete bored by the same old thing, the ethical individual gains satisfaction in the struggle to maintain a general equilibrium in himself and society.

> When the ethical individual has completed his task, fought the good fight, he has reached the point where he has become the one man. There is no man altogether like him. At the same time he has become the universal man. To be one man is not in itself so great, but this is the art of living.[24]

The ethical individual is, however, constantly living under the demands of self-perfection through wisdom, the application of an ethical code, and all the constraints of social life; this can lead to interior psychological conflict.

One pitfall for the ethicist is that although joy is found in the pursuit of duty, it need not lead to psychological happiness even though hardship may be withstood. More seriously, there can arise a conflict between the individual conscience and populist morality. We can become part of the crowd to repent at leisure; crowd morality has nothing to do with true morality but everything to do with the herd instinct. Overall, the problem for the ethicist is that by commitment, there is always the obligation to self-judgment. Even though the ethicist knows nobody is perfect, the ethicist always lives in the shadow of guilt. "It is only when I choose myself as guilty that I choose myself absolutely ... It is the expression of the strongest assertion of existence."[8] The all-pervasive nature of sin means that the only answer is the leap into the next stage of the religious. Those who choose to remain in the ethical stage may think they can be saved through adherence to an ethical code or are self-righteous. Good and evil do not exist as abstractions but are tied up with concrete reality and the free existence of the individual.

The Religious Sphere

Crucifixus est Dei Filius ; non pudet, quia pudendum est;
Et mortuus est Dei Filius ; prorsus
credibile est, quia ineptum est;
Et sepultus resurrexit ; certum est, quia impossibile.

The Son of God was crucified: there is
no shame, because it is shameful.
And the Son of God died: it is wholly
credible, because it is absurd
And buried, He rose again: it is
certain, because it is impossible.
(emphasis added)
—Tertullian, *De Carne Christi* (The
Incarnation of Christ)[14]

In this stage, the individual finally finds contentment and satisfaction. It is the highest sphere of living because it requires faith in the transcendent, which the other spheres do not.[3] It also involves being in the ethical sphere where we have seen that people are given some hope and meaning to life by committed personal ethical codes of commitment: the inner self becomes more important, shaping one's identity and character, and one strives to be a better person.

However, moralists will see they cannot live up to their own standards, the state St. Paul described in Romans. Sensitive people are always critical and will judge themselves guilty or not by their own standards before they judge anyone else, unlike the Pharisees, who could not bother to take the plank out of their own eyes. This self-scrutiny, although engaged in by an integrated personality, may then be more than they can bear. Just as self-despair forces people from the aesthetic into the ethical sphere, it forces people from the ethical into the religious. A prime example of this is Martin Luther, who found he was not really getting right with God by trying to lead what was at that time considered the highest form of ethical living in a monastery and discovered relief in justification by faith after reading the book of Romans.

In some of the previous works discussed above, two of the pseudonyms are given—the designators religion A and religion B. It becomes clear why that is when the religious sphere is reached, for it is possible to have a genuinely religious life that is not Christian (**religion A**); perhaps Socrates fitted this; and one that truly embraces a Christian commitment (**religion B**). Religion A is the pagan, pantheistic, or at least non-Christian conception of religion and is characterized by apparent intelligibility (which in the end it is not, as the foolishness of God is better than the wisdom of men), **immanence**, and recognition of continuity between temporality and eternity—that is a failure to see the great gulf between sinful humanity and God.

Other classic examples apart from that of Socrates could well be that of the Buddha, who found a non-theistic enlightenment, or the old Hindu of high caste, who after spending most of his life as a householder in the ethical stage of life was expected to disappear into the jungle to end it in religious contemplation. Sadly, such a religiosity does not lead to the foot of the cross and cannot lead to eternal life.

False religion whether aesthetic, ritualistic; ethical, moralistic or pharisaical; when it attempts to gain salvation by self-effort, mystical or otherwise, is doomed to failure. The Devil tries every psychological trick to get men and women from getting to the point where they are driven to accept and submit to divine grace.

Abraham and Isaac 1635
Rembrandt (1606–1669)
Hermitage Museum,
St. Petersburg

Religiousness B, however, was dubbed **paradoxical religiousness** by Kierkegaard and represents the essence of Christianity. It posits a radical divide between immanence and **transcendence**, a discontinuity between temporality and eternity, and a recognition that there is a great gulf between humanity and God, but it also claims that the eternal came into existence in time. This is a paradox and can be believed only "by virtue of the absurd."[3]

These concepts of religion B are of course direct allusions to a famous quote from the maverick church father **Tertullian**, himself a master of style, as quoted above. This is in an approximate translation; unless you are a Latin scholar, you may miss his ironic nuances, and he has perhaps been misquoted. For example, the Latin word *ineptum*, from which we get inept, can only be clumsily translated in its nearest form as "unsound" or "having no sense of what is fitting" and may also be translated as "foolish," "silly," or "just plain daft." One could also translate it perhaps as "laughable," so it is often translated with considerable justification as absurd. This is one aspect of the humor Kierkegaard said lay in the crossover from the ethical to the religious spheres. Only those who can rest in the apparent meaninglessness of life, as *Qoholeth* did, can find peace in submission.

But there is added force in Kierkegaard's arguments as he examines what happened to Abraham, for whom faith was counted as righteousness. The story of Abraham and Isaac was the major theme of *Fear and Trembling*. The title was a reference to a line from Philippians 2:12: "You must work out your own salvation with fear and trembling," itself a probable reference to Psalms 55:5, "Fear and trembling assail me." Kierkegaard wanted to understand the anxiety that must have been present in Abraham[12] when "God tested him and said to him, take Isaac your only son, whom you love, and go to the land of Moriah and offer him as a burnt offering on the mountain that I shall show you."

The story is found in Genesis chapter 22 onward. God had promised Abraham a son in his old age and that he would be the father of a great nation, although he hedged his bets by getting his slave girl Hagar pregnant. But the son was not born to Sarah until fifteen years later. She had first laughed when she learned she would conceive when she should have been past it, and she laughed again when Isaac was born (the humor of transition to faith). Almost immediately, Abraham was told by God to take Isaac, whom he loved, up to Mount Moriah and sacrifice him to God as a burnt offering. At the last moment, the angel of the Lord appeared and told Abraham that he had passed God's test of faith and that a ram caught in a thicket was to be sacrificed instead.

Was Abraham ethically defensible in keeping silent about his purpose? On the face of it, Abraham's conduct was indefensible, for he paid no heed to the intermediate ethical behavior expected.

But in the face of his concealment, we are in the presence of a paradox that cannot be mediated, for it rests on the principle that the individual is higher than the universal. Abraham had a choice to complete the task or forget it. He resigned himself to the three-and-a-half-day journey and to the loss of his son. The task God gave Abraham was so horrifying that he could tell no one about it because no one would understand him. Ethics as well as aesthetics forbade it. He said nothing to Sarah, nothing to Eliezer. Who, after all, would have understood him, for did not the nature of temptation extract from him a pledge of silence? He split the firewood, he bound Isaac, he lit the fire, and he drew the knife.

What was the most Abraham could do in his relationship with God? Remain faithful to his commitment to God. He accomplished that by actually lifting the knife with the intention of carrying out his mission. In short, he *acted*; the intention was more important than the result. He had faith and had to go no further to please God. Because he had kept everything to himself in hiddenness, he "isolated himself as higher than the **universal.**"[9]

Kierkegaard envisioned two types of people in *Fear and Trembling.* One lived in hope— Abraham, who looked for a transcendent, "out there" happiness; and the Young Man of the aesthetic stage, Constantine Constantius, the pseudonymous author of *Repetition* in the ethical stage who live in the immanent. Abraham had suspended the ethical and failed to follow the universal.[12] Kierkegaard wrote, "Hegelian philosophy culminates in the thesis that the outer is the inner and the inner is the outer."

Abraham had to choose between the ethical requirements of his surroundings and what he regarded as his absolute duty to God. [3] Kierkegaard's pseudonym, the agnostic John of Silence (whom as remarked above parallels the story from Grimm) is horrified.

> That man was not an exegetical scholar. He did not know Hebrew; if he had known Hebrew, he perhaps would have easily understood the story of Abraham. [Kierkegaard was saying the story was plain enough even if, like himself, one does not know Hebrew].

He cannot understand it, and yet is obsessed with it he dreads it in the deep psychological sense which will be explained below. He has a "**sympathetic antipathy**" and an "**antipathic sympathy**" for the story[12] He dreaded it—a psychological state we will examine later.

However, there is to John at least a partial analysis: Abraham's act in obeying God is a "**double movement**" of "**infinite resignation**" (to the will of God) and "**a movement of faith**" (when he acts on that will). In the former case it is a negative movement where he gives up Isaac and in the second a positive reception, where he gets him back.

Herein lays the paradox of faith. In giving up Isaac Abraham became a **knight of resignation** and in the movement of faith whereby he gets him back he is a **knight of faith.** At the back of his mind he could not really believe God would require Isaac of him, as God had already promised that through Isaac a nation would be founded .

> Even as the knife glittered he believed that God would not require Isaac ... He believed by virtue of the absurd; for all human reckoning had long since ceased to function.[9](emphasis added)

All faithful believers in the covenant God are children of Abraham, who is described as "the father of us all."

John of Silence considered the ethics of Abraham's situation. [9] He pointed out that the situation was an outrage: "Abraham enjoys honor and glory as the father of faith whereas he ought to be prosecuted and convicted of murder" (or at least attempted murder!). The agnostic John then suspected that there was a common misunderstanding of the story when it sometimes it was said of him that "he loved God so much that he was willing to sacrifice to him of his best." John then imagined an impassioned sermon given on this theme.[12] Consequently, one of the congregation went home and killed his only son. At the next sermon, the preacher lambasted the man (who presumably has not been arrested yet), "O abominable man, off scouring of society, what devil possessed you to murder your son?"[9] So the question becomes, can it ever be a holy act to murder your son? Here we come to a point of ethics; it is wrong to murder, yet Abraham was willing to kill Isaac. Abraham annulled the commonly perceived ethical for a higher purpose. Kierkegaard called this moral annulment **the teleological suspension of the ethical.**[12] He wrote of Abraham,

> If the task had been different, if the Lord had commanded Abraham to bring Isaac up to Mount Moriah so that he could have his lightning strike Isaac and take him as a sacrifice in that way, then Abraham plainly would have been justified in speaking as enigmatically as he did, for then he himself could not have known what was going to happen. But given the task as assigned to Abraham, he himself has to act; consequently, he has to know in the crucial moment what he himself will do, and consequently, he has to know that Isaac is going to be sacrificed.[9]

Christian theology understands that the story of the sacrifice of Isaac prefigures the crucifixion of Christ and the atonement. The point remains that the feelings that God the Father experienced must be like those that father Abraham experienced. Can we objectively know that?

What is definitely true for Christian thinkers is that it is difficult to see how they can be anything other than subscribers to **divine command theory.**[27] What this basically means is that things are right because of the fiat or command of God, because he says so, not merely that God just does what is right. Simply, before the eternal God, there was nothing, not even ethics and morality, and within the strictures of historical time, he can predestine events (including miracles) to fit his plan even if to human eyes they seem unpleasant or evil. This does not mean God is not a God of order, a standard of righteousness or of consistency and love; it also means he is not trapped by some preexistent moral code. He can suspend the "ethical" if He wants to fit into his teleology (end plan or end game). In fact, as God is Lord of time and history, each event is planned within his omnipotent will.

Faith is indeed a paradox. Abraham was resigned to the will of God as a knight of resignation. He needed to make a **movement of faith** to become a knight of faith; at the back of his mind, he could not really believe God would require Isaac of him, as God had already promised that through Isaac a nation would be founded. On Mount Moriah, "even as the knife glittered he believed that God would not require Isaac ... He believed by **virtue of the absurd;** for all human reckoning had long since ceased to function."[9] (emphasis added)Abraham was holding two mutually exclusive ideas in his mind at the same time; a "dialectic tension." Common sense would indicate that his actions were unintelligible, but they were not.

By virtue of his unintelligible act, he became the father of faith. In the end, John of Silence praised Abraham.

> Abraham was greater than all, great by reason of his power whose strength lies in impotence, great by reason of his wisdom whose secret is foolishness, great by reason of his hope whose form is madness, great by reason of the love which is hatred of oneself. (emphasis added)

Abraham's actual experience, although it could be described objectively, was nevertheless something that could be intelligibly felt and driven only inwardly and subjectively. Faith such as his is something peculiar to each individual and cannot be communicated in full exactitude to another mortal.

Mark C. Taylor, of Fordham University, wrote,

> The Abrahamic God is the all-powerful Lord and Master who demands nothing less than the total obedience of his faithful servants. The transcendent otherness of God creates a possibility of a collision between religious commitment and the individual's personal desire and moral duty. Should such a conflict develop, the faithful self must follow Abraham in forgoing desire and suspending duty-even if this means sacrificing one's own son or forsaking one's beloved [which in Kierkegaard's case would have been his justification for breaking his engagement with Regine Olsen]. The Absolute Paradox occasions an absolute decision by posing the absolute Either-Or. Either believe or be offended. From the Christian perspective, this crucial decision is of eternal significance.

Pagan calculation of the meaning of sacrifice, human or otherwise, is completely different. It is strictly done on a nonpersonal basis: "You scratch my back (the gods providing the goods) and I'll scratch yours (provide a sacrifice)." It is a completely automatic "law of nature," and faith in any form has nothing to do with it.

Seen in this light, the absurdity of life experienced and expressed by *Qoholeth* and Job makes sense: the eternal and unchangeable will of God meets the person and will of the individual destined for salvation and communion with the divine, as faith, in a state of dynamic dialectic tension in their personalities between hope and the fear of God. As the old hymn put it "With many a trembling many a doubt, O Lamb of God I come."

> Faith is the highest <u>passion</u> in a person. But the person who has come to faith (whether he is extraordinarily gifted or plain and simple does not matter) does not come to a standstill in faith. Indeed, he would be indignant if anyone said to him, just as the lover resents it if someone said that he came to a standstill in love; for, he would answer "I am by no means standing still. I have my whole life in it."[9](emphasis added)

Faith is not static it is a dynamic and ongoing thing. In addition the knight of faith is obliged to rely upon himself alone, he feels the pain of not being able to make himself intelligible to others, but he feels no vain desire to guide others to experience things in exactly the same way. Kierkegaard tasted his first love in Regine and he said it was "beautiful and healthy, but not perfect."[24] Regine, his first love was his second love; it was an infinite love. But he resigned it in order to serve God. The double meaning of "Fear and Trembling" is clear, Abraham is both the father who brings his son as an offering, and Kierkegaard who offers Regine.[12]

137

In other words, one must give up all earthly possessions in infinite resignation and must also be willing to give up whatever it is one loves more than God. Jesus put it more plainly in Luke 14:26: "If any man comes to me and does not hate his own father and mother and wife, children, brothers and sisters, yes even his own life he cannot be a disciple of mine." There are many people across the world coming into the faith from cultures violently opposed to true Christianity who are finding this way of martyrdom without having to ask for it. Kierkegaard said that everyone had a choice in life; freedom consists in using that choice. We each have the right to speak or not and the right to act or not. Toward the end of the book, Johannes Silentio compared those who merely wanted a comfortable temporal existence with those who were willing to step out in faith.

> With a solid pension and sure prospects in a well ordered state; they have centuries and even millennia between them and the concussions of existence. On the other side are those single individuals—Mary, Mother of Jesus; the Apostles; above all, Abraham— who in their own lives have suffered such concussions. These special individuals, their psyches stretched on the rack of ambiguity, have become febrile. Minds inflamed with absurdity, their lives burn with an unearthly glow. But for the man also who does not so much as reach faith, life has tasks enough, and if one loves them sincerely, life will by no means be wasted.

Summary of the Religious Stage

It is not really possible to imagine any religion without some kind of morality, which is why Kierkegaard combined his latter two stages into an ethico-religious stage.[12] Faith does not do away with ethics or lead to **antinomianism,** for as St. Paul put it, "The law is put on a firmer footing" (Romans 3:31). This is important to note because it is evident that many people can shift from the grossest aesthetic stage of life to a truly Christian religious stage through a conversion experience often marked by deep conviction of sin. The individual in Christianity is paradoxically "before God" in an unacceptable state of sin as the awareness of guilt makes plain. If people are not to whip or fast themselves to death in a monastery or the like, their self-awareness has to accept that God himself has to be infinite and is the only measure the individual can rest in. The state of humankind is to recognize individual and corporate sin as children of Adam. Guilt exists as a totality, and the anguish bound up with this consciousness leading to the foot of the cross is the highest form of existential pathos.

Kierkegaard's exposition of the fall was an ingenious display of depth-psychology found in his examination of angst; the bottomless freedom of Adam's innocence was for him a kind of curse in a state of such nameless dread. The possibility of freedom leads the dread to a high pitch. Once dread was activated in the fall, the pathway to deeper sin lay open: "However deep the individual has sunk, he may sink deeper."[12] The knowledge from the tree of good and evil led to deeper dread, sin and grief. As St. Paul put it, "The good which I want to do, I fail to do; but what I do is the wrong which is against my will" (Romans 7:19), or the dread leading to sin is a sympathetic antipathy and an antipathetic sympathy. In the last analysis, sin is against God himself, who is the source of creation and Holy Wisdom. King David found this out when confronted with his murder and adultery when he confessed, "Against You only have I sinned" (Psalm 51:4). The consciousness of sin is absolutely necessary in Christianity. It was completely lacking in the paganism of King David's time and is still a sign of it today: "Abolish the awareness of dread and you might as well close all the churches and turn them into dance halls."[24] The answer to the consciousness of sin is not to counter it with greater ethical virtue but to "submit in faith to the answer provided by God in the righteousness of Christ."[24] The greatest danger for someone under this conviction is not to believe in the possibility of forgiveness; it can lead directly to committing the sin against the Holy Spirit of not only abandoning Christianity altogether but warring against it as a lie and myth.

St. Paul was a young ethical Pharisee when he had his Damascus road experience; his dramatic conversion showed that this hothead had presumably not gone past the point of no return. The leap from the ethical to the religious is seen as twofold—there are two "parallel movements." First, there has to be a movement of "infinite resignation" in which all self-righteousness and indeed anything else you may be clinging to is abandoned, and second, an act of faith in which one regains the innocence one has lost. This double movement takes place simultaneously.

In some respects, the story of Job offers some insights into the transition from the ethical to the religious sphere, involving as it does Job and his friends as Wisdom teachers, although Kierkegaard would not consider Job a knight of faith but only of resignation. The suffering the religious sphere involves is characteristic of it; one must "take up one's cross" against the world in passionate hope without any visible reason for such a hope. For the truly religious Christian, "Revelation is signalized by mystery; happiness by suffering; certainty of faith by uncertainty; the ease of a paradoxical religious life by its difficulty and truth by its uncertainty."[1] Anything else is false religion. The remedy for sin must be radical and the medicine strong. Of course, the believer is not totally free from sin, but the very drawing closer to God ignites suffering, which leads to forgiveness and peace through the intermediary Wisdom of the advocacy of the Holy Spirit. As Pascal put it, "Suffering is the natural state of the Christian."[14] Difficult as this may seem at times, it is but the outworking of God's infinite love shown in severity, gentleness in harshness, peace in war. If one is not God's child, one is not subject to his chastisement.

> Infinite resignation is that shirt we read about in the old fable. The thread is spun, the cloth bleached and sewn in tears, yet it is better protection than iron or steel armor. The secret is that everyone must sew it for themselves. Here is the reason for joy that nothing can happen ... can shake the belief that God is love ... when a man suffers continuously before God because of guilt ... he is assured that God is love and he is prevented from falling into doubt.[1]

The New Testament View

The life of Jesus Christ the man covered all three stages. He was no gratuitous ascetic. He enjoyed the legitimate pleasures of good company, with men and women, food and drink to the extent of being accused of being a glutton and a wine bibber (Matthew 11:19; Luke 7:24), and he wore a smart seamless robe, but the aesthetic sphere was not the one he majored in. When one looks at the wisdom of Christ in his parables, his teaching, and the way he rebuffed attacks and solved dilemmas such as that of the woman caught in adultery, we see someone who in his life was fully one of *Mashal* in the ethical sphere. He described himself as "wiser than Solomon" (Matthew 12; Luke: 11).

In the epistles, Paul was in line with the Wisdom teachers of the past, but in 1 Corinthians, he referred to a secret Wisdom and used it as a descriptive category of Christ himself. Christ is more than Wisdom—the agent of creation became part of creation.

In Colossians 1:30, Paul stated that Christ is God's and our Wisdom prefigured in the Wisdom Literature: creation and salvation were held together in the person of Jesus Christ through the Holy Spirit. Christ was the Wisdom of God. In 1 Corinthians 2:3, Paul distinguished between divine Wisdom, which was seen as foolishness by the world, and that of the wisdom of the world, seen as foolishness by God. Paul was not thinking of these things in a detached, objective way but in the subjective terms of his personal experience of salvation through Christ as mediator between humanity and God.

Did Jesus the man, as well as being a devout Jew, move into a religious stage of resignation? If we are to avoid any hint of **docetism**, the answer has to be yes. There is enough scriptural evidence to support this. He remarked that his will was to do the will of his father in heaven, and although well aware of his destiny, he submitted to his agonizing passion and death, praying that "the cup be taken from him." However, at the same time, he knew that after his sacrifice, he would be raised on the third day. In this way, he fit into the double movement of resignation and faith in his humanity. The faithful action of Abraham on Mount Moriah prefigures this.

Theology

The Fall Revisited and the Nature of Dread

The fundamental purpose of the first few chapters of Genesis is fairly straightforward: it is that one eternal God has created everything out of nothing (exactly how, as Job found out, is not a good question); that God created humans as special creatures with a spiritual dimension to their being; that they used the freedom they were given to disobey their creator and suffered the consequences and that God set in motion his great scheme of salvation, which is what the rest of the Bible is about. The purpose of this chapter is to examine the fall and to look at the way Adam's disobedience has a bearing on the human condition in the here and now, existentially.

Of several areas to look at, perhaps the first is in the recent field of **phenomenology**,[23] which emphasizes our consciousness and direct experience of the world over and above any abstraction; second, the nature of dread in itself as another psychological aspect of the fall and how it affects us now; and third, the nature of consciousness itself and the direct bearing it had on the fall.

Edmund Husserl (1859–1938) Photo 1890

To begin with, phenomenology is sometimes called "a descriptive philosophy of experience."[18] It was also seen as important that the consciousness is intentionally focused on something outside of itself to experience life so that humans, who express themselves creatively in artifacts many of which are copied from nature, nevertheless do not create the universal natural reality but interact with it.

The initiator of this field was Franz **Brentano** (1838–1917). He had a special interest in Aristotle and scholastic philosophy, studied theology, and was ordained a Catholic priest. However, between 1870 and 1873, Brentano was heavily involved in the debate on papal infallibility. A strong opponent of such a dogma, he eventually gave up his priesthood and his tenure in 1873 and in 1879 left the church. Brentano reintroduced of the concept of **intentionality**, a concept derived from the scholastic philosophy (Latin *intentio*, referring to ideas or representations of things formed by the mind); the main characteristic of mental phenomena, by which they could be distinguished from physical phenomena." Intentional inexistence" indicates the status of the objects of thought in the mind.[27] In short, objects in the neurocenters of the mind exist only as a mechanism of perception and may not be objects of desire.

The major phenomenological philosopher **Husserl** took up the precise analysis of mental processes in his *Logical Investigations* by attempting to find what was intrinsic to mental processes but avoiding any rationalism theories or presuppositions, transcending any objects and focusing on experience itself. He felt that the meanings and sense of being everyone has can be linked by what he called transcendental **intersubjectivity** by a process of reduction.[27]

The main idea of phenomenology in short is to put aside all question of the existence of any outside object, impression, or assumption, "bracketing" them, and examine any life experience from a fresh, unbiased perspective. The word **epoché** has been recoined for this, from the Greek, implying a suspension of judgment.[2] What is particularly significant in the case of Adam is that the first phenomenological process that has been noticed is one of naming. Adam as a freshly created being was like a newborn in that all experiences were new to him (in fact, he had not even had any experience in the womb), so he was completely focused outside himself. The name *Adam* is cognate with the Hebrew words for "dust" and "blood."

What made him different from the rest of the created order was his ability to communicate verbally, initially with his Creator. After God had warned him not to eat the forbidden fruit (Genesis 2:17), the next thing he did was to bring living creatures to Adam to name (2:19–20). In chapter 1, both male and female humans were created and told to be "fruitful" (1:28). The important thing to reiterate is that the newly created humans were focused on the world around them and not on themselves. They interacted with the reality around them that they were able to refer to through the process of naming without trying to create one of their own. A phenomenological analysis of Adam's state after the fall will be examined below. Let us now move on to his consciousness in his state of innocence.

The actualizing of original sin was analyzed by Kierkegaard in *The Concept of Dread* (1844), written by the pseudonymous Vigilius Haufniensis, "Watcher of the Marketplace" (Copenhagen means "marketplace" in Danish). The "dread" that is examined is angst, the fear without an object, which is only roughly translated as anguish or anxiety. According to this analysis, although Adam was in a state of innocence before the fall, he was also subject to such a dread. He had a gut-felt fear of the possibilities of his own freedom, what he may do; the primary act of prohibition from his creator against eating the tree of knowledge had induced this dread.[12]

Freedom is *never* just a possibility; as soon as it is suspected, it becomes an actuality.[12] This is what St. John meant when he said that, for example, when a man hates his brother, he is in a position to murder him (1 John 3:15, 4:20, as indeed happened with Cain to Abel). Please note that God put this forbidden tree in the middle of the garden, near the tree of life (2:9) and not in some out-of-the-way place. Temptation was never out of Adam's way, and it just grew stronger in his innocence. We can now introduce the technical definition for this kind of dread that John of Silence expressed in *Fear and Trembling*, a "sympathetic antipathy" and an "antipathetic sympathy." It is a *desire* for what one fears and a *fear* of what one desires. I often call this the "wet paint syndrome"; one can't resist touching fresh paint to see if it is dry. It has also been designated by John Staff as **contrasuggestibility**; it is also probably what St. Paul had in mind when he stated, "Sin gains its power from the law" (1 Corinthians 15:56). So once Adam knew he could disobey God, he desired to do so, yet he dreaded his own desire because he knew that as a free being, there was nothing to stop him from committing the first sin. Adam and Eve managed to resist sin until the Devil got to work, so what was the process that led them to it?

The word *consciousness* is in fact cognate with the word *conscience* and once meant much the same thing. The philosopher John Locke gave consciousness its present connotation in *An Essay on*

Human Understanding. Formerly, consciousness usually referred to communication between people—what people understood they were saying to each other, but after the seventeenth century, it increasing became to mean inner consciousness, especially self-consciousness.[27]

Let us go back to the phenomenology of naming. Once we have named something, as Adam did with the birds and beasts, we have replaced their sensibly received immediate reality with the opposition of "otherness." The thoughts and words we have for something in our neural mind produces the possibility of contradiction. Unlike the Cartesian notion that consciousness overcomes doubt, consciousness *is* a form of doubt because it can lead to double mindedness.[7] So for example, if we are aware of a god or God who is there and we have given him a name, the opposite possibility immediately arises: that the god or God we have named is *not* there. This is probably why the Old Testament God is YHWH—a name that is too sacred to mention; instead, he was referred to as *Adonai*, "Lord," which could apply to any superior being, thereby avoiding the twin traps of atheism and polytheism, because if one cannot name someone, one cannot deny that person's existence. We humans realize as verbally thinking beings that the world is in a constant state of change; as **Heraclitus** observed, "You can't step in the same river twice." The negative and the possibility of contradiction are present in all consciousness, and it can be reflected on our consideration of the divine. Doubt accentuates this negative; the only cure for it is a genuine, subjective faith that sustains thought yet realizes the world is uncertain and not justified by any objectivity.

We maintain the relationship between the real world and the conception of it in our consciousness through the belief that it really is there. Again, this is unlike Descartes' idea of radical doubt of the external world but being assured of our own thinking selves. There are two possibilities: either one accepts that normal states of consciousness are a strange mixture of doubt and belief that accept and believe *by faith* that the outside world is real and are very like religious states of consciousness in which God really is and can be communicated with, or one runs away and hides just like Adam and Eve did in the garden,[22] pretending that one's acceptance of reality and belief does not depend on a wrestling with one's conscience over the possibility of contradiction that lies within one. Children, unlike sophisticated adults, find it far easier to believe in things and have faith.

A salient point about the fall is that it must have taken place in an altered state of consciousness, when the psychological guard of our first parents was down. Eve, whose name in Hebrew, *Ishshah,* means "source of life" and puns with the name for man, *Ish*, had been created from Adam while he was in a trance. Also, *min,* "from" in Hebrew, puns with the word for "kind." So Adam was saying that Eve was created from him but of the same kind.[26] So a changed state of consciousness had already been induced in Adam by God for her own creation. (2:21–23). Later, she was approached by the Father of Lies in the guise of the serpent who in reply to Eve's stating "[If] either of us eat or touch the fruit we shall die" (3:3, 4), said, "Of course you will not die ... your <u>eyes will be opened</u> ... you will become like gods knowing <u>both</u> good <u>and</u> evil" (3:5, 6). They then committed the sin of disobedience by eating the fruit. "Then the <u>eyes of both of them were opened</u>" (3:7).(emphasis added)

It seems that the act was also committed in an altered state of consciousness, except this time induced by the hypnotic allure of Satan. So today, shamans and others usually through the use of drugs and abandon try to get to another state of consciousness to contact the spirit world.

After their act of disobedience, they became fully awake. Whereas before they had been conscious of each other's nakedness but without shame, they became *self-conscious*, aware of their nakedness, and the possibilities of doubt, disbelief, and contradiction arose in them. The reaction was to run away and hide both from themselves and their maker under a useless heap of leaves. (Children playing hide and seek often think if they can't see someone, the seeker can't see them). God's remark to Adam was, "Who told you you were naked?" (Genesis 3:11). Adam did not answer, but the correct answer would have been that he realized it himself. Before, they had been innocent; then, there was an awful awakening to a full state of consciousness and conscience in which human freedom meant it became possible to deny the reality of the inner and outer world even to the point of denying their creator.

A phenomenological analysis of this state would be the way that the world was changed to our first parents in a state of **embodied consciousness** that takes into account the subjective quality of the lived, the subjective quality of someone's experience. [2] Embodiment represented then as it does now the subject's view of his or her body as it has to be lived with subjectively, the exact opposite of one's body as perceived by other observers in the outside world. The inner perception is often at variance with the perception seen by others in a painful way, giving rise to dysfunctional behavior between the self and others. The human race would be condemned to this lot until the appearance of the second Adam, Jesus Christ. The human race was not condemned to *ignorance* but to *knowledge* that could be passed from generation to generation. This knowledge would not have been available to Adam and Eve in their innocence, but such knowledge could be used for both good *and* evil.

Perhaps another phenomenological thinker who followed Husserl, Martin **Heidegger** (1889–1976), had this in mind. He developed the idea of **dasein**, "being there," to indicate not merely humankind's presence in the world but its involvement in it. A fundamental aspect of this notion is that unlike animals or inanimate objects, we are aware and concerned about our place in the world and above all *our mortality*. This awareness heightens our sense of dread about our existence and the bottomless range of possibilities for good or evil open to us. It has to be offset by the day-to-day *care* for the world about us that dasein[22] brings. To illustrate, take another pun that seems to come out in the Genesis passage and was surely in the mind of the writer: the word used for serpent in Hebrew is very close to the word for copper, *nahas*. The bronze-age writer would have been only too aware that although useful tools could be made from the metal, so could vicious weapons. Not just that, but as humankind fell further away in communion from its creator, so polytheism and idolatry grew up, often using idols made of such metals.

In a way, there was a certain awful inevitability about the fall, but God was not to blame. He created a creature with freedom with whom he desired communion; this freedom led to humanity's downfall through the lying spite of the Devil. Adam called Eve *hawwa*, "living thing" (Genesis 3:16). (**LXX,** *zoe*) to indicate her new status as an object; this may also pun with the Aramaic word *hiwya*, "serpent."[26] So the consequences of the fall were twofold: first, awareness of guilt and shame and separation from God shown in pointlessly hiding from him and wrapping up in leaves whereas before there had been unimpaired communion, and second, in the curse of toil, sorrow, pain in childbirth, and eventually in death, humans now become perverted creatures who had lost their true selves, that is, the image of God in which they had been created.

However, as mentioned above, the image of God is still stamped on humans as is shown in their pursuit of scientific knowledge, its use in engineering and technology, and the development of art, culture, and civilization. These achievements, however, are subject to frustration, as people who do not love the invisible God do not love their fellows and vice versa. The image of Satan, the great, destroying hater of humanity, is also stamped upon them; humanity after the fall has known both good and evil.

When confronted by the gospel, people must choose good or evil. In the New Testament, the psychological effects of the fall were outlined by St. Paul in Romans 1; everybody, no matter how bad they are, knows the truth about God and themselves deep in at least their unconscious selves, but they wickedly suppress the truth despite the fact of their own existence and (despite how the evolutionists try to muddy the argument) the created order around them. So again, humanity's situation is not one of ignorance but suppression of knowledge; people prefer darkness to light and refuse to glorify God, leading to intellectual vanity. Or as St. Paul put it, "All their thinking has ended in futility and their misguided minds are plunged in darkness" (Romans 1:21).

The fall was not the end; from all eternity, a redeemer had been planned for humankind and a better state than humanity in its original innocence. The cross on which Jesus died was another tree that this time gives life; we need to be clothed in the righteousness of Christ to cover our moral nakedness in the same way Adam and Eve were clothed in skins by the Lord; and as Adam means blood and Eve life, so we should consume Christ's body and blood spiritually.

The Western church has often restricted itself to St. **Augustine's** idea that somehow the fall was and is transmitted by concupiscence or carnal desire; on the other hand, Eastern

Orthodoxy realized that Augustine was not the only church father whose opinion had weight and rejected the idea that the guilt of original sin was passed down genetically by the sexual act. It based its teaching in part on Ezekiel 18:20, which said a son was not guilty of the sins of his father.

The Eastern Church teaches that in addition to their conscience and tendency to do well, men and women are born with a tendency to sin due to the fallen condition of the world; the situation is behavioral, psychological, and cultural. It follows **Maximus the Confessor** and others in characterizing the change in human nature as the introduction of a "deliberative will" (*theleema gnomikon*) in opposition to the "natural will" (*theleema physikon*) created by God, which tends toward the good.[14] Thus according to St. Paul in his epistle to the Romans, non-Christians can still act according to their consciences. Nonetheless, as a consequence of Adam's sin, seen merely as the prototype (since human nature has been degraded) of all future sinners, each of whom, in repeating Adam's sin, bears responsibility only for his own sins, humans became mortal.

Adam's sin is not comprehended only as disobedience to God's commandment but also as a change in man's hierarchy of values from theocentricism to anthropocentrism, driven by the object of his lust, outside of God, in this case the tree that was seen to be "good for food" and something "to be desired." So instead of God being the center of the individual's desire, it is the human self or other created objects.

To go back to one of Husserl's concepts, "original sin" is shared by all humankind through a process of transcendental intersubjectivity. Furthermore, the recent development of the notion of **functionalism** rather than mere behaviorism gives this approach to the fall extra weight in that it sees human behavior resulting from a whole complex of clusters of interactive mental states. Functionalism holds that types of mental states are definable in terms of the causal roles played by their tokens in an interconnected network.[2]

Another point the Western church in the last millennia has been at fault over has been to blame Eve rather than Adam for the fall, ensuring that the female sex is seen as a source of guilt and sin. In this more-enlightened age, perhaps the view of our old English and British ancestors who saw more weight in Paul's injunction in 1 Corinthians 7 of Christian wives to their unbelieving husbands and saw that the wise counsel should be expected and respected should be paid attention to.

In the anonymous Anglo-Saxon translation of Genesis, known as Genesis B, the story of the fall, the Devil disguised as a serpent but claiming to be an angel, goes first to Adam to persuade him to eat the forbidden fruit. But as the serpent didn't look like any angel he had met before, Adam refused. The defeated snake moves on to Eve, who was taken in by his claim to be a divine messenger with a new line of argument: he appealed to her as a wife whose duty it was to do the best for herself, her husband, and her children. He told her God would be *angry* with them both if they refused to eat. "Coax Adam carefully," he told her, "so that he carries out your counsel lest you should both be forced to be hateful to God your Ruler." Eve was thereby conned by a disguised liar into playing both the role of believing wife and "peace weaver." She asked Adam, "What will it avail you, such shameful quarrelling with our Lord's messenger." She talked with him day and night until eventually he changed his mind. Nevertheless, the writer was asking for sympathy for the loyal Eve, who acted out of the best intentions and did not try to portray womankind as the source of wickedness and falsehood. It was Adam who sinned.

Man Is Not a Machine (Cybernetics and Neuroscience)

There is a long history of machines that mimic human behavior as automata, and the science fiction of the twentieth century contains many stories of man-made intelligent machines originally designed to serve humanity who then developed wills of their own and decided to rebel against their creators. The original one was *Rossum's Universal Robots*, a 1920 Czech story from which we get our word *robot*, meaning "worker" (although the robots in the story are not completely mechanical and perhaps could be called cyborgs).

After the development of computers, later stories put forward the idea of superintelligent computers that could develop wills of their own and take over, like Hal in the film *2001: A Space Odyssey*. However, in more recent years, the realization has grown up that machines like this are not likely to ever exist, and hardly anyone writes such stories now.

The object of this section is to show how recent advances in knowledge have diminished any ideas of **mechanical determinism**[25] that sees the human brain as some kind of highly sophisticated computer that cannot decide anything for itself, that the human being as a whole is not a machine but also that machines could never be human. There is, however, an epistemological conundrum in dealing with psychology in that the object of study—the mind—is being examined by the mind!

It gets even more problematic when issues of linguistics are being discussed because not only is the mind involved with the processing of linguistic information, but also, the means by which it is communicated—language—is itself the subject of study! It makes objective sense then to make a start in this area to see how "intelligent" machines unaffected by the human psyche might operate and to go on to look at human anatomy and physiology.

Cybernetics is a discipline closely related to control engineering, systems theory, and information theory; the word coined from the Greek *kubernos*, "steersman" by the American mathematician Norbert Weiner after his work as an engineer on antiaircraft tracking systems in World War II. He had to make continuous adjustments to their guns' trajectories to hit their moving targets. The basic working notion in cybernetics is that of the **feedback loop**: self- regulation that applies to every controllable system from mechanical servos right up to the nervous systems of animals and the human brain. External influences are sensed and communicated to subsystems, and the results monitored. The two essential requirements are that there is efficient communication between constituent subsystems and that there are control mechanisms to regulate operations.[23]

To see how this might be seen to be acting in the human mind, take the act of plucking an apple. There is an interactive sensor motor cycle in which the information supplied to the eye about what the hand is doing is fed back to the nerves and brain controlling the hand; the brain then corrects the movement of the hand, and the process is repeated until the task is complete. This is all well and good, and most animals seem capable at it though robots seem to be clumsy at tasks like this.

What happens, though, when we apply this to the area of **artificial intelligence?** The central criteria for an intelligent machine then would be first that it could conceive and integrate abstract concepts, drawing conclusions from incomplete data, and second, that it could exhibit consciousness,[23] that is, the awareness that it existed and had consequential behavior, something lower forms of animal life like insects don't seem to manage. Both aspects would seem to be essential in autonomous language and communication.

A test that has been proposed to find if a machine is capable of human levels of intelligence is the **Turing test**, after the mathematician and computer pioneer Alan Turing in 1950. It works like this: a human asks questions electronically by keyboard to two hidden correspondents, one human and one mechanical. If the questioner cannot determine whether the answers given are from another person or a machine, the machine is intelligent.

Turing predicted that in fifty years such an intelligent machine would exist.[25] Despite the fact that computers are much more powerful now than Turing could have imagined and are capable of a multitude of tasks, to date, no machine has passed this test with any certainty, and it looks as if none ever will. Even if a machine could be developed that was capable of abstract thought, it would be capable of developing only universal ideas that could be used as propositions in objective thinking. For a machine to be fully human, it would have to develop the kind of consciousness that was aware of its own existence through subjective statements and self-reflection. Such a machine is unlikely to be developed (and who would want it anyway?). In addition to the failure of the Turing test, there is also the corollary of **Gödel's theorem**, which shows the impossibility of proving the consistency of natural number systems in the same system: machines depend on natural number systems.[25] The admittedly speculative inference is that any theory that takes the human mind to be a mechanical deterministic system is bound to be false.

The architecture and indeed workings of the human nervous system are completely different from any intelligent machine that has ever been devised. The brain gives rise to twelve pairs of cranial nerves largely concerned with sensory input. The whole of the nervous system, including the spinal cord and the nerves that run off it, is composed of the spider-like cells of the neuralgia supporting the main star-shaped neurons within them. The posterior nerve roots passing into the spinal cord are sensory bringing sensations from all parts of the body, while farther forward are the motor roots bringing impulses of movement to the body muscles. Within muscles and similar tissues away from the spinal cord, these two types mingle to give instant response.[18] So far, it is easy to see that at a basic level, a cybernetic system is organized in the body, but of course there is far more to human physiology than that.

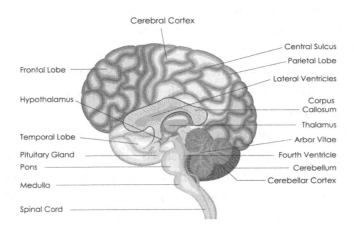

Cerebral Cortex

Central Sulcus
Parietal Lobe
Frontal Lobe
Lateral Ventricles
Hypothalamus
Corpus Callosum
Thalamus
Temporal Lobe
Arbor Vitae
Pituitary Gland
Fourth Ventricle
Pons
Cerebellum
Cerebellar Cortex
Medulla

Spinal Cord

BRAIN

The brain operates on two levels: simpler actions and more-visceral emotions are experienced by the hypothalamus, which in many ways is the seat of the unconscious mind. The large, walnut-shaped cerebral hemispheres, which are the largest part of the brain, are the seat of our cognitive functions and have some control over the functions of the hypothalamus, which is more prominent in more-primitive animals. Some large animals such as elephants or gorillas may have a large cerebellum, but the ratio of cerebral to hypothalamic activity is always higher in humans. In any case, the development of the temporal lobe, which controls language, is different.

There are two cerebral hemispheres, one of which tends to be dominant in humans—usually the left, which is why most people are right handed. This dominance is present in animals but less so. Different parts of the cerebellum control different mental functions as illustrated in the diagram; perception, memory, motor skills, and above all, language, are some. Damage to specific areas of the cerebellum results in corresponding disorder, and dementia affects more, including any ability to reason. Having said this, as the brain is an organic structure, it has some ability to repair some of these functions as in any body tissue through regeneration and the "rewiring" of neurons, something no machine has so far been designed to manage.

Primitive or **ordinary reflexes** such as suddenly removing the hand from a hot surface or sharp object do not involve the brain at all but result from the instantaneous feedback from large nerve bundles called ganglions in the spinal cord. This explains why a headless chicken can still run around. These differ from a **conditioned reflex** as in the famous Pavlov's dog experiment.

The idea of **behaviorism** in psychology, largely introduced by B. F. Skinner, is based on the notion that all the higher activities in the brain, such as language for example, can be explained behaviorally. This somewhat mechanistic notion has been largely displaced by the cognitive ideas of Chomsky,[23] but there is no doubt that a degree of conditioning goes on in the brain, as any practical teacher knows.

In philosophy, this has been given extra weight in recent years by the development of **functionalism** as mentioned above, which recognizes that behavioral input can occur as a complex and that the idea of universal notions such as beauty may be abstracted from the number of beautiful objects experienced.[25] There is a morbid difference between a physically damaged spinal cord and a badly damaged or poisoned brain. In the first case, there is a flaccid paralysis, whereas in the second case, all reflexes are exaggerated and the lower centers of the brain are unleashed to act in an uncontrollable way. The cerebellum is affected like this in drunkenness—the first thing to go is people's inhibitions. What is interesting is that the hypothalamus also operates the **autonomic nervous system**; this controls the purely automatic functions of the body that, when we are in a state of relaxation, we are usually unaware of. It has two components—the sympathetic and the parasympathetic. The former usually prepares us for "fight or flight" under the influence of hormones, and the latter prepares us for rest.

The part of the brain responsible for emotions can therefore influence things such as our blood pressure. The cerebellum then is engaged in a constant relationship of control with the hypothalamus and indeed with the whole body.[18] What makes humans distinct from animals and of course with any conceivable intelligent machine in this respect is that whereas in the former, hypothalamic operations, including the "fight or flight" response in reaction to a predator, last only while the threat is real, in humans, the power we have to form concepts, symbols, and language in our cerebellum to represent feelings and emotions that spring from the hypothalamus and the glands of the endocrine system can be long and drawn out; a "bad day at the office" can last all through the evening. Too much of this sort of thing with the raised blood pressure associated with it can lead to fatal heart attacks.[18]

On the other hand, a calm attitude leads to increased resistance to disease and pain even in child bearing: "A quiet mind means a quiet womb." In a word, people are subject to **psychosomatic** influences. It is generally accepted by physicians that all conditions both mental and physical are to a degree psychosomatic; the body and mind are closely intertwined, and the human needs to be considered holistically—body, soul, and spirit. If anyone wants a mechanistic analogy, one could say that the body is the hardware, the soul is the software, and the spirit is the electricity that makes it all go. A good physician will always treat a patient as a whole and will not focus merely on his or her disease.

An important upshot of these considerations and much of the rest of this is that the **mind-body problem** first put forward by Descartes[22] does not exist. He thought there was a distinct mental or spiritual sphere separate from the physical, that there were two types of substance, "mind" and "matter," and a question arose on how these could interact.[23] Simple questions such as, "How do I know I have hurt myself with this pin?" which may have been a problem to him in the seventeenth century, look trivial in the light of modern science, but the debate has gone on.[25] However, along with what we know about neurology (which on its own might lead us to a purely mechanistic view of human nature), we have the insights of phenomenology, which concentrates on the intentionality of human consciousness: the mind does not create reality but interacts with it, and what matters in the last analysis is relation and relationships. The relation between a subject and its object is most important, for example, the "I-thou" relationship between lovers or between worshippers and their God examined by **Martin Buber** in his eponymous book.[17] The two main parts of the brain, the cerebellum and the hypothalamus, are engaged in their own state of feedback intimately linked with the rest of the body; however, the decision to act consciously based on considerations that can rise to the ethical and religious and acting on it is what makes people spiritual beings.

The Object of Christian Faith and Life

(According to H. V. Martin, *Wings of
Faith*,[30] with added comments)

Many Christian thinkers point out in regard to Kierkegaard's ideas
that faith requires an object and that as the most important truths
for him were subjective; it needs to be shown that Kierkegaard,
as well as aligning himself with the classical rules of logic, did
indeed present Jesus Christ as the object of faith. This section
covers his view of Christ as the object of Christian faith and what
he thought the nature of that faith should be. It comes out more
as passionate personal expression in his *Journals* rather than his
other writings, but it is there.

The Object of the Christian Faith Is Jesus Christ: Himself and not His Teaching

Unlike Socrates' idea in which as a living soul an individual
"recollects" the truth within him as a living soul and part of
the eternal reality, Kierkegaard clearly indicated Christian faith
depended on an *event* in space and time in which God became
incarnate. For rationalists including Kant, the historical existence
of Jesus was not really relevant as he was interested only in
ethical principles; it was not relevant to the idealist Hegel either
as he saw only the possibility of "finite and Absolute spirit."

164

But to Kierkegaard, the historical fact of incarnation was vitally important and fundamental. The relationship between God and an individual can be personally appropriated only by faith. "The object of faith is not a doctrine, for then the relationship would be intellectual" *(Concluding Unscientific Postscript)*. This means of course that Christian faith does not depend on an individual's intelligence, mental health, or age. In addition, faith answers not to our reason, which would be the concern only of thinkers, but to our very existence and the nitty-gritty of life, which is everyone's concern. Also, **apologetics** is downplayed, as either Jesus was or was not (a misguided madman or fool) whom he claimed to be. There is no rational proof or disproof of the incarnation of God any more than there is of God's existence. The Bible merely assumes these are true, and either you believe Jesus was divine or you do not.

As Fully God and Fully Man

It would have been easier for Christianity to start in Greece or Rome, where gods were conceived as human or emperors divine rather than in monotheistic Jewry! "The contradiction between being God and being an individual man is the greatest possible, the infinitely qualitative contradiction" *(Training in Christianity)*. Perhaps the usual extreme language is used by the word *contradiction*, but to recognize this paradox and to accept it must be better than to endlessly and pointlessly argue about the issue or to subscribe to one of the heresies that has emphasized either the divinity or humanity of Christ. The particular danger from the nineteenth century (thanks to Hegel and others) onward has been to think that there is not in fact a gulf between humanity and God that could be bridged only by this divinely costly paradox: "The fundamental misfortune of Christendom is ... the fact that the doctrine of the God-man is taken in vain, the qualitative distinction between God and Man is pantheistical abolished" (*Sickness unto Death*). Perhaps Tertullian should have the last word on the above issue: *Credible prorsus est, quia ineptum est,* "It is credible because it is absurd."

Incognito

Rather like a prince who disguises himself as a beggar to see if the woman he has chosen as his bride will love him for himself rather than his magnificence or majesty, so Christ came to woo his church. Jesus came as an ordinary man in an ordinary family. Although he made divine claims for himself, he never said, "I am God," preferring to call himself the "Son of Man," and he actually kept a lower profile, if one reads the Gospels, than some imagine. However, the incarnation was a unique event in time and space: Jesus was not like the Hindu **avatars** of Vishnu who keep appearing in bodies or forms that are just disguises for the divine spirit; that is a **theophany**, although it is quite possible the second person of the Trinity appeared as such as the angel of the Lord as in the sacrifice of Isaac or the mysterious "man with no name" who wrestled with Jacob. These events were preincarnational.

There was a complete fusion of the human and divine in Jesus Christ though his godhood was completely veiled by his manhood. Some, like Peter, who in answering the Lord's question, "Who do you say I am?" (Mark 8:9) and all the Synoptic Gospels recognized him; others did not. "He came to his own and his own people would not accept him" (John 1:11). Great moral teaching, kindness, wisdom, and even miracles will not convince those who do not recognize that God has come as a man, and there *must* be this mystery or else there can be no true faith.

Faith does not act by human sense or sight. "The mystery is the expression for the fact that the revelation is a revelation in the strictest sense, so that the mystery is the only trait which it is known" (*Concluding Unscientific Postscript*). Christ's response to Peter when he said that he did recognize him as the Messiah shows that faith was working in Peter through his incognito. "You did not learn that from any human being; it was revealed to you by my heavenly Father." (Matthew 16:17).

The Sign of Contradiction

Some say Kierkegaard wanted to deny any objective information God wanted to convey to us, so when he highlighted that when God imparted himself to people indirectly and without any immediacy, it is easy to see why he has been misunderstood. But he was saying that Christ's divinity cannot be experienced directly as knowledge, it can be apprehended only through the sign of his humanity.

The study of signs, **semiotics**, has developed over the last century, but the Jews of old were not averse to it as they were always asking Jesus for a "sign" as to who he was, and St. Paul noted the Jews wanted a sign as much as the Greeks wanted wisdom from him about Christ. A sign is something other than what it stands for: for example, a white flag waved on a battlefield is just a piece of white cloth but a *sign* the people waving it want to surrender. Kierkegaard was basing his claim that Christ was "a sign of contradiction" in the context of the infant Jesus' purification at the temple; the seer Simeon blessed the holy family and said to Mary, "This child is destined to be a *sign that will be*

R.I.Johnston

rejected [the Greek *antilegomenon*, "reject," can also be translated "spoken against"]; and you too will be pierced to the heart. Many in Israel will stand or fall because of him, and the secret thoughts of many will be laid bare" (Luke 2:34).

So the sign of the incarnation is ambiguous and has two contrary meanings: Jesus in his immediacy is a man, but his presence as a man seemingly contradicts his claim to be God. The communicator of Christianity, Jesus, not the communication, is the main point about the message. This should ring a bell in this day and age: as Marshall McLuhan put it, "The medium is the message"![15] The revelation of Christ comes with the possibility of rejection Simeon foresaw—either he would be rejected, or people would give him their allegiance. There is no sitting on the fence about Christ, as loyalty to him comes with the force of a royal command. As St. Paul put it when preaching to the men of Athens,

> The God who created the world and everything in it,
> Lord of heaven and earth ... God has overlooked the
> age of ignorance; but now he COMMANDS men and
> women everywhere to repent, because he has fixed a
> day on which He will have the earth judged, and justly
> judged by a man of His own choosing; of this He has
> given assurance to all by raising him from the dead.
> (Acts 17:24–31)

Some of those hearing laughed, some decided to leave it for further discussion, but some did believe. The first two refused the divine command and were guilty of offense; only the last showed saving faith. The decision of these people did not rest on any unintelligibility—"Faith must not rest content with unintelligibility" (*Concluding Unscientific Postscript*); please note that Paul made intelligible remarks about Christ mentioning his resurrection rather than his sacrificial death to these gentiles.

In His Eternal Contemporaneousness

To put it simply, "Jesus Christ the same: yesterday, today and forever" (Hebrews 13:8). Faith is far more than a matter of historical witness, important though that is. The challenge to faith is the same to people now as it was on the Areopagus of Athens twenty or so centuries ago. Humanly speaking, it is only the present that really exists when a person in his or her temporality can meet in spirit with the crucified, risen, and alive forever God-man, Jesus Christ. The nature of Jesus the man is rooted in history; his nature as God the Christ is contemporaneous with all eternity. Jesus was aware of his eternal nature, and all who are inclined to him in space and time desire him. For example, Jesus said, "Your father Abraham was overjoyed to see my day; he saw it and was glad" (John 8:56). This gives some insight into the problem of those who could not hear the gospel because they lived before the Christ event, or those who live and die in those lands where the gospel has not been proclaimed; they instinctively see Christ in their spirits and come to him when the gospel *is* proclaimed.

What is also important is that although Kierkegaard did not focus on the crucifixion and was refreshingly free from stressing any particular atonement theory, Jesus must have been seen to die and there must have been evidence for a bodily resurrection for any contemporaneous spiritual contact with Christ to make sense.

Again, in emphasizing this point, Kierkegaard was fighting against two things started by Kant and Hegel and carried on by German theologians that are still showing their deadening hand today—first, the tendency in philosophical theology to minimize or negate the historical character of Judeo-Christianity, and second, the tendency to conceive of Christian revelation as the mere communication of knowledge.

What St. Paul called "the appointed time" in Galatians 4:4, Kierkegaard developed into what he called the "moment" or the "instant." Here, the divine revelation rooted in history breaks through the ages as an instant of faith, impacting subjectively upon the believer. It has the character of an "atom of eternity" (*Concept of Dread*). It has to be remembered that history is the sphere of the human race but eternity that of God. People are merely creatures existing in space and time; this might lie behind one of Kierkegaard's typically extreme and provocative remarks, "God does not exist; He is eternal."

A final point with regard to all of the above is that just because Kierkegaard played down the historical facts of Jesus' earthly life to make his main points does not mean he thought they had no significance: "The successor believes by <u>means</u> of the testimony of the contemporary [witnesses to the life, death and resurrection of Jesus], and <u>in virtue of</u> the condition he himself receives from God" (*Philosophical Fragments*).(emphasis added)

The Nature of Christian Faith is -

(According to H. V. Martin, *Wings of Faith*,[30] with added comments)

Absolute Trust

Kierkegaard takes the position of the Protestant reformers in that people are not "made righteous" by faith in God (by means of imparted grace, the Roman Catholic position), but that they are *reckoned* righteous (by means of imputed grace). So an individual is fully and freely justified in God's sight in heaven's place of judgment—the mercy seat—by faith in Christ. Nevertheless, such an act of faith cannot and must not be a mere nodding intellectual assent; it must be infused with subjective passion. The trouble with state Lutheranism by the time of Kierkegaard was that it had lost the sense of transforming passion that had made all the difference at the time of the Reformation and had gone cold. It was this subjective passion, that of the heart aflame, that he sought to reestablish.

Different in Origin from Reason

"Faith gives substance to our hopes and convinces us of realities we do not see" (Hebrews 11:1); so where there is certainty, true faith cannot arise. Faith cannot be based on proof but must be precipitated from the feeling of despair over one's alienation from one's Creator God driven by the Holy Spirit. This kind of true faith is always going to be in a state of dialectic tension with normal common sense and reason.

Kierkegaard is often misunderstood as being antirational on this point, but he was being no different from Luther about this specific type of reasoning about an ineffable God and his works. Luther could be just as extreme in his language; in his *Commentary on Galatians*, he wrote, "Faith kills reason and slays that beast" and that reason was "that cruel and pestilent enemy of God." He was more extreme elsewhere when he called reason "the Devil's harlot." What he was fighting against was the **scholastic** medieval tendency to approach the whole problem of revelation intellectually. What both he and Kierkegaard were saying was that reason was inadequate in spiritual matters. This did not mean reason was useless elsewhere; Luther stated that the enlightened reason of the regenerate man in his *Table Talk* was "a fair and glorious instrument and work of God" even though he also stated therein, "Reason is the greatest enemy that faith has; it never comes to the aid of spiritual things but ... struggles against the divine Word, treating with contempt all that emanates from God."

One of the leading skeptical figures of the Enlightenment, David Hume, perhaps could back up Luther when he wrote, "Reason is and only ought to be slave of the passions." So it is not absurdity in itself that is the basis of Christian faith; it is only that the eternal truth and paradoxical nature of the Christ event must appear to be absurd to existing human creatures and it must be believed in spite of that. Where reason plays a part is bringing the Christian humbly up against the inscrutability of this ultimate reality. "The effect of reason is in fact to know the paradox negatively but not more" (*Journals*). It is a corrective necessity to expose the futility of using reason to give a sense of the absolute in this day and age: "And so the whole generation is stuck in the mud banks of reason: and no one grieves over it, there is only self-satisfaction and conceit, which always follow on reason and the sins of reason" (*Journals*).

A Passionate Leap of Life-Decision

To create nuclear fusion, a proton shot at an atomic nucleus has to overcome the repulsive electrical force of the nucleus before it can become attached to it by the much larger binding force that acts only over a glue-like distance. In the same way, the absolute paradox of the Christ event acts as a repulsive force in the will against the natural immediacy of faith. The leap the believer makes powered by the Holy Spirit is usually made in terms of a struggle against this repulsive force. Strangely enough, for less-reflective people and probably young children, this is easier to do, as they do not recognize the paradox so much (as George Formby famously said, "It's grand being daft."). But the more reflective, educated, and worldly wise you are, the more difficult it is, and the will needs to be broken.

Faith can arise only "when all conceivable human certitude and probability pronounces" (*Repetition*), and with the usual extreme language, "Only a man of iron will can become a Christian, for only he has a will that can be broken." Christianity then becomes an answer to the tragedy of the human situation rather than an answer to philosophical problems. Someone who puts faith in a doctor does not want an explanation of symptoms as much as a cure. Such is the cure that Christ the Great Physician offers. Only those faced with the vital anguish and bondage to their temporal existence are willing to make "The Leap" at the abyss of decision. "Without risk faith is impossibility."

173

R.I.Johnston

However, such a leap is more into the arms of a loving, heavenly Father than into an uncertain darkness. Inward assurance of faith once the decision has been made may be a work of the Holy Spirit along with a psychological process. But faith to the believer is never taken for granted; "I believe, help my unbelief" (Mark 9:24). This is not doubt but fear and trembling in reaction to despair: "Doubt is a despair of thought; despair is a doubt of the personality" (Either/Or).

A good illustration of Christian assurance of salvation is that of a swimmer in a deep ocean; the scary fact that there is a deep abyss below is there in the mind, but the water bears the swimmer up. In the same way, the despair believers struggle against bear them up in their fear of sin, and the inward joy and peace of the Holy Spirit sustains them.

Another analogy might be that of a bird alighting on the frail twig of a tree that may break; it cheeps its song anyway, knowing it has wings. Anyone who has been up in a glider knows that the sound of the creaking airframe and the knowledge it has no engine is inclined to stiffen with fear, but after a while, confidence in the aircraft's flight performance leads to an increasingly relaxed but alert attitude.

An Act of Individual Freedom

The act of Christian faith is a personal, individual decision of the human will, but this does not and cannot happen unless it is driven by the divine determination of the individual by the Holy Spirit. There can be no amoral "decision for Christ" without the conviction of sin that he induces any more than there can be the kind of lazy acknowledgement of the doctrine of predestination that does not see that it must involve the

174

freedom of the individual. The irresistible purpose of God and the limited will of the individual exist in dialectic tension. "[By] having unquestionably arisen in order to relate freedom and God's omnipotence [predestination theories] solve the riddle by denying one of the concepts, and consequently explain nothing" (*Journals*). But "A pure and unadulterated *liberum arbitrium* [arbitrary autonomous free will] is a chimera" (ibid.).

It is not unknown for evangelists to make an appeal to people either alone or in the midst of a congregation to make a decision for Christ. Actually, any decision to the ethical or religious has to be a moral decision to make any sense; one cannot become a Christian without accepting a specific moral code, in summary, of loving God with all you have and anyone you come across in life as yourself. What is more, it has to be individual and subjective and not made as the result of any peer pressure: It cannot be the result of a Dionysian or sensuous religious atmosphere, fine rhetoric, or the desire for purely emotional expression that may be expressed externally but has not been felt and held passionately deep in the heart. It leads to a new personality.

It is also not uncommon for some Christians to say with perhaps a little too much force that God has given them free will. Free will (apart from the idea of a free will offering) is a concept found nowhere in scripture. It is not so much that our wills are free; they are not, as the philosopher John Locke observed, walking about on two legs like a weird doppelganger; it is people who are free. The Christian recognizes the ultimate irony—to be free is to be a slave. In the case of the Christian, this is to be the slave of the kindest master of all, God himself.

Conversion happens at a place and time when the individual's experience of the pathos of existence overcomes cool reason against the paradox of the Christ event. At this point, **the**

moment, there is no undetermined free choice, but the kind of people individuals have become determines the choice they make. There is no psychological "will to believe" that some thinkers and preachers would have us believe. But at the moment, the individual cannot remain neutral in the face of God's command to repent and believe in his Son.

> Christianity says to a man: you shall choose the one essential thing, but in such a way that there is no question of a choice ... If you drivel on any longer, then you do not in fact choose the one essential thing ... the very fact that in this sense there is no choice expresses the tremendous passion and intensity with which it must be chosen.[24]

> However astonishing it may seem, one is therefore obliged to say that only "fear and trembling" only constraint, can help a man to freedom. Because "fear and trembling" and compulsion can master him in such a way that there is no longer any question of choice—and then one chooses the right thing.[24]

So people are not really free to choose to believe when and where they like but only on "the day of visitation," when there can be no question of indecision and where time meets eternity in the existence of an individual.

> The most tremendous thing which has been given to man is; the choice, freedom. If you desire to save it and preserve it, there is only one way; in the same second, unconditionally and in complete resignation to give it back to God, and with it yourself.

Thus, there is on the face of it formal freedom, in relation to "selving" oneself in Christ when the "moment" comes, but the truth is, it does not happen just when and where one pleases. In addition, where there is indecision, one is struggling only with the illusion of freedom. Almighty God demands allegiance when it is demanded: "Choose here and now whom you will serve" (Joshua 24:15).

An Involvement in Suffering

This is more than the normal human suffering of life every human being experiences, or even the persecutions and scorn Christians thrown at them by the world and the Devil; it means realizing that one exists in the face of an utterly transcendent, holy God through the act of faith. One's autonomy has been crucified. Again, animals cannot have this awareness "but to know that one exists before God and not to go crazy or brought to naught" (*Sickness unto Death*).

Perhaps there has been a little too much "worm theology" in which evangelical believers have expressed their unworthiness, but it is corrective to look at the call of some of the prophets, that of Isaiah probably being the best example. On seeing the Lord "high and lifted up and his train filling the temple," he cried, "Woe is me! For I am doomed" (Isaiah 6:5). But an angel touched his lips with a live coal from the altar, and he went on to a long, distinguished career.

The heart of the believer continually longs for "just a closer walk with thee," as the hymn puts it, that is far more than just religious awe that may have nothing to do with desire for a relationship with the object of that awe. It is through fear and trembling; "It is really terrible to have anything to do with God who neither can nor will give one direct certainty or a legal relationship."[24] True Christian faith leads to a lifelong increase in a sense of unworthiness, not the kind of Religion A with its apple-pie increase in peace, worldly joy, and security so beloved of the prosperity gospelers. The old Adam in a person must die so the new man', the new creation, in Christ may be made alive: "Faith is on the other side of death" (*Self Examination*). For true believers, this world is not home, and to live as spiritual beings in this world of space and time must involve suffering.

Like Pascal, Kierkegaard deliberately refrained from anything that might have led others to attach themselves to him in affection. This was no doubt one reason why he broke his engagement to Regine Olsen and deliberately incurred the scorn of Goldschmidt. "To believe is to venture out as decisively as possible, breaking with all a man naturally loves in order to save his own soul, that in which he naturally has his life" (*Attack on Christendom*). Thus, "to be loved by God and to love God is to suffer."[7]

It would be grim indeed in the earthly life of the Christian if the above was all there was to the matter, but the heavenly joy and peace through the Holy Spirit in believing in Christ and in full faith and assurance in imputed righteousness through him and the love of and from God that can flood the heart make all the difference. Dying in Christ leads to being raised with him, just as his crucifixion led to his resurrection. A Christian must be baptized into Christ's death, be conformed to it, and be crucified unto the world (see Romans 6:3, Philippians 3:10, and Galatians 6:14). God kills but only to make alive. [30]

Logic and Grammar

"Philosophy, rightly understood, is not a
set of theories but an <u>activity,</u>[emphasis
added]_the clarification of propositions. The
propositions which philosophy clarifies are not
themselves propositions of philosophy but non-
philosophical propositions about the world."
—Ludwig Joseph Wittgenstein,
Tractus Logico-Philosophicus

Classical Logic Overview

In the allegorical portrayal of the seven liberal arts in the Middle Ages, it was not uncommon to have the three linguistic arts, **grammar, logic, and rhetoric** (as were the mathematical ones of arithmetic, geometry, astronomy, and music) displayed as three young women. Whereas grammar and logic were shown as prim and properly dressed with their hair modestly put up, the persuasive art of rhetoric was generally shown as a young woman with her hair enticingly down.

Existential philosophers and novelists, not least among them Kierkegaard himself with his rather strange books, make rather extensive use of the persuasive allure of lady rhetoric, but in this section, I hope to demonstrate the fundamental sense of subjective truth by an appeal to both grammar and logic. There are two reasons for this. First, I want to show how Hegel tried to change the tried-and-tested rules of classical logic, and second, in the "The Tyranny of the Transitive," how subjective thought has been ignored but should be taken seriously.

In addition, much will have to be a Cook's tour of what has become the extensive subjects of logic and grammar before I get on to what I believe to be my most pertinent points about subjective truth and intransitive utterances. Perhaps those already familiar with the study of formal and classical logic may miss out some of what follows.

All objective knowledge from the time of Aristotle onward, with his intensive initial coverage of the subject, has relied on the extensive use of **deductive** and **inductive** reasoning and by **propositions.** A proposition is defined as a statement, utterance, or sentence that has a **subject** and an **object** or **predicate** usually joined by a verb in the grammatically **indicative mood.** A simple example in English is, "All dogs have four legs." "Dogs" is the subject and "four legs" is the object or predicate. These are joined in **relation.** A proposition can be **true** or **false.** So the proposition "All dogs have five legs" is patently or **immediately** false, whereas the proposition "Some dogs have three legs" is true (Let's face it; sometimes they lose one in an accident). Statements beginning with "All" are called **universal** as they contain all subjects in their set; statements beginning "Some" are called **particular** because they do not. There are also **universal** negative propositions such as "No dogs fly" and **particular negative** propositions such as "Some birds don't fly" (like ostriches and penguins).

Other forms of speech, like questions (even **rhetorical questions**, which are posited to provoke a yes or no agreement or disagreement, such as, "Is not England a rainy country?") are not.[10]

Deduction is a way of arguing from the **universal** to the **particular,** a process of narrowing down. The fundamental way this is done is through the device of the categorical **syllogism.** [5] Take this example.

> All swans are white birds
> The queen owns swans
> Therefore, the queen owns white birds

The initial proposition is called **the major premise;** the second proposition is called the **minor premise.** The term common to both of them, swans, is called the **middle term** and is the subject of the major premise and the object of the minor premise, the process eliminates the middle term and leads to the final proposition or **conclusion.** This conclusion has followed the rules of logic and so is said to be **valid.** It is also **true** in that the queen does own white birds. However, although the major premise is good on the face of it, it is not true because we know that some Australian swans are black and the Queen might well own some! An argument is said to be **sound** if both premises are true and it is valid. The conclusion must be true. An argument not following the rules of logic is said to be **invalid.**[5] Take this example:

> Knives are weapons
> The cook has a weapon
> Therefore, the cook has a knife.

We know cooks have knives, so the conclusion may be true, the premises can be true, but the conclusion is invalid; the weapon we have been informed the cook has may be a gun (aspiring sleuths take note!). In the above, we have an example of an **undistributed middle term,** "weapon," which is the same term, in this case the object or predicate. For a syllogism to be valid, the middle term must be the subject in one premise and the object in the other.

Here is another example; in this case, the invalidity of the syllogism leads to a conclusion that is obviously untrue as well as invalid.

> All dogs are animals
> All cats are animals
> Therefore, all dogs are cats.

And finally, here is an example of a syllogism that has two sound or true premises with a properly distributed middle term, "cats," leading to a sound, valid conclusion.

> All cats are animals
> All Devon Rexes are cats
> Therefore, all Devon Rexes are animals.

It is fairly easy in English to spot the subject, verb, and object because English is what is known as an SVO language, that is, in terms of its word order, the subject comes first followed by the verb followed by the predicate. Danish is not so different. On the other hand, a language such as Latin is an SOV language; the verb comes last and the subject needs to be distinguished through its **nominative** case ending and the object by an **accusative** case ending.

There are many syllogism variations; in fact, Aristotle and his followers identified 256 of them, but only 24 of them can be said to be valid.[10] Please note as well that as well as the positive universal "All" type proposition examples given above, there may be totally **negative** propositions, such as "No planet is a star," **particular** propositions such as "Some men are bald," propositions that are both **negative** and **particular**, such as

"Some birds don't fly" or, "Not all birds can fly." There are also **individual** propositions that apply to only one being or person, like, "My cat kills mice" or "Socrates was not beheaded." Here is an example that contains a particular proposition.

Some temples are in ruins
All ruins are fascinating
Therefore, some temples are fascinating

Here it can be seen that a particular "some" premise leads to a particular conclusion. But in addition, in this example, it may be true only for you if you are interested in ruins as a matter of personal taste. Generally speaking then and subjectivity aside, if premises are true in a categorical syllogism and the rules of logic are followed, the conclusion is true.

Let us discuss what is meant by the transitive in grammar and more to the point in logic. The word comes from the Latin meaning "to carry across," and transitive verbs carry across meaning from a subject to a predicate in a sentence, of which there are plenty of examples above. A transitive verb is a verb that takes a direct object or predicate, and all propositions must have one because they need an object as well as a subject.

In mathematics, transitivity is always **commutative**,[10] that is, if I say $X = Y$, I can also say $Y = X$. But as we have seen in the logic of language this may not be the case. However, transitive verbs act as a bridge in a similar way to equality and the equals sign in math even if relations in logic may be noncommutative. To illustrate, if I say all dogs are animals, that does not mean all animals are dogs, whereas in math if we put $1 + 100 = 101$, it is perfectly alright to say $101 = 1 + 100$.

Over the last two hundred years, the study of logic has led to the development of **symbolic logic**, which uses symbols as algebra does in math. In addition to statements that can be said to be true or false, there are grey areas leading to definitions of **fuzzy logic**[10] and the consideration of the subjective and intransitive statements I shall consider below. But where symbolic logic has started to deal with intransitivity, it is usually linked with theories of probability, that is to try to find out to what extent a subjective or intransitive statement can be reduced to a probable transitive one. This is, however, beyond the range of this book.

Let us see how one syllogism or logical statement in combination with others can lead to more than one conclusion in a line of reasoning; by adding another premise, another conclusion can be arrived at, and so on, to form a chain or **catenary.** A favorite of mine is the Chinese one.

> If there is peace in the individual, there will be peace in the family;
> If there is peace in the family, there will be peace in the neighborhood;
> If there is peace in the neighborhood, there will be peace in the city
> If there is peace in the city, there will be peace in the country;
> When there is peace in each country, there will be peace in the world.

Such propositions are **hypothetical** beginning as they do with the word "if" (and in the case above a big if!). The initial proposition in such cases is called **antecedent**, and the following proposition the **consequent**. There are other arguments that do not use the hypothetical in logic, but which incorporate **modal verbs** such as "will," "would," or "should" in their transitivity, the prescriptive, predictive and counterfactual for example that may or may not lead to a catenary.

Hypothetical syllogisms are traditionally represented in the form.

> If P then Q
> If Q then R
> Therefore, if P then R

which as can be seen is still "iffy."

The rule in propositional logic, *modus ponendo ponens* (Latin for "the way that affirms by affirming") affirms the antecedent, allowing one to reach a less "iffy" conclusion. It is often abbreviated to MP or *modus ponens* or **implication elimination** and is a valid, simple argument form and rule of inference.[5] It can be summarized as "P implies Q; P is asserted to be true, so therefore Q must be true." For example,

> If it rains, I will get wet (antecedent)
> It is raining
> Therefore, I will get wet

Or,

> If P, then Q
> P, therefore Q

This reasoning is invariably valid and not "iffy." However, in this kind of argument, one has to watch one's P's and Q's because of the danger of **affirming the consequent**, sometimes called **converse error** or **fallacy of the converse**,[5] a formal fallacy of inferring the converse from the original statement. The corresponding argument has this general form.

> If P, then Q.

Q.
Therefore, P.

An argument of this form is invalid; the conclusion can be false even when statements 1 and 2 are true. Since P was never asserted as the only sufficient condition for Q, other factors could account for Q while P is false. For example,

If it rains, I will get wet.
I will get wet.
Therefore, it is raining.

It may well be raining outside; on the other hand, you may have noticed you were about to be attacked by a gang of children with water pistols or a man with a hose!

There is a corollary to the above called the *modus tollens* or *modus tollendo tollens* (also called **denying the consequent**); Latin for "the way that denies by denying", which is also a valid argument form and rule of inference.[5] It is the inference that

1. If P implies Q, and the second premise, Q, is false,
2. then it can be logically concluded that P must be false.

Or

If P, Q
Not Q
Therefore, not P

For example,

If you had shot me, you would have killed me.
You wouldn't have killed me.
Therefore, you didn't shoot me.

The accompanying fallacy is

If P, Q
Not P
Not Q

For example,

> If you had shot me, you would have killed me
> You didn't shoot me
> You wouldn't have killed me.

Or maybe you didn't get the chance because the gun jammed!

I am now moving into those areas of transitive logic that are closer to existentialist thinking. The first considers the **absurd**. This is a Latin word, again, and really means a remainder, something that can be reduced no further. To the existential thinker, this is the very fact of their own personal existence, the "bottom line."

In logic, there is another rule of inference, *reductio ad absurdum* or reduction to the impossible remainder (Latin: "reduction to absurdity" or "reduction to the impossible"). It is a common form of argument that seeks to demonstrate that a statement is true by showing that a false, untenable, or absurd result follows from its denial, or in turn to demonstrate that a statement is false by showing that a false, untenable, or absurd result follows from its acceptance. This technique has been used in both formal mathematical and philosophical reasoning.[5] Let us look at a *modus tollens* argument that a thinker such as Sartre might use and then challenge it with *reductio ad absurdum*.

> If life is meaningless, death is the end of existence.
> Life is meaningless.
> Death is the end of existence.

To counter this,

Suppose death is the end.
If death is the end, why have so many people staked
their lives on the resurrection?
It is absurd to think that people would do this if this
life were all there was.
Therefore, death is not the end of existence.

We can now move on to another type of valid argument reflected in the title of Kierkegaard's first major work, *Either/Or*. This is the either/or method of the **disjunctive syllogism** (also known as **disjunction elimination** and **or elimination**,[5] or abbreviated **VE**) and is a valid rule of inference. If we are told that at least one of two statements is true and also that it is not the former that is true, we can infer that the latter is true: if either P or Q is true and P is false, then Q is true. The reason this is called "disjunctive syllogism" is that, first, it is a syllogism, a three-step argument, and second, it contains a logical disjunction, which simply means an "or" statement. "Either P or Q" is a disjunction; P and Q are called the statement's disjuncts. The rule makes it possible to eliminate a disjunction from a logical proof.

In Ps and Qs, this may be expresses as:

Either P or Q.
Not Q.
Therefore, P.

For example,

Either he believes in God or he doesn't.
He isn't an atheist.
So He believes in God.

This requires that an entire issue be brought down to two possibilities, and if that can be done, it is very useful indeed. However, it should be noted there are two kinds of logical disjunction.

- **inclusive** means "and/or"—at least one of them is true, maybe both.
- **Exclusive** ("x/or") means exactly one must be true, but they cannot both be.

The distinction between "or" and "or" when it means "and/or" is not always that clear in English or for that matter Danish, but it is clearer in Latin, which has separate words for it as Kierkegaard must have been aware. Of course, the distinction is very important in computing these days, but please observe that the disjunctive syllogism works whether "or" is considered "exclusive" or "inclusive" disjunction. The widely used English language concept of *or* is often ambiguous between these two meanings, but the difference is pivotal in evaluating disjunctive arguments. In the above case where things are positive or negative and mutually exclusive, the distinction does not matter because one cannot be a believer and an atheist at the same time! We are largely concerned with exclusiveness. This is not like the kind of inclusive disjunct below.

> Either the victim was shot and/or suffocated.
> He was shot.
> [But he could have been suffocated first!]

With the inclusive meaning you can draw no conclusion from the first two premises of that argument. This argument,

> Either P or Q.
> Not P.
> Therefore, Q.

is valid and indifferent between both meanings. However, only in the *exclusive* meaning is the following form valid.

> Either P or Q (exclusive).
> P.
> Therefore, not Q.

Affirming a disjunct is the fallacy that goes with this form of argument, also known as **the fallacy of the alternative disjunct** or a **false exclusionary disjunct**.[5] This occurs when an argument takes the form,

> A or B.
> A.
> Therefore, it is not the case that B.

The following argument indicates the invalidity of affirming a disjunct.

> Fido is a dog or [and/or] Fido is a mammal.
> Fido is a dog.
> Therefore, Fido is not a mammal.

This inference is invalid. If Fido is a dog, then Fido is also a mammal. (Remember "or" is defined in an inclusive sense, not an exclusive sense.)

So we have seen that it is only in the exclusive sense that valid conclusions may be drawn from disjunctive syllogisms, but the fact that an entire issue may be brought down to two possibilities, only one of which may be right, makes either/or a powerful tool of logic despite what Hegel did. Let us take another example of the use of this type of syllogism:

> Either Jesus was who he accepted what others said he was—the Messiah, Son of his heavenly father, or he was in a state of crazy megalomania.
> He wasn't crazy because he exhibited too much wisdom.
> Therefore, he was who he said He was.

Actually disjunctive syllogisms are commutative: I could equally say that Jesus was a wise blasphemer and prove the opposite; both conclusions would be equally valid as they cannot deny the antecedent or the consequent. The important and indeed crucial thing to notice, as Kierkegaard would have done, is that only one or the other can be true. There is no other alternative that is the possibility of a **false dilemma**.[5] Opponents arguing a case can shoot *reductio ad absurdum* and opposing disjunctive syllogisms at each other forever.

This leads to the final type of deductive argument I wish to discuss because I believe a distortion of it leads on to Hegel's idea of dialectic synthesis and all the dreadful thinking that has resulted: **the constructive dilemma**. It is the inference that if P implies Q and R implies S, and either P or R is true, then Q or S has to be true. In sum, if two conditionals are true and at least one of their antecedents is, then at least one of their consequents must be too. Constructive dilemma is the disjunctive version of *modus ponens,* whereas **destructive dilemma** is the disjunctive version of *modus tollens.*[5] It takes this form.

> Either P or Q.
> If P, then R; if Q, then S.
> Therefore, either R or S.

> Either swans are white or black.
> If swans are white, they are old world.
> If they are black, they are Australian.
> Therefore, swans are either old world or Australian.

(A false dilemma could arise if there were other alternatives such as blue or green swans, making the initial premise unsound, but that is not the case!)

An example of the destructive dilemma might be:

> If I win the lottery, I will donate it all to charity.
> If my friend wins the lottery, he will keep it all himself.
> Either I will win the lottery or my friend will win the lottery.
> Therefore, either charity gets all the money or gets none of it.

The dilemma derives its name because of the transfer of disjunctive **operands**.[5]

It can be seen that by superimposing further propositions to the conclusions in the case of these disjunctive syllogisms, arguments may be continued in a catenary. But there is plenty of opportunity for invalidity if care is not taken even if the premises are true. The longer the chain of reasoning with hypothetical propositions, the greater the possibilities for error.

I have discussed deductive logic in some detail leading up to either/or. This is a way of arguing from the universal to the particular—of narrowing down the reasoning. If we wish to argue from the particular to the universal, there are three options open.

The first is the **inductive method** particularly useful in science for arriving at laws and principles. Suppose you were an early biologist and were classifying mammals; you might state as a law that they have hair, give milk, and are viviparous (give birth to live young from the womb). These would include dogs, cats, mice, elephants, seals, and bats. This principle was arrived at by a process of induction by observing every known mammal. However, this "law" had to be changed when it was found the Australian platypus and the echidna were hairy creatures that suckled their young but laid eggs!

Induction does not give cast-iron proofs, but it is usually an excellent way of finding principles in the "hard" sciences and with simple systems and induction is flexible when anomalies are found.

The second, similar option is the process of **arguing by analogy**, that is, drawing conclusions by similarities.[5] Here, the boundaries between scientific and nonscientific issues and the persuasiveness of rhetoric can become blurred. Look at this example of such reasoning.

> Darren and Shaun are both hoodies.
> Darren and Shaun are both from broken homes.
> Darren and Shaun both live with their girlfriends on a run-down estate.
> Hoodies coming from broken homes and living with their girlfriends on run-down estates are usually on benefits.
> So Darren and Shaun are on benefits [probably].

It is easy to see how our prejudices or sympathies can be aroused by arguments like this and how the conclusion is only a probability. The best thing to do is to try to turn them into deductive syllogisms. In the above case,

> Darren is partnered financially to his girlfriend in the same way Shaun is to his.
> Darren is on benefits.
> Therefore, Shaun is on benefits with his girlfriend.

This conclusion may be somewhat unsound but at least it is valid.

Third is **abduction**[27] a commonsense inference: the queen is expected in town today; I see an armored limousine with a motorized escort. I abduce it is her.

Two final points need to be made about sentences in logic: first, in some languages, there is no verb "to be" normally used, so for in Arabic, for example, you wouldn't say "The table is white," you would say "The table white." The related Semitic language of Hebrew is similar. There is a special verb "to be" in Hebrew, and where it is used, it has an especially strong meaning, as where Jesus said, "Before Abraham was I am."(emphasis added) Second, some languages have future tenses that can get involved in syllogisms; where Aristotle had problems with the syllogism, the classic example was over the putative prediction of a sea battle. But Germanic languages such as English (and Danish) do *not* have a future tense but only ways of referring to the future; this makes the substantiation of the laws of logic clearer, as we shall see below. Hegel, of course, was a native speaker of German, so he should have known this.

After our tour of the realm of classical logic, we need to go back to what the first principles of this science, as originally defined by Aristotle, are: he defined three basic **laws of thought**. [10] First, the **law of identity**, or A is A. So a dog is a dog, Socrates is Socrates, God is God—pretty axiomatic, or so you would think.

Second, the **law of noncontradiction**, or What is A cannot be non-A. So a dog cannot *not* be a dog, Socrates cannot *not* be Socrates, and God cannot *not* be God; again undeniably axiomatic.

Third, the **law of the excluded middle.** So, (i) A is A, (ii) whatever is A cannot be not-A, so (iii) Everything is EITHER A OR not-A.

Although Hegel tried to deny the lot (inadvertently immediately contradicting himself by breaking rule ii, it is on rule iii that the battle lines of thought are drawn, as even Aristotle considered the law of the excluded middle somewhat shaky. What about statements such as, "It will rain tomorrow" (due to the future tense conundrum in Greek). Although such statements imply an unspoken opinion and conform to the test of a proposition that it can be considered either true or false, it can still be considered questionable.

There is also the danger of the false dilemma, in which more than two possibilities exist, such as, "Suppose it snows tomorrow." So opinion and above all faith have important parts to play in basic reasoning. The basic laws can be laid down axiomatically, but they cannot be proved. The recent development of Gödel's theorem gives weight to this. Actually, even Hegel should have been aware of the contribution of the philosopher Leibnitz, who in the previous century had declared the principle that nothing occurs without sufficient reason for it to be that way or another.

Let us look at how Hegel tried to change classical logic in his three-volume work *The Science of Logic* (1812). He disliked the idea that some things are unchangeable and can be seen in only black or white, preferring shades of grey. First, he attacked the law of identity by positing that everything is always <u>more</u> than itself. Second, he attacked the law of noncontradiction by declaring that everything <u>is both itself and not itself</u>. And finally, he attacked the law of the exclusive middle by declaring that even in an exclusive "or," everything is BOTH A *AND* NOT A(emphases added). All this allows for a multiplicity of possibilities that are simply not allowed by Aristotelian classical logic.[12] It also allows for a "god" who is never the same and can be not himself if he feels like it—even a liar presumably.

Kierkegaard was firmly against all this, particularly Hegel's attack on the excluded middle, which although on the face of it may seem somewhat shaky, can be seen from an examination of disjunctive syllogisms to be pretty sound. He thought that Hegel had dissolved all distinctions and turned philosophy "into that night in which all cows are black." He had also removed the possibility of decisiveness between opposites and thereby of all freedom; Hegel had declared war on consequent human freedom and subjectivity.[12] *Either/Or* rules okay!

Before leaving our look at classical logic, I want to take a brief look at **philosophical logic.** This is not a field of logic as such but one that examines those areas concerning the relationship between philosophy as a whole and the study of logic. It is a fairly recent field, going back to the beginning of the twentieth century and concerned with such issues as the proposition, analyticity, necessity, existence, truth, meaning, and reference. The only question it asks that I want to examine is in the area of "existence, propositions, and descriptions": the question of whether "exists" is a true predicate.

Kant was helpful here in pointing out that although in a sentence it acts grammatically as an object, in fact, in terms of logic, it does not act as one at all[21]; it is a sort of "dummy" word acting a bit like the zero does in mathematics, standing for nothing. We have dummy words in English. For example, whereas in English, we ask, "Do you drive?" in other languages, the form "Drive you?" would convey the same meaning. If I say, "Dogs exist," it doesn't really tell me anything about dogs; although the concept of "dogs" is there, it adds nothing to the concept.

To sum up, "exists" is not a predicate first because nothing *new* is added to the concept of the subject of such propositions, and second, because nothing is said in such propositions that has not been implicitly said already. Three exceptions have been discerned concerning this. First, the subject term of such a statement may refer to something fictional such as unicorns or Harry Potter; second, it may be things that have existed only for a time but don't exist now such as the Crystal Palace, and third, we may be referring to a dream, phantom, or hallucination. This has been called **referential contradiction**.[21]

So as long as the subject of existence is not a fiction, the product of an altered state of consciousness or having a being only in the past, for which in the latter two cases a degree of qualification may be needed, I can refer to the existence of a thing. But unless I give the existent subject some qualities, it really only signifies that the subject is there.[21] If I say "God exists," I have to say what he is like—his attributes (his loving kindness lasts forever; Hebrew *Sadaka*, he is just, omnipotent, etc.)—to invest my statement with any meaning; otherwise, I may just as well say, "God is." It all boils down to existence on its own being not being capable of further explanation and the importance of subjective statements where meaning lies only in the subject, as there is no object or else "exists" is only a dummy word.

Well now, Lady Logic, perhaps a younger relative of Lady Wisdom, has had a bad-hair day. She has had her hair disheveled enough by Hegel. So let us let her retreat to her chamber to rearrange her dignity and let Lady Grammar take the stage so we may examine subjective truth, which although it may not be subject to rationality and syllogisms, may nevertheless have propositional statements made about it. We shall overcome any shyness she may have in appearing before philosophers, who often ignore her, with an old joke.

The Tyranny of the Transitive

My dog has no nose.
Really! Then how does he smell?
Awful!

This joke relies on its humor on the different ways the verb "to smell" can be used. In this instance, how my dog might smell to me or how it might have a somewhat more appealing smell to other dogs is known as an example of **qualia**.[27] but that is not the main point. As we shall see, there are two kinds of verbs regarding truth. This is more than mere ambiguity: there are **transitive** verbs, which take an object (these were the only ones considered in our discussion of classical logic) and **intransitive** verbs, which do not or cannot take an object. Some verbs are capable of being transitive and intransitive. An **action verb** with a **direct object** is transitive, while an action verb with no direct object is intransitive. Some verbs, such as come, go, arrive, sit, swim, and sleep are always intransitive; it is impossible for a direct object to follow. Other action verbs, however, can be transitive or intransitive, depending on what follows in the sentence. And this is how the joke above works: "My dog smells a bone" is a transitive statement in which the bone is the object. This joke, however, works on two expectations on the word play of the verb "smell" used intransitively: the question "How does he smell?" is expecting a process whereby the dog can smell, but the punch line gives the adverb "awful." "My dog smells awful" is intransitive, and "awful" is merely an adverb that describes the smell! "I drink in the evening" is intransitive, but "I drink whisky" is transitive, and as it is true or false, it may be taken as a proposition capable of rational manipulation. So in a lot of languages, English particularly, a verb can act both transitively or intransitively, "to smell" being but one example; these verbs are **ambitransitive**.

It is important to note that "What?" questions are not applicable to intransitive statements; a "what" question is seeking an object that works only on transitive statements. To the statement "My dog smells a bone," the question "What does he smell?" produces the answer "a bone." It does not make sense to ask "What does he smell?" to "My dog has no nose," but it *does* make sense to ask "How?" because this question implies either a process as an answer or an adverb—in the case of the joke an unexpected one!

Let us look at the shortest verse in the Bible: "Jesus wept" (John 11:35). The statement is intransitive, not subject to taking any further in rational argument or subject to a "what" question, as there is no direct object. On the other hand, it may be suitable to augmentation by adding "because his friend Lazarus died," and we might fairly speculate on how he wept. Such questions work with intransitive statements. What we cannot do is put a measurement on his sorrow. Objective measurement does not work in the realm of subjectivity as it does with transitive statements such as "This lightbulb generates sixty watts of energy."

Aristotle himself noticed that an explanation of everything that exists could be found by asking four basic questions, who, why, what, and how. This is known as the **doctrine of the four**

causes.[27] Suppose one looks at a human being as the focus of these questions in Christian terms. An answer to a "who" question gives the **efficient cause**: Who made man? God. An answer to the "what" question gives the **material cause**: What are people made of? Flesh and blood. An answer to the "why" question gives the **final cause**: Why do people exist? To glorify and enjoy God. An answer to the "how" question gives the **formal cause**: How do they exist? In a state of inward passion.

I have given an answer to the formal cause in terms of the arguments Kierkegaard was presenting. If I were to ask the question about something like a saucepan or bicycle, it would be easy to give answers to the why and how questions as these inanimate objects exist to fulfill their functions as utensils or machines. Again, with animals, it is not too difficult to give final and formal causes because they exist to eat and reproduce. However, as a non-Christian, Aristotle had some difficulty giving final and formal causes to human existence and eventually came to the conclusion that humans exist to be happy through the exercise of reason. This is an astonishingly weak conclusion for a great mind like Aristotle, not least because animals can reason albeit in a nonverbal way and happiness is an elusive butterfly that defies definition. Nevertheless, he hit on a very important question in seeking formal causes. These causes at a human level are largely found in the realms of subjectivity and intransitivity.

Although intransitive utterances are not open to the rules of logic, they are not beyond understanding. The problem is that predication is often sought for any statement that does not have an object. It is fair to say that the areas of utterance that are not subject to the rules of reason and logic have been generally ignored by most thinkers who wish to dismiss what they consider to be merely "irrational." Indeed, this is so much the case that it is virtually impossible to find a philosopher or theologian who operates outside the sphere of propositional logic. It is all too prevalent in theology. In the case of Catholic theologians, it gave rise to scholasticism and people such as Thomas Aquinas and it exists today. In the case of, particularly, Reformed Protestant theologians, we have those who see the Bible as "God's propositional revelation" and try to build systematic theologies.

This may explain why both Luther and Kierkegaard used some strong language regarding the uselessness of objectivity and rationality in spiritual matters though they respected objective thought in other areas. However, the whole, largely unexplored field of subjective truth available through the examination of the largely intransitive statements expressing active passion lies before us, the principles of which may indeed then be delineated through propositional principles.

Before we proceed with this section, let us examine in more depth how faith clashes with reason in what is known as **fideism**. [27] This notion held by Luther, Pascal, and Kierkegaard is the idea, unlike that held by medieval intellectuals such as the Jewish Moses Maimonides and the Christian Thomas Aquinas, that religious faith and reason are incompatible with each other: that religious faith is separate from reason and cannot be reconciled with it. According to fideism, faith involves a degree of absolute certainty and personal commitment that goes beyond any evidential reason.

The essence of true Christianity is that people are saved by faith alone (*fide sola*). All humanity's faculties, including reason, have been corrupted by sin and are untrustworthy, so God's direct revelation must be believed instead. If one could prove the existence of God, as medieval scholars thought they could, faith would not be necessary or relevant.

So in response, Kierkegaard declared that because faith was characterized by absolute certainty and passionate personal commitment, it could never be supported by reason.

Almost in ironical response to the three classical arguments for the existence of God (the ontological, cosmological, and teleological), Kierkegaard put forth three fideist arguments of his own: approximation, postponement, and passion (APP!). As outlined by Robert Adams of Princeton University in his 2012 paper "Kierkegaard's Arguments against Objective Reasoning in Religion,"

> Approximation: because arguments can never prove things with absolute certainty since there may be faults in the evidence or reasoning of the argument Faith on the other hand must go beyond this and wants total certainty.

> Postponement, because of his belief that there is always the possibility of new data or evidence that will invalidate previous conclusions, as in inductive reasoning: if we were to base our faith on scientific inductive investigation, we would have to wait until the end of time until all the data is in! A quicker choice is needed.

> Oddly, the above two thoughts are in line with the latest concepts in epistemology: the **Falsification Principle**[27]

> Thirdly, the Passion Argument: emphasizing the crucial personal commitment that in inherent in faith. With only imperfect evidence at our disposal, like the spiritual gambler in **Pascal's Wager**[27] there must be risk involved in believing any conclusion. Indeed, the faith that goes against all known evidence, as with Abraham willing to sacrifice Isaac, is the most

valuable because it is the riskiest faith of all. Should
we prove God's existence through evidence or reason,
then faith would be unnecessary, not to mention
bland and boring.

It is a common mistake to assume that subjectivity is a
concept limited to the first person and is just a matter of their
opinion over matters that may in fact be solved by a logical
and measurable process, but that is not the case. As we have
seen, these statements can apply in the first, second, or third
persons of a verb in the singular or plural. Furthermore, as I
have noted, because intransitive statements have only the verb
acting on the subject, they are not subject to quantifying or
measurement. A prime example of this is pain. Naturally, this is
a matter of concern to physicians and clinicians. Take childbirth.
For many women, it is an excruciating chore, whereas for a tiny
minority, it is the ultimate erotic experience. To give some idea
of degrees of pain like this, a subjective pain scale measured in
"dols" (Latin *dolor*) was devised the unit based on studies of pain
during the 1940s and 1950s. One dol was defined to equal to "just
noticeable differences" (JNDs) in pain.[18] The unit never came
into widespread use, and other subjective methods are now used
to assess the level of pain experienced by patients; subjective
scales are notoriously difficult to establish.

In grammar, the number of objects or predicates the subject
is transferred to by the verb is called the **valence**, so if I say
"Dogs are animals," the valence is one, and if I say "We have
both kinds of music here, country and western," the valence is
two, and so on. As we have seen, intransitive statements do not
have an object, so the valence is always the same.

Also in grammar is a construct called the **passive voice**.
Here, a transitive verb can take on an intransitive form. If one

wishes to avoid saying who did something, this is a way of **promoting** the object to the subject. For example, suppose we have the proposition "Romeo kissed Juliette"; this statement, like all propositions, is said to be in the **active voice**. Let us now promote the object of the statement, "Juliette," in the passive voice; this becomes "Juliette was kissed," thus hiding who kissed her! This statement is intransitive because there is no object. If we want to say it was Romeo who was responsible, we may continue with an **agent**: "Juliette was kissed by Romeo," but there is still no direct object, and the statement is still intransitive. What or who was she kissed is a non-question. How was she kissed? Well ...

The grammatical plot thickens when we take into account the many forms the passive voice takes in different languages. Some languages have a middle voice and two forms of passive voice; Icelandic is a prime example. Others have an impersonal passive voice or can be passivized to remove the subject. Some languages even have an anti-passive voice in which the subject of a transitive verb is promoted to the object of the corresponding intransitive verb. (This is almost impossible to give a decent example of in English, so I won't try. Suffice it to say that languages such as Basque have it). Perhaps one aspect of ambitransitivity that should be mentioned is **ergativity** (from the Greek for "work") I which the alignments are changed. English has a few verbs that behave in this way, an example might be: "She changed cars." "Cars were changed." In the first case, the verb is transitive and the lady is the agent; in the second case, she becomes the patient and is affected by the action.

There are some languages, notably many Native American languages and Basque, as above, that are fully ergative and differ from European languages where there subject and object are distinguished by case endings or else by word order, but a full explanation is beyond the range of this book. I mention this because again there is a difference in other languages, particularly Romance languages such as Spanish and Italian; this is expressed by **pseudoreflexive verbs**. For example, in English, we would say in an ergative, intransitive form, "The cup broke." but in Spanish, this is "La taza se rompio," "The cup broke itself."

One final point: the possibility, as in the case of English, of intransitive verbs taking **cognate objects**, that is objects, formed from the same root as the verb itself. For example, with the intransitive verb "sleep," I could say, "She sleeps," but I could also say, "She slept a drunken sleep." This is the same as saying, "She slept, and her sleep was drunken." Here, the verb takes on transitivity.

Let me now say a few words about the truth or falsehood of intransitive statements. First, it is meaningless to refer to their validity or invalidity as they cannot follow the rules of logic. Second, an intransitive statement can indeed be true or false about the subject: "Jesus slept in a boat in a storm" (Matthew 8:24) is true if you believe it, but to say, "Jesus slept in an aircraft" is not. In these cases, the subject as patient can be observed by a third party; when I observe "My dog smells," I know it. But the highest form of subjective truths are, as Kierkegaard noticed, those that are inwardly and passionately held by the individual in the first person and are not, however, available to objective detection by an observer. It is difficult to convey an intransitive truth such as my belief in God absolutely no matter how I try; it can be true only for me if I know and feel it, or false, in which case I would be faking it. Also, in the cases of intransitivity giving rise to subjective truth, the verb in the sentence acting on the subject sometimes implies the most intense passion, such as "to die" or "to hurt."

From all of the above, we may observe that there are principles that can be expressed as propositional statements that we may make about intransitivity and the subjective truths it expresses. I may have exceeded the necessary bounds of simplicity below, but I leave it to others to whittle it down:

- Utterances involving a subject may be transitive or intransitive and are either true or false.
- Transitive statements are objective and have a subject and direct object. Intransitive statements are subjective and have no direct object
- Only transitive statements can be said to be valid or invalid.
- Transitive statements may take a "what" question directed to its object or predicate to give what Aristotle called a "material" cause.
- Intransitive utterances cannot take a "what" question as they have no object or predicate.
- Intransitive utterances may take a "how" question directed to the intensity or manner in which the verb acts on the subject (an adverb) or else any process the subject may undergo to give what Aristotle called a "formal" cause
- An intransitive utterance has zero valence as there is no object.
- As transitive statements are limited to having an object, intransitive statements are more fundamental, being free from this requirement. Additionally, utterances tend to have a default from transitivity to intransitivity through a change from active to passive, ergative, and pseudoreflexive verbs. Consequently, subjective truths are more basic than objective truths.

- Intransitive utterances are not logic propositions and so cannot be used in syllogisms or catenaries. They cannot be said to be valid or invalid and are unsystematic.

- Some verbs are subject to ambitransitivity and so may be used for transitive statements subject to logic. They are also multivalent.

- A transitive utterance may be changed from its active voice form to one in the passive voice, losing its transitivity and becoming intransitive.

- Intransitivity and the presentation of subjective truth is language and culture sensitive because there is a wide variety in the ways objective and subjective statements may be conveyed through modes of active, middle, and passive voice—reflexitivity and ergativity in different languages.

- Ergativity and the consequent way in which subjective truths are presented, are more common in arcane and ancient languages such as Sumerian, Basque, Native American, and Australian aboriginal languages

- The subjective truth of intransitive statements in the second and third person may be established by observation by a third party.

- Subjective truths experienced in the first person and expressed by an intransitive utterance cannot be established by a third party and are manifest by the passion or feeling of the individual concerned.

I hope the above discussion on logic and grammar will help explain Kierkegaard's attack on Hegel and his point that subjective truth is more important than objective truth as it relates to the individual. As he put it, "Truth is Subjectivity, not axioms or systems" and "Truth [with a big "T"] is an objective uncertainty held in an appropriation-process of the most passionate inwardness." The objective accent falls on what is said, but the subjective accent on how it is said. Not just the "accent," but as I have shown above, there is a whole range of utterances, mainly intransitive, that cannot be reduced to predicated propositions. Human passion and emotion cannot be disregarded any more than rationality. Solid grammatical grounds can be established for the superiority of subjective truth. Kierkegaard, as shown, was no enemy of classical objective logic and had even considered studying physics under Ørstead, who then headed the university, as mentioned above. Unfortunately, he did not explain in depth why he understood the importance of subjectivity.

Some more of the things Kierkegaard would discern were,

> In religion, belief makes it objective true but indeed it is that subjective become truth. A subjective reflection makes its way inwardly in inwardness. Inwardness culminates in passion ... The subjective truth is a paradox. A paradox is rooted in its having a relationship to an existing subject; An objective reflection is directed objectively to the truth. Reflection is not focused upon the relationship, but upon the questions of whether it is the truth to which the knower is related, God is a subject thus only exists for subjectivity ...

> God is a subject thus only exists for subjectivity. It is impossible to bring God to the light objectively ... God exists only for subjectivity in inwardness ... A definition of truth and objective uncertainty ...

> A definition: An objective uncertainty held fast in an appropriation-process of the most passionate inwardness is the truth, the highest truth attainable

for an existing individual ... The sum of all this is an objective uncertainty ... Without risk there is no faith ... If I am capable of grasping God objectively, I do not believe, but precisely because I cannot do this I must believe. If I wish to preserve myself in faith I must constantly be intent upon holding fast the objective uncertainty.

At its maximum this inward "how" is the passion of the infinite, and the passion of the infinite is the truth. But the passion of the infinite is precisely subjectivity and thus subjectivity becomes the truth, and the subjective "how" constitute the truth.

The highest form of subjective truths are, as Kierkegaard noticed, those that are inwardly and passionately held by the individual in the first person and are not available to objective detection by an observer. It is difficult to convey an intransitive truth such as a belief in Christ dying for me personally. It can be true for me only if I know and feel it, or false in the case of faking it. To quote Kierkegaard, "Truth is an objective uncertainty held in an appropriation-process of the most passionate inwardness."

Epilogue

It would be remiss to finish this work without a least an outline of how the way of thinking that Kierkegaard—the father of existentialism as he has been called—has played out. By and large, it has been taken up by people with whom he would have not aligned himself, and this has not helped his work or memory. As has been mentioned, his works were not rediscovered until the end of his century and did not really start to have an impact in translation until the end of the First World War.

The peak of his influence on other thinkers was in the postwar era, in the middle of the twentieth century, and has since faded somewhat. He was prophetic in being aware of the "mass man" subject to the "universal" control of despotic regimes that arose at that time with their downplaying of the value of the individual. But there are two lines of thinking he affected: first, the sacred or at least theological, and second, the blatantly secular philosophical. Both fields have influenced scholars and their scholarship. It was only between the wars that the word **existentialism** was coined by Karl **Jaspers** to describe the thinking of Heidegger,[4] though Heidegger denied he was such!

During the time Kierkegaard had been forgotten, the Protestant church had thrown up liberal theologians such as Schleiermacher, Ritschl, and von Harnack. Following the horrors of the First World War, liberalism in all its forms was discredited, and Protestant theologians, including Karl Barth and Dietrich Bonhoeffer, turned to "neo-orthodoxy." Rudolf Bultmann, an excellent Bible scholar in his own right, decided as a theologian that to get to the heart of the Christian faith, it needed to be "demythologized"[14]; in this sense, he was influenced by Kierkegaard, to whom the contemporary presence of Christ was what mattered and only the bare bones of historicity, but he went far beyond him in saying that knowledge of the historical Christ was not only unnecessary but also illegitimate! In many ways, he influenced the notorious *Honest to God* of Bishop John Robinson. (SCM press 1963), who stated as did Paul Tillich, that modern secular man needs to recognize that the idea of "God out there" is an outdated simplification of the nature of divinity. Rather, Christians should consider, like Tillich, God to be 'the ground of our being' and embrace 'religion-less Christianity' as God's continuing revelation within human culture..[14]

Perhaps it could be argued that Bultmann and Heidegger, by whom he was influenced, wanted to keep their jobs while Germany was under the idolatrous Nazi regime, whereas Bonhoeffer, who was killed by the Nazis, has gone down in Christian circles as a martyr.

Paul Tillich was another theologian influenced by his own take on existentialism. He defined God as "the ground of our being." Despite its deep insights, Tillich's approach was wholly philosophical in character and didn't seem to consider Scripture much at all. He was strong on existential themes, particularly anxiety and subjectivity, to the extent that he defined grace as the subjective feeling of acceptance that one gets in a crisis.[4] Some Catholic theologians such as Gabriel Marcel have had their own take on existentialist thought.[4]

Schools of secular existential thought were clustered in different countries. Existentialism was, initially at least, a continental movement that included Karl Jaspers (1883–1969) in Germany, who as mentioned above originally coined the term, and to a limited extent Heidegger. There were other thinkers in other continental countries before the movement filtered across to Britain and crossed the Atlantic. The largest and most influential was based in France during and after World War II and included the writers Albert Camus, Frantz Fanon, Maurice Merleau-Ponty, Jean-Paul Sartre, and his feminist partner Simone de Beauvoir. Most of them were atheists and heavily influenced by Marxism. Sartre was undoubtedly the most influential and is famous for his saying, "Existence precedes essence."[4] Put simply, to him, there was "nothing there," and one has to find one's own meaning to life in its meaningless emptiness! Not to face up to this was "bad faith."

It is interesting to note that at the end of his life, Sartre became more sympathetic to theism, although de Beauvoir (who had refused his proposal of marriage more than once), after behaving like a bereaved widow at his somewhat jazzy funeral, in response to his disavowal of atheism, asked, "How should one explain this senile act of a turncoat?" The blind, decrepit, but fully sane Sartre had said in 1980 on his deathbed, "I do not feel that I am the product of chance, a speck of dust in the universe, but someone who was expected, prepared, and prefigured. In short, a being that only a Creator could put here: and this idea of a creating hand refers to God."[4]

Afterword

Literary and Theological Conclusions

I have been moved to write this book by what I believe is a need: the themes that Kierkegaard covered in his books (and indeed the themes of many of the thinkers who have tried to follow in his footsteps) are the ones that the inspired Scripture of the Bible covers. The God of history loves the human race and is concerned about people not so much *en masse* but as individuals. Christianity links subjective, inner experience and truth with the objective, supernatural events of history, most crucially the resurrection of Jesus Christ. In doing so, a cohesive worldview can be presented that has had universal appeal; the only satisfactory explanation of the historical and forensic evidence is Christianity.

Kierkegaard's greatest weakness was perhaps that even in his devotions, he was more concerned with a relationship with the present and living Christ than considering the crucial, historical, objective facts about his Christianity. In addition, because he wanted to protest against the rise of the mass man as well as "Christendom," which he saw, as in the Danish state church, a perversion of true Christianity, he did not emphasize any distinction between the true, invisible church of individual believers and the visible, external church, and he ignored its essential communal nature.

However, he was absolutely correct to emphasize the gap between intellectual assent to Christianity and commitment to a Christian way of life, although perhaps he should have realized that objectivity is the best starting point. Perhaps we should forgive him; it is almost as difficult now as it was in his day for Christians who are God's elect to find soul mates.

It should also be recognized, as he did, that not all the divine utterances in the Bible are given in propositional form or in transitive statements, so therefore a completely systematic theology is not possible. It ought to be pointed out as well that the Wisdom books of the Bible are not historical books other than at certain points about the historical context in which they were written; they are timeless and in many ways could have been written in any day or age: they are not event dependent except when Holy Wisdom became incarnate in the historical person of Jesus.

I hope I have been able to demonstrate two things: first, by an examination of the Bible, that if one accepts it, it is perfectly commensurate with the development of Christian faith for the individual as expressed by the central idea of the three spheres or stages of life. Second, the importance of subjectivity as means of *suprarational* rather than *irrational* approach to inner truth. I have attempted to do this through an analysis of intransitive grammar, which I believe as far as I can ascertain, may be breaking new ground. Pilate asked, "What is truth?" (John 18:38) at the trial of Jesus when the truth in the person of Jesus was standing before him as an active subject, and Kierkegaard put the nature of important individual truth in his dictum, "Truth is subjectivity not axioms or systems ... Truth is an objective uncertainty held in an appropriation-process of the most passionate inwardness."[1] If people make merely objective propositions about God, we make him merely an object. He does not want mere activists, no matter how worthy the cause. He wants to have an active relationship with us, his worshippers.

Unfortunately, what Kierkegaard tried to achieve has been misunderstood from Bible believers to atheists, and his legacy has largely been distorted except by those willing to wade carefully through his purple prose. His legacy among true believers tends to be seen through the distorted lens of philosophers such as Sartre and theologians such as John Robinson. This is a shame; his work needs to be reassessed and put on more of an evangelical footing.

It also needs to be recognized that his legacy has had a positive effect in other areas that have been mentioned above: analyses in psychology and neurology such as logotherapy (as discussed below); phenomenological studies that examine pure, personal relationships as in dasein; critical attacks on **positivism**; attacks on the idealism of Hegel and others; and above all, the rejection of the ideas of materialism. Let Kierkegaard's true legacy stand, and with a clear understanding of what he was trying to say, let it advance.

Appendix A

Some Pastoral Applications

It is profitable to consider personal pastoral problems in the context of life phases, especially where it can be connected with scriptural references. In the first place, there is a need to distinguish those genuine spiritual and problems people suffer from any psychosomatic or psychiatric problems. A prime example of this is the depression, clinical or reactive, that many suffer from today; it has been called "the common cold of modern psychiatry," and despair or dread, which are spiritual problems. After all, some great Christians, such as the poet William Cowper, were depressives. To tell these people they can't be Christians because of their condition is of course unhelpful, to put it mildly.

Christianity and the "Pleasure Principle"

The aesthetic level is particularly prominent when we are young. Youths, Christian or not, are generally out to have fun and need to be warned of the deadly boredom, lack of satisfaction, and above all the uselessness of being submitted to the "pleasure principle." This emptiness can strike even the most refined intellectual pursuits if self- centered. As *Qoholeth* put it,

"Remember your creator in the days of your before the evil days come" (Ecclesiastes 12.1).

A Freudian analysis of neurotic despair is of little use, and it needs to be seen for what it is—a spiritual problem that can be met in only two ways: first, the partial solution to a morally committed way of life in community or marriage, or better still, to make a leap of faith straight through the ethical stage into full faith in Christ. This takes careful evangelism, but it is often more successful with the young than those who are entrenched in the cares of life.

It is important to warn of the dangers of marriage purely for aesthetic, romantic reasons, which can easily end in a broken relationship if a serious, lifelong commitment is not sought. Furthermore, if there is a "sublimated leap of faith" straight into a Christian commitment without going through an ethical stage, there should be a concern that the importance of a desire to inculcate Wisdom is recognized, something the "babe in Christ" needs; St. Paul recognized this. The spiritually mature Christian Wisdom of the new age and covenant is seen as not immediately available to the newly "born again" (1 Corinthians 3:9) but only to those growing spiritually who respond to it as a gift of the sanctifying Holy Spirit. Sanctification should follow a sublimated conversion.

Christianity and Life's Duties

In the ethical stage, say with solid citizens who may realize they have "God- sized holes" in them, as Pascal put it, the problem is less flexible. It may be that they have been trying to lead good lives but have been convinced of their shortcomings. Dangerous guilt can set in. The ethical individual is constantly living under the demands of self- perfection through wisdom, the application of an ethical code, and all the constraints of social life, which can lead to interior psychospiritual conflict even though any hardship may be withstood.

Seriously, there can arise a conflict between the conscience of the individual and general populist morality that can lead to a fractured personality. The problem for the ethicist is that by that commitment, there is always the obligation of self-judgment. The ethicist always lives in the shadow of guilt. Genuine conviction of sin is both a matter of a careful exposition of the gospel and a matter of the work of the Holy Spirit.

Human nature is given to rejection, though. Paul was an example of a zealous ethicist; he was saved from his self- righteousness on the Damascus Road. Often, persecution is more severely carried out by those who have an inner conviction they are wrong.

What is essential is an understanding that mere acknowledgement of the historical facts of Christianity and a nodding acceptance of orthodox doctrines, as Kierkegaard realized, is not enough without a living relationship with the risen Christ, who is the same "yesterday, today, and forever." This cannot be achieved without a subjective passion that is individually true. The basic existential category of the freedom of the individual together with the irrepressible working of the Holy Spirit on a properly presented knowledge of the gospel is perfectly capable of generating true Christian faith that is commensurate with the statements about predestination that Paul presented in Ephesians and Romans.

The Dangers of Immanence

It is of course quite possible to develop a religious commitment to a faith that is other than Christianity, and where this has happened in a Christian culture, it may have been the result of a poor spiritual upbringing.

The gospel should be proclaimed globally, but whereas there is an increase in true Christianity outside Europe, within it, it seems, as Kierkegaard put it, to have been "abolished by expansion"[1] even if people do not assume (as some do) that they are Christians because they live in a Christian country.

There is a problematic overemphasis on the immanence of God in some churches today, accompanied by intoxicated and superficial worship without a serious consideration of sinfulness. Religion A exists in Christendom; it is as well that a preceding confession of sin in most forms of formal eucharistic worship has not been swept away. There is a great need in many churches to instill an appreciation of the great gap between the sinful individual and a transcendent and holy God that can be bridged only by believing the absurd foolishness of God in the Christ event and not just in its historical truth but also in its ever-present finished reality that is individually and subjectively true. Infinite resignation can then be followed by a movement of true faith. God our Father deserves our awe as much as he desires our fellowship with him.

Appendix B

Viktor Frankl[16]—A Knight of Faith

Viktor Emil Frankl, MD, PhD (1905–1997) was an Austrian psychiatrist and neurologist born in Vienna. While still a medical student between 1928 and 1930, he organized and offered a special program to counsel high school students free of charge. The program involved the participation of psychologists such as Charlotte Buhler, and it paid special attention to students at the time when they received their report cards. In 1931, not a single Viennese student committed suicide.

Between 1933 and 1937, Frankl completed his residency in neurology and psychiatry at the Steinhoff Psychiatric Hospital in Vienna. He was responsible for the so-called *Selbstmörderpavillon*, "suicide pavilion," where he treated over 30,000 women prone to suicide. In 1937, he established an independent private practice in neurology and psychiatry at Alser Strasse 32/12 in Vienna. Frankl's practice was highly effective; he didn't lose a single patient.[16]

Starting after the Nazi takeover of Austria in 1938, he was prohibited from treating "Aryan" patients due to his Jewish identity. In 1940, he started working at the Rothschild Hospital, where he headed its neurological department. This hospital was the only one in Vienna to which Jews were still admitted. His medical opinions saved several patients from being killed through the Nazi euthanasia program.

In December 1941, he married Tilly Grosser. On September 25, 1942, Frankl, his wife, and his parents were deported to the Nazi Theresienstadt ghetto. There, Frankl worked as a general practitioner in a clinic. When his skills in psychiatry were noticed, he was assigned to the psychiatric care ward in block B IV, establishing a camp service of "psychohygiene" or mental health care. He organized a unit to help newcomers to the camp overcome shock and grief. Later, he set up a suicide watch and offered a series of lectures on such diverse subjects as Sleep and Sleep Disturbances, Body and Soul, Medical Care of the Soul, Psychology of Mountaineering, "How to keep my nerves healthy, Medical ministry, Existential Problems in Psychotherapy, and Social Psychotherapy. Meanwhile, his father, Gabriel, died of pulmonary edema and pneumonia at Theresienstadt.[16]

On October 19, 1944, Frankl and Tilly were transported to Auschwitz, where he was processed. He was then moved to Kaufering, a Nazi concentration camp affiliated with Dachau, on October 25, 1944. There he spent five months working as a slave laborer. In March 1945, he was offered to be moved to the so-called rest camp Türkheim, also affiliated with Dachau. He decided to go to Durkheim, where he worked as a doctor until April 27, 1945, when he was liberated by the Americans.[16]

Tilly had been transferred from Auschwitz to another camp, where she died. Frankl's mother, Elsa, was killed by the Nazis in the gas chambers of Auschwitz, and his brother Walter died working in a mining operation that was part of Auschwitz. Apart from him, among Frankl's immediate relatives, the only survivor of the Holocaust was his sister Stella.

Frankl was to describe how human beings were to be stripped of all elements of their humanity spare their bare existence; many ridded themselves of any scruple just to exist. Though in the providence of God, Frankl survived, he knew many good men did not. Naturally, some survivors, unlike Frankl the trained psychiatrist, could not talk of their experiences. The first emotional experience in camp was one of shock, sometimes followed by a psychological condition known in the profession as "delusion of reprieve," the idea that things might get better after all, such as happens to a worldly man approaching death or to a condemned man just before his execution.[16]

On leaving the transport, though, nine out of ten of Frankl's fellow travelers were immediately sent to the gas chambers. A long and painful psychological journey followed; any remaining possessions, including things like wedding rings, were taken away at pain of a whipping. In Frankl's case, it was a precious research manuscript. The prisoners had their heads shaved. They became mere, humiliated nonentities.

Shock was replaced with cold curiosity; what could possibly happen next? What would the consequences be? Sometimes, this defense mechanism turned to surprise, for example, that standing around in the chill air did not lead to catching cold. For Frankl, other surprises were how little sleep he needed, that gums did not suppurate on the meager diet, nor did sores and abrasions in dirty skin and ragged clothes.

Eventually, after a brief spell of suicidal thought, prisoners sank into a state of relative apathy, an emotional death that served to deaden both the inner pain and that dealt out by the guards. It was a necessary protective shell for all. Adults suffer physical pain in the same way as children, but in spite of what some think, Frankl considered that they were more susceptible to a sense of insult, injustice, and unreasonableness when they saw it as gratuitous.

Some of Frankl's colleagues in the camps, who had also been psychoanalysts but cast in a Freudian mold, interpreted the desires of a prisoner in this state as **regression,** that is, a retreat to a more primitive form of life. In true Freudian fashion, this should have shown itself in dreams. Disappointingly for the Freudians, sex did not appear in any of the prisoners' dreams, but the prisoners did dream about food, drink, stimulants, and hot baths. Once, Frankl was tempted to awake a prisoner who was having a horrific nightmare until he realized that the real nightmare was the life within the camp; he stopped himself.[16]

Physically, of course, the men were reduced to skin and bones; in addition, through constant standing, they suffered edema, swelling in the feet and legs; there was also the constant risk in the winter of frostbite as well as lowered immunity to infections such as typhus.

Any cultural interest died, resulting in a kind of cultural hibernation we see in oppressed people; only rumors or news about the war caused any stimulation.[4]

Frankl gave a surprising observation: after all this, spiritual and religious interest became "the most high imaginable." In other words, stripped of all the pleasures and comforts of life and being in an ethically appalling situation, the men were drawn into a religious sphere of life. It must be admitted that sometimes this had aberrant manifestations; the worst state of delirium suffered by a patient (a friend of Frankl's) occurred when he believed he was dying, wanted to pray, but could not find the right Hebrew words.

A more sinister occasion occurred when Frankl was obliged to observe a spiritist séance—spirits did not appear, but someone who had a blank piece of paper in front of him found that he had quite involuntarily drawn the letters V, A, E, V, not knowing what they meant as he did not have any Latin. Frankl was more educated, though, and understood that this was an abbreviation for *vae victis*, "woe to the vanquished,"[16] although in Frankl's skeptical opinion, he thought the writer had probably come across it before and had tucked it away in his unconscious mind. Perhaps these events were examples of Kierkegaard's Religion A.

There were more-encouraging signs of spirituality though. Frankl also observed that sensitive men who may have been thought to be poor survivors, through withdrawing into a richer, inner world of spiritual freedom, did better than those of a rougher, apparently more-robust nature. In his own mind, he experienced this on an excruciating march out to work one day. A fellow prisoner said to him, "If our wives could see us now! I hope they're better off." Frankl's separated wife was brought into remembrance in his mind in the pink light of a fading, starry night. He imagined the face of his six-month bride more luminous than the sun that was about to rise and suddenly realized that love was the greatest thing there was, and "the salvation of man is through and in love."

In his suffering, he found meaning in the contemplation of his beloved. Within this aesthetic thought was a religious one, and he understood the meaning of the words "the angels are lost in the contemplation of an infinite glory." True love is indeed "stronger than death," as the Canticle says, and it went beyond even the physical existence of his wife, who unbeknown to him then, was indeed dead.

Numinous spiritual experience could also be experienced in contemplation of nature; here, an aesthetic state immediately sublimates into a religious or spiritual state in consciousness of our own mere existence. For example, in viewing the Salzburg summits on the journey from Auschwitz,; viewing the setting sun in the Bavarian woods with a sky above with multicolored clouds—at the time, Frankl glanced at a light of a distant farmhouse in the gathering dusk. He felt his spirit penetrate the gloom and heard a *Yes* to the question of the existence of an ultimate purpose to everything; the words *et lux in tenebris lucet* sprang from his unconscious mind—"the light shines in the darkness" (John 1:5).[16] St. John's gospel continues, "and the darkness has not mastered it." Frankl's faith stretched beyond the veil of existence. He felt the presence of his wife, that he could grasp her hand. To him, that was subjectively, she really was there.

Suffering and joy both have gas- (ghost-) like qualities; they both fill their containers from surface to surface. A little suffering can completely fill the human soul and consciousness; the same is true of joy. Examples of this modicum could be shown in the grater spirituality seen in the camps. Frankl told of a young woman he met who knew she would shortly die. "I am grateful that fate has hit me so hard," she said. "In my former life, I was spoiled and did not take spiritual accomplishments seriously." She pointed through a window to a tree. "This tree is the only friend that I have in my loneliness." The chestnut tree had one branch with a couple of blossoms on it. "I often talk to this tree," she said. "It said to me, 'I am here I am here—I am life, eternal life.'"[4]

How different this is to a similar but fictional existential experience described by the character Merseault in Albert Camus' *The Stranger*. Merseault was due to be executed the following day for a crime he did not remember committing. He went to the window of his cell and smelled the roses he had never bothered to truly smell and appreciate before. He looked at the moon that he had never wondered over before. These existential experiences convinced him that he had lived, but not before he had violently thrown a priest out of his cell, which to him was his first truly human act! Here was someone who was spiritually dead but came alive for a moment before extinguishing his true self without recognizing the eternity he was about to lose.[12]

Frankl was content to let fate, as he saw it, take its course, but this did not stop him from being truthful to himself or others; he was prepared to meet death in a dignified and courageous way. He did not trip over himself to survive, but survive he did; his decision to live selflessly gave him peace. He knew only too well that people were influenced by their surroundings and soulish or carnal factors—the biological, psychological, and environmental factors—but thought it must be believed that man was more just soul (Latin *anima*, Greek *psychē*). People also have a spiritual dimension in relation to their Creator in psychic and physical stress that can lead them to overcome anger, apathy, and conformity and to act heroically. People are not animals even if they can act like demons, as the SS and kapo guards in the concentration camps did.[16]

To behave spiritually is not just a once-and-for-all decision; truly spiritual people, he came to see, had to take up their cross daily; as Frankl put it, "Suffering is an ineradicable part of life, even as fate and death. Without suffering and death human life cannot be complete. The way in which a man accepts his fate and all the suffering it entails the way he takes up his cross gives ample opportunity even in the most difficult circumstances to add a deeper meaning to his life."[4]

It is germane in this day and age to say that the "provisional existence" experienced in a concentration camp is an extreme example of the distorted time experience suffered by the newly unemployed or retired after a long period of regular work. If they are to survive, they need to find meaning in life and some kind of goal. Actual historical life can be seen only in the past, but to live there is dangerous and foolish. Life must be lived forward, breaking through into the future. Imagination has its uses here, as when Frankl disgusted on a cold and miserable workday imagined himself in a cozy lecture theater, giving a talk on the psychological impact of concentration camps![16] "With no one in authority people throw off all restraint" (Proverbs 29:18) or "Where there is no vision the people perish" (ibid., AV).

Everybody's destiny is different, but it is more important to know the "why" of life than the "how," and here, the Christian faith has clear answers about our ultimate destiny. But life makes demands on us that do not necessarily meet our expectations. How we react to life's challenges in pursuance of our goals, not in planning them, but in doing right by them is what leads to rewarding Christian virtue, whether we are called to passively bear our cross or respond actively.

Incidentally, unselfish tears are nothing to be ashamed of, as when Christ wept over Lazarus;: it shows we have the courage to suffer. Jesus did not throw away his life needlessly; he always had in mind the responsibility toward the elect the Father had given him, and he was willing to take any "how" of his earthly existence. When he was finishing his work by crucifixion, those who were nearest to him were John and Mary, and she understood suffering too. In the world of mere material success, a sacrifice like that would appear pointless.

The end of Frankl's nightmare came with the liberation of the camps by the advancing allied armies. A final note needs to be sounded about the psychological reactions of any released prisoners or holocaust survivors. Frankl noted,

> Human kindness can be found in all groups, even those which as a whole it would be easy to condemn [like the SS] the boundaries between groups

overlapped [there were some prisoners who were sadistic] and we must not try to simplify measures by saying these men [the prisoners] were angels and those [the Germans] devils ... From all this we may learn that there are two "races" of men in this world and only two: the race of decent people and the race of those who are not.

In a similar way to telling apart the similar sheep and goats on judgment day, Frankl sometimes found a decent fellow among the guards, even at the bottom of the abyss that was a concentration camp.[16]

At the time of their liberation, the prisoners dragged themselves to the gates and looked around, but they had lost the joy of appreciating their freedom and the beauty of the spring world around them. Aesthetic feeling had gone and had to be relearned; they had experienced depersonalization. Naturally, their bellies had no such inhibitions, but once they had had a chance to get things off their chest through talking to a friendly ear, their psychological fetters fell off.

The joy of creation became real to Frankl; in a moment of prayerful meditation in a flowery meadow, he dropped to his knees and repeated the same sentence in his mind, "I called to the Lord from my narrow prison and He answered me in the freedom of space" (Lamentations 3:55, Frankl's English translation of the Hebrew). However, with the release of pressure, some prisoners suffered the psychological equivalent of an attack of the bends and became intent on using their freedom for licentious ruthlessness; they were no longer oppressed, so they felt they should become the oppressors. There were also many who, returning home, found bitterness and disillusionment, although their suffering was not as intense as before.[16] These days we know about post-traumatic stress syndrome. Frankl would not have been aware of the term in his day and found suitable therapy for it difficult. Nevertheless, his advice would be to use this kind of suffering as a stimulus to further meaning and goal, as many people who have gone through the trauma of serious accident or illness these days set up or work with organizations to help similarly afflicted people.

Frankl was a "knight of faith," though perhaps he was denied choice in the circumstances that gave rise to it. In the concentration camps, where existence was stripped to the bare minimum, he became resigned to his losses, even of those dearest to him, and became a "knight of resignation." He was forced to renounce "fineness," which means renouncing the world. He had to give up his societal rights and obligations, his familial duties, and the love that went with it, and he had to live in a "dog-eat-dog "world. Yet in doing so, he got it all back again just as Abraham and Job did, with the added bonus of the true faith he found himself moving toward.

The Logotherapy of Frankl[16]

Unlike Freud, who poked into peoples' subconscious past and saw everything through the "will to pleasure," or Adler, who saw psychological or neurotic problems springing from a frustrated "will to power," Frankl concentrated on the individual's future and breaking down the feedback mechanisms that a morbid obsession with the past brings. He tried to make people aware of their potential life tasks and give them an existential **will to meaning** (*logos*). Life can be lived only from moment to moment, and its challenges are specific to the individual, who alone is responsible for his or her destiny related to his or her personality and character. Its categorical imperative (to use a Kantian term) is "To live as if you were living already for the second time

AND AS IF YOU HAD ACTED WRONGLY THE FIRST TIME ANYWAY." Nothing had in fact changed except future possibilities."[16] One cannot change the past: the thing is to confront one's existence in the here and now.

Unlike **Sartre,** who thought as an atheist that we all invent our own **essence** from our own existence (summed up in his famous saying that existence precedes essence), theists such as Frankl can accept that it is quite acceptable that the meaning of our existence is not self-invented but detected in ourselves as part of our created being.[16] If we are not Pharisees who act morally (within the ethical sphere) only to salve our own consciences and to feel good about our own inflated egos, we should rather be pulled along by the love of God and others in line with the greatest of the divine commandments.

According to Frankl, neurosis is not psychological but is **nögenic,** that is, not a conflict of basic animal drives as in Freud and Adler but one of moral and spiritual problems. Despair, as Kierkegaard pointed, out is a spiritual distress, not a mental disease like depression. Frankl also introduced the notion of **nödynamics,** which he described as an inner tension held in equilibrium that is essential to mental health.[16] It lies between those things one has already achieved and those things one still could accomplish; the gap between being and becoming—a dialectic tension, if you like, parallel to the subjective dialectic tension which Kierkegaard described the religious individual holding within them as faith. A therapy of a tensionless, **homeostatic** state lulled or drugged into a neurotic individual, then, is not then the best way to mental or spiritual health. Frankl used the analogy of a decrepit arch on the point of collapse that could be strengthened by the addition of an extra compressive load to that of a neurotic whose psychological mortar is weak.[16]

Let us not forget that this kind of morbidity is related to humanity's loss of original innocence, manifest initially as Kierkegaard noticed by a state of boredom. In short, by treating suffering creatively, no life, no matter how long or short, need be a failure. Animals that are made to suffer by people can never see any meaning to it, as they live entirely in the aesthetic sphere. But for the spiritual Christian, suffering need not be meaningless. As the psalmist said, "God preserves all our tears" and as Paul put it in Romans, "All things work together for good for those who love God." Leaving our footsteps in the sands of time, "what is crooked cannot be made straight," as *Qoholeth* put it, but these past events can still be seen actively and positively in the light of an awareness of an omnipotent providence. In addition, the individual needs to move away from any self-centered or narcissistic attitudes.

The clinician Gordon Allport (*The Person in Psychology* 1968) [31] wrote, "The neurotic who learns to laugh at himself may be on the way to self-management, perhaps to cure." It is often by doing the opposite of what we want in a hopeless state that we can be cured. Frankl gave the example of a man who was suffering from writers' cramp who, instead of trying to be legible, was encouraged to just scribble and was then cured. No doubt this kind of confidence was engendered in the Israelites by God when he told them to march around the walls of Jericho blowing their **shofars** rather than trying to work out a siege plan. This kind of effect Frankl called **paradoxical intention**. Frankl gave several examples of those suffering from neurotic and compulsive disorders being helped. He also pointed out that at least in a clinical sense, it did not matter what the etiological (that is, the causal) basis of the patient's condition was; complexes and mental trauma could be symptoms rather than causes. In analogy, he said, "A reef which appears at low tide is not the cause of the low tide, but the low tide causes the reef to appear."[16]

Frankl's approach to neurotic and pastoral therapy shown above is nondeterministic, anti-nihilist, anti-materialist and shows up the weakness of psychotherapy or pastoral concern that sees only the basic instincts at work in the distressed. People can rise above the level of beasts or even demons, and with the spiritual dimension they have to their lives can rise to transcend themselves. No matter how lowly and untalented people may be, they can gain joy in doing things for God's sake and glory.

Is unrestrained freedom all that matters? Frankl's most striking suggestion was, "The statue of liberty on the East coast of America should be complemented by a statue of responsibility on the West coast."[16]

Glossary

Abduction—The kind of reasoning used by detectives and spies based on observation of facts that has eliminated any unwarranted assumptions.

Absolute mind—In Hegelian philosophy, an undistorted, rational view of the truth. Philosophy is the ultimate expression of the "Absolute Mind" and so is superior both to art (the aesthetic) and to faith (the religious).

Absurd—That which cannot be rationally explained or justified in any way, and which transcends all human and intelligible possibility. The term appears in *Fear and Trembling* to describe the movement of faith Abraham made to regain Isaac. There was no reason at all that Isaac should be returned to Abraham, and yet, by virtue of the absurd, it happened.

Acrostic—A poem or other form of writing in which the first letter, syllable, or word of each line, paragraph, or other recurring feature in the text spells out a word or a message. Common in Jewish writings.

Active voice—In grammar, the voice is the relationship between the action or state that a verb expresses and the participants (subject and object). A direct transitive statement is active: "Romeo kissed Juliette" is in the active voice. English also has the passive voice, which is intransitive.

Aesthetic—The lowest of Kierkegaard's three "stages on life's way": the aesthetic, the ethical, and the religious. The aesthetic is primarily concerned with individual experience and individual sensory experience in particular. An aesthetic experience could range from animal lusts to a deep appreciation of music, say, but it always relates the single individual to something else. Because it works on the level of the individual, the aesthetic values privacy and hiddenness.

Affirming a disjunct—In logic, a fallacy that arises from confusing "and/or" with simply "or." Disjunct means "not joined," which applies with the exclusive use of "or" but not the inclusive use of "and/or." For example, to say Bonzo is a terrier or Bonzo is a dog, Bonzo is a terrier, therefore, Bonzo is not a dog is invalid.

Affirming the consequent—The converse error.

Akhenaton—King of Egypt (1375?–1358?BC) who rejected the old gods and initiated a monotheistic worship of the sun god Aton.

Allegorical approach—One of the four main ways of interpreting the Bible.

Amenemope—(ca. 1100BC; the son of Kanakht); the ostensible author of the "Instruction of Amenemope," an Egyptian wisdom text. He was a scribe and sage who lived during the twentieth dynasty of the New Kingdom and resided in Akhmim, the capital of the ninth Nome of Upper Egypt. His discourses were presented in the traditional form of instructions from father to son on how to live a good and moral life, but they are explicitly organized into thirty numbered chapters.

Antecedent—In logic, a proposition beginning with "if" in a hypothetical syllogism.

Anthropic principle—The idea that observations of the physical universe must be compatible with the conscious life that observes it.

Antinomianism—The notion or doctrine that being a Christian frees one from moral obligations.

Antipathic sympathy—The fear of what one desires.

Antithesis—In Hegelian thinking, the opposite of a thesis that when combined with it gives a synthesis.

Anxiety—One translation (the other option is "dread") of the Danish word *angest*. Kierkegaard used it to denote the peculiar kind of fear that was directed at no particular object, except perhaps at our own freedom. We feel anxiety when we are made aware of our freedom to choose our own fate and to define ourselves with our choices. For instance, Abraham felt anxiety because he knew he could retreat into the ethical at any moment. In not doing so, he defined himself as a religious, rather than as an ethical, hero.

Apocalyptic—A genre of prophetic literature that detailed the authors' visions of end times as revealed by a heavenly messenger. The apocalyptic literature of Judaism and Christianity embraces a considerable period, from the centuries following the Babylonian exile (e.g., Daniel) down to the close of the Middle Ages.

Apocryphal—Books not accepted as part of the Hebrew Bible because of their uncertain origins.

Apollo—A very important god to the ancient Greeks, a sun god. Apollo had been variously recognized as a god of light and the sun, truth and prophecy, healing, plague, music, poetry, archery, and more. Apollo was the son of Zeus and Leto and had a twin sister, the chaste huntress Artemis.

Apologetics—From Greek "speaking in defense"; the discipline of defending Christian faith and doctrine particularly in a systematic and rational manner; not the approach of subjective truth.

Aramaic—A set of languages and dialects closely related to formal Hebrew.

Arguing by analogy—In logic, using perceived *similarities* as a basis to infer some further similarity that has yet to be observed. As a method, it gives good evidence but not absolute proof. For example: monkeys look like people; they can use their hands like people. People can talk, so monkeys can probably talk too.

Arianism—A theological teaching attributed to Arius (AD 250–336), a Christian leader from Alexandria, Egypt. The Arian notion is that Christ the Son of God did not always exist but was the first being created and is therefore distinct from God the Father.

Aristotle—(384–322 BC); tutor to Alexander the Great and an ancient Greek scholar of vast scope, known in the Middle Ages as *the* philosopher. He is credited with the earliest study of formal logic, and his conception of it was the dominant form of Western logic until nineteenth-century century advances in symbolic and mathematical logic.

Artificial intelligence—The idea that the claim that central properties of humans, intelligence, consciousness, and autonomy can be so precisely described that they can be simulated by a machine.

Autonomic nervous system (ANS)—This regulates the functions of our internal organs including the heart, stomach and intestines. It is part of the peripheral nervous system, and it controls some of the muscles. We are often unaware of the

ANS because it functions involuntary and reflexively. For example, we do not notice when blood vessels change size or when our heart beats faster. However, some people can be trained to control some functions of the ANS such as heart rate, menstrual timing, or blood pressure.

Avatars—The manifestation of a god, usually Vishnu, in Hinduism. The Sanskrit noun *avatāra* is derived from the verbal root to, "to cross over," joined with the prefix *ava*, down. Avatars only *appear* to have bodies. The Christian heresy of Docetism (Latin "appear") states that Jesus only appeared to be human is similar.

Babylonian captivity—The period in the history of the Jews when the inhabitants of Judah, after its conquest by Nebuchadnezzar, were forced into exile in Babylon. This occurred in three phases attributed to c. 597 BC, c. 587 BC, and c. 582 BC respectively. The forced exile ended in 538 BC, after the fall of Babylon to the Persian king Cyrus the Great, who gave the Jews permission to return to his Jewish province and to rebuild the temple in Jerusalem. Pioneers returned around 536 BC though many Jews stayed in Babylon. The prophet Jeremiah had prophesized this captivity period.

Brentano, Clemens Honoratus Hermann (1838 –1917)—An influential German philosopher and psychologist, important for introducing the idea of intentionality and theories of perception and judgment.

Buber, Martin —(1878 –1965): Jewish philosopher best known for his *philosophy of dialogue*, a form of existentialism centered on the distinction between the I–Thou relationship and the I–It relationship.

Catatonia—An abnormal state variously characterized by stupor, insensibility, and either rigidity or extreme flexibility of the limbs.

Categorical imperative—The main concept in Kant's ethics. A moral law that is unconditional or absolute for all rational beings that does not depend on any ulterior motive or end. "Thou shalt not murder," for example, is categorical as distinct from the hypothetical imperatives associated with desire such as, "Do not murder if you don't want to be hung." Expressed in a number of ways, the best known of which are, "Act only according to that maxim by which you can at the same time will that it should become a universal law" or less formally, "So act as to treat humanity, whether in your own person or in another, always as an end, and never as only a means." More simply it is his take on the Golden Rule of "do as you would be done by."

Catenary—A chain of immediate reasoning.

Cognate objects—In grammar, objects formed from the root of the verb.

Cognate—A word having the same or a similar meaning in a similar language.

Common grace—In Protestant, particularly Calvinistic thinking, benefits of benign, divine providence experienced by or intended for the whole human race without distinction between one person and another. It is "grace" because it is undeserved and sovereignly bestowed by God. It includes any talents unsaved people may have.

Commutative—Statements where the relationships may be inverted. Say, if X = Y, then Y = X. This is more applicable in math than verbal logic.

Conclusion—A final remark. In syllogisms, the result of the interaction of two or more premises.

Conditioned reflex—The conditioned response is the learned response to the previously neutral stimulus. For example, suppose that the smell of food is an unconditioned stimulus, a feeling of hunger in response to the smell is an unconditioned response, and the sound of a dinner bell is connected with the smell. A response can be triggered by such a bell in the absence of any dinner, as was the case in the experiment Pavlov carried out with dogs.

Consciousness—In the simplest terms, anything we are aware of at a given moment forms part of our consciousness; the quality or state of being aware of an external object or something within oneself. It includes the states of awareness, subjectivity, thought, and self- control along with the awareness of one's own existence and the ability to experience and feel these things in a state of wakefulness.

Constructive dilemma—In logic the inference that, if P implies Q and R implies S and either P or R is true, then Q or S has to be true. In sum, if two conditional propositions are true and at least one of their antecedents is, then at least one of their consequents must be too.

Contrasuggestible—Responding or tending to respond to a suggestion by doing or believing the opposite.

Converse error or **fallacy of the converse**—In logic, a formal fallacy of inferring the converse from the original statement. The corresponding argument has the general form: If P, then Q. Q, therefore P. For example: If a man is drunk, then he is incoherent. The man was incoherent. So he was drunk.

Crop rotation—In Kierkegaard's aesthetic stage, the technique the aesthete uses to avoid boredom by moving from one means of self-satisfaction to another.

Cybernetics—A broad field of study, with the essential goal of understanding and defining the functions and processes of systems in both biology and machines that have goals and that participate in circular, causal chains and feedback, moving from action to sensing to comparison with desired goal, and again to action.

Dasein—In German, *dasein* is the vernacular term for existence, "being there." Not definable as self-consciousness, it involves awareness of the outside world and temporality including mortality; its usage goes back to Hegel; Heidegger and Jaspers used the word in different ways.

Deduction—In logic, reasoning from the universal to the particular.

Denying the consequent—In logic, another name for *modus tollens*.

Destructive dilemma—In logic, the rule that if two conditionals are true but one of their consequents is false, one of their antecedents has to be false; this is the disjunctive version of *modus tollens*. For example, If it rains, we will stay inside. If it is sunny, we will go for a walk. Either we will not stay inside, or we will not go for a walk. Therefore, either it will not rain, or it will not be sunny.

Dialectic—In Hegelian philosophy, the process by which a thesis and an opposing antithesis resolve themselves into a synthesis. The classic example is the thesis of being and the antithesis of nothingness resolving into the synthesis of becoming. According to Hegel, all thought and all history move forward according to the dialectic, slowly progressing toward a better and better state.

Divine command theory—The doctrine that states that what is moral is determined by what God commands, and that to be moral is to follow his commands. This is an answer to the Classical Euthyphro dilemma, which asks whether an action is good because God commands the action, or that God commands an action because it is good. If the first is chosen, it would imply that whatever God commands must be good. Even if he commanded someone to inflict suffering, inflicting suffering must be moral. If the latter is chosen, then morality is no longer dependent on God, defeating the divine command theory. Additionally, if God is subject to an external law, he is not sovereign or omnipotent.

Doctrine of the four causes—Aristotle's idea that an explanation of everything that exists could be found by asking four basic questions: who, why, what, and how.

Double movement—The movement required of the knight of faith. The first movement is the movement of infinite resignation, which the knight of faith shares with the tragic hero. In this movement, the knight of faith gives up everything he holds dear and reconciles himself with this loss. The second movement, the movement of faith, which takes place only by virtue of the absurd, is the movement according to which the knight of faith regains everything he gave up in the movement of infinite resignation. These two movements combined make up the double movement of faith.

Efficient cause—The "who" question in Aristotle's **doctrine of the four causes.**

Embodied consciousness—The subject's view of his or her body as it has to be lived with subjectively, or the idea that human consciousness is part and parcel of the body and can be viewed objectively. The term was used differently by Jaspers and Heidegger. Our analysis takes Heidegger's definition.

Empiricism—Philosophical school taking after Aristotle that relies on observation and experiment rather than pure thought to establish objective facts or truths.

Enlightenment—Intellectual and cultural movement in the seventeenth and eighteenth centuries in Europe and the

Americas. Its purpose was to reform society using reason, challenge ideas grounded in tradition and faith, and advance knowledge. It promoted scientific thought, skepticism, and intellectual interchange; it opposed superstition, intolerance, and abuses of power by church and state.

Epistemology—The branch of philosophy that deals with the study of knowledge and justified belief.

Epoché—"suspension" is an ancient Greek term which, in its philosophical usage, describes the theoretical moment where all judgments about the existence of the external world, and consequently all action in the world, is suspended

Ergativity—(from the Greek for work) **ambitransitivity** in which the alignments are changed. English has a few verbs that behave in this way, an example might be "She changed cars" and "Cars were changed." In the first case, the verb is transitive; she is *the agent* and causes the action; in the second case, the car is *the patient* and is affected by the action. Some ancient languages are fully ergative.

Essence—A Latin term originating from Aristotle's as "the what it is." Closely related to the definition of a thing, it is more exactly attributes that make an entity or substance what it fundamentally is and which it has by necessity, without which it loses its identity. Essence is contrasted with accident: a property that the entity or substance has contingently, without which the substance can still retain its identity. For example, Jesus was substantially holy and one with God the Father in his essence. But his seamless robe was accidental to his being. For Kierkegaard, it was the individual who is the supreme moral entity, and the personal, subjective aspects of human life are the most important. For Kierkegaard, all this had religious implications. **Sartre** changed the classic meaning of essence with his dictum "Existence precedes essence," arguing that existence and actuality come first and the essence is derived afterward.

Eternal consciousness—A term that would have greater importance in Kierkegaard's later philosophy, eternal consciousness is essentially an awareness of one's unending selfhood.

Ethical—The second of Kierkegaard's three "stages on life's way": the aesthetic, the ethical, and the religious. The ethical is the expression of the universal, wherein all actions are done publicly and for the common good. One acts for the betterment of others rather than for oneself. Hegel considered the ethical to be the highest form of life, and Johannes agrees that it is the highest that can be understood. *Fear and Trembling*, in a nutshell, argues that there is the third category of the religious and that the religious is higher than the ethical.

Ex nihilo—The Judeo-Christian doctrine that God created the universe, time, and space out of nothing.

Exclusive—In logic, where "or" is used in a sentence, it means just that and not and/or. Such as "something can be either true or false."

Exegesis—A critical explanation or interpretation of a text, especially a religious text, from the Greek for "leading out."

Existentialism—A difficult term to define especially as many of those considered to be existentialists do not wish to be called so! But by and large, existentialists believe that subjectivity is the basic category, the individual is the most important thing, and life must be lived and not just talked about.

Ezra (480–440 BC) —; Jewish leader and scribe largely responsible for editing the Old Testament after the Babylonian exile.

Faith and doubt—Descartes' idea of opposites as opposed to the existential opposites of faith and objective certainty.

Faith—That which is required to make the leap into the absurd, which is required for the religious. Faith is spoken of dismissively by Hegel, who suggests that it is a lower, irrational form of thought that must be moved beyond. Johannes asserts that faith is in fact higher and that it cannot be understood by simple reflection; faith demands passion.

Fallacy of the alternative disjunct—In logic, the fallacy of concluding that one disjunct must be false because the other disjunct is true; in fact, they may both be true because "or" is defined inclusively rather than exclusively.

False dilemma—Stating that only two possibilities exist when there may be more.

False exclusionary disjunct—The **fallacy of affirming the disjunct**.

Falsification principle—An epistemological principle connected with the philosopher Karl Popper that any hypothesis must be inherently falsifiable to be sound.

Feedback loop—In cybernetics, the section of a control system that allows for feedback and self-correction and that adjusts its operation according to differences between the actual output and the desired output. Feedback can be positive or negative; positive feedback amplifies the output operation while negative feedback diminishes it. Positive and negative feedback play valuable roles in maintaining and regulating the body's natural set point and biological functions, such as sweating (negative) or fighting infections through fever (positive). Feedback also occurs at a psychological level such as praising success in learning (positive).

Fichte, Johann Gottlieb (1762 – 1814)—German idealist philosopher who followed Kant, Fichte was important due to his original insights into the nature of self-consciousness or self-awareness.

Fideism—From *fides,* Latin for "faith"; the notion that in religion, faith is superior to reason.

Final cause—The "why" question in Aristotle's **doctrine of the four causes.**

Formal cause—The "how" question in Aristotle's **doctrine of the four causes.**

Functionalism—A theory of the mind in philosophy developed largely as an alternative to the full behaviorism of Skinner and opposed to the mind-body problem of Descartes and crude materialism. Its core idea is that mental states are constituted solely by their functional role (causal relations to other mental states, sensory inputs, and behavioral outputs). It is only concerned with the effective functions of the brain, through its organization or its "software."

Fuzzy logic—Probabilistic logic dealing with reasoning that is approximate rather than fixed and exact. Rather than stating if propositions and conclusions are absolutely true or false, a probabilistic value is given.

God's grace—The undeserved favor of God.

Gödel's theorem—The mathematician and philosopher proposed three main theorems; there are two incompleteness theorems largely applicable to math but also to intelligent machines. The second incompleteness theorem, an extension of the first, shows that such a system cannot demonstrate its own consistency.

Grammar—A way of systemizing the rules of a language. Different languages at a superficial level have different grammars, although the human brain must be "wired" for a "deep" grammar, which is common to all languages.

Hegel, Georg Wilhelm Friedrich (1770 –, 1831)—Very influential German idealist philosopher who reintroduced the method of dialectic in his philosophy of "absolute spirit" and challenged the rules of classical logic. He influenced Marx and was in many ways the proponent of the absolutist political state.

Heidegger, Martin (1889 –1976)—German philosopher known for his existential and phenomenological explorations of the "question of being." His membership of the Nazi party is the most controversial aspect of his personal life, but it seems to have little to do with his philosophy.

Hellenistic era—Period in ancient history from 300 to 100 BC, between the conquests of Alexander the Great and the dominance of the Roman Empire, during which Greek culture spread and became dominant.

Heraclitus (535–c. 475 BC) —: Pre-Socratic Greek philosopher from Ephesus famous for his insistence on ever-present change in the universe as stated in the famous saying, "No man ever steps in the same river twice."

Heuristic -; Greek for ", "find" or "discover" refers to experience-based techniques for problem solving, learning, and discovery to speed up the process of finding satisfactory solutions via mental shortcuts. Examples of this method include using a rule of thumb, an educated guess, an intuitive judgment, stereotyping, profiling, and above all common sense.

Hezekiah—(king of Judah c. 715–686 BC); mentioned in the genealogy of Jesus in the gospel of Matthew. According to the Bible, Hezekiah witnessed the destruction of the northern Kingdom of Israel by Sargon's Assyrians c. 720 BC and was king of Judah during the invasion and siege of Jerusalem by the Assyrian Sennacherib in 701 BC. Isaiah and Micah prophesied during his reign.

Homeostatic—Greek, *homios,* "constant," and *stasis,* "stable." Something that is homeostatic is stable. In psychiatry in particular, *homeostasis* is a state that can be achieved by relaxing or tranquilizing.

Husserl, Edmund Gustav Albrecht (1859 –1938)—German philosopher and mathematician who believed experience was the source of all knowledge. He worked on a method of phenomenological reduction by which a subject may come to know an essence directly. He criticized positivism and historicists such as Marx.

Hypostasis—The underlying state or substance; it is the fundamental reality that supports all else. In philosophy, it means something that penetrates basic states. In Christian theology, a hypostasis or person is one of the three elements of the Holy Trinity. The figure of Holy Wisdom comes close to hypostasis but is not a separate person of the Godhead.

Hypothetical—In logic, propositions starting with "if."

Idealist—Philosophies that assert that reality, or reality as we can know it, is fundamentally mental, mentally constructed, or otherwise immaterial. It shows skepticism about the possibility of knowing any mind-independent thing and is strong on showing how beliefs and values shape society. As an extreme doctrine of pure being, idealism goes further, asserting that all entities are composed of mind or spirit.

Immanence—In philosophy and religion, the concept that the divine is seen to be manifested in or to be encompassing the material world; this is in contrast to transcendence, in which the divine is seen to be outside the material world. Christianity sees God as both immanent and transcendent, while Hegelianism and pantheistic religions such as Hinduism consider only the immanent.

Immediately—Conclusions that can be reached without recourse to further facts, such as, "All roads lead to Rome, so some roads lead to Rome."

Implication—Reasoning by similarities as in **analogy**.

Inclusive—In logic, where "or" is used in a sentence to mean "and/or."

Indicative mood—In grammar, a mood is a verbal form that allows speakers to express their attitude toward what they are saying. The most common indicative mood or evidential mood is used for factual statements and positive beliefs. Other moods are the imperative, which expresses a command such as "Stop!"; the subjunctive, which expresses uncertainty or suggestion as in, "If I were you, I wouldn't do that," and others less common in English.

Inductive method—Arguing from a series of particular propositions to a universal proposition.

Innatism—An early form of rationalism, characterized by Plato, who thought most problems in science could be solved by thought alone, as opposed to Aristotle, who was an empiricist.

Intentionality—As opposed to its common meaning, in philosophy, it is defined as the power of minds to be about, to represent, or to stand for things, properties, and states of affairs, the ability of the mind to form representations. The term dates from the Middle Ages but was resurrected by Franz Brentano and adopted by Edmund Husserl.

Intersubjectivity—In philosophy and psychology and related fields, the psychologically aware relation between people as distinct social beings in contrast to being aware only of one's own existence.

Invalid—A conclusion that has been arrived at by breaking the rules of logic; despite this, the conclusion may be true.

Jamina—A town in Palestine where the final canon of Jewish Scripture was decided by a council of rabbis.

Jaspers, Karl Theodor (1883–1969) —; German existentialist philosopher who had a strong influence on modern theology, psychiatry, and philosophy.

Kant, Immanuel (1724–1804) —:German philosopher who was the central figure of modern philosophy and set the scene by which all subsequent thinkers have worked. His works included three "critiques" on pure reason, practical reason, and judgment. Probably the last great thinker of the **Enlightenment,** he proposed international cooperation and looked forward to world peace.

Knight of faith—To Kierkegaard, the person who exemplifies the religious way of life; the knight of faith is not at all distinguished in appearance since he exists, like the aesthetic hero, as an individual and delights in the finitude of this world. Still, the knight of faith has undergone the double movement of infinite resignation and the leap of faith into the absurd by which the knight regains everything he has lost. He can delight in the finitude of this world as someone who has learned to appreciate it through loss.

Knight of infinite resignation—Those who have given up worldliness as an act of self-recovery. By destroying the world's dominion and placing themselves in a position of self-definition, they can go on to be knights of faith.

Law of identity—The first of Aristotle's three laws of thought: A is A.

Law of non-contradiction—The second of Aristotle's three laws of thought: What is A cannot be not-A.

Law of the exclusive middle—The third of Aristotle's three laws of thought: Everything is either A or [exclusively] not-A.

Laws of thought—Foundational and essential rules of classical logic annunciated by Aristotle.

Leap of faith—The idea that because religion is absurd and cannot be understood, it cannot be approached rationally. There is no way we can think matters through and convince ourselves that it is the right step to make. Instead, we must put our faith in God and make the leap. The use of the word *leap* suggests that Kierkegaard believed faith in God was a matter of personal choice that each person must make or not make; this is counter to earlier rationalism. Kierkegaard probably got the notion of the leap from Schelling's idea that God made a leap in creation.

Logic—The study of the rules of reasoning largely confined to the manipulation of transitive propositions.

Luther, Martin — (1483 –1546) Sixteenth century reformer and founder of the Lutheran churches. His main tenets— salvation by faith alone, Scripture as authority alone, and glory to God alone—were held by Kierkegaard.

LXX— The Septuagint, the Greek translation of the Old Testament.

Major premise—In logic, the starting proposition in a syllogism.

Masoretic text—To Jews, the officially accepted Hebrew text of the Bible.

Mass-man—The common man, especially one held to be typical of a mass society, characterized by the absence of unique values or distinct personality traits and a sense of individuality, subject to the universal, and readily manipulated by social forces such as dominant regimes and mass media.

Material cause—The "what" question in Aristotle's **doctrine of the four causes.**

Maximus the Confessor—(c. 580–662); Christian monk, theologian, and scholar; in his early life, Maximus was a civil servant to the Byzantine Emperor.

Mechanical determinism—The notion that explains man purely as a machine subject to physical laws.

Mediation—According to Hegel, the process according to which the dialectic functions: two opposing positions are mediated into a synthesis, so all movement takes place according to mediation. What progress we perceive is really a process of mediation. Because mediation takes places on the level of ideas, it takes place on the level of the universal. Thus, mediation is firmly bound up in the ethical and the universal and cannot help make sense of the religious or of faith.

Metaphysics—A main branch of philosophy so called because Aristotle put the topic in a volume *after* his physics. It attempts to answer two basic questions in the broadest terms: what actually exists, and what is the basic nature of things. Previously, speculative science, now studied empirically by observation and experiment, fell into this category of study and was called natural philosophy. Now, metaphysics concerns itself with two main purely speculative areas: ontology, the investigation into the basic categories of being and how they relate to each other, and cosmology: the study of all phenomena in the universe. The latter sometimes passes itself off as science when it is actually dealing with speculation.

Middle term—In a syllogism, the term or noun phrase that is common to the major and the minor premise.

Mimetic method—In rhetorical speech and writing, the art of imitation to convey truth. Jesus used parables that mimicked nature or human behavior to convey spiritual truths and values.

Mind-body problem—A problem largely put forward by Descartes that states the mind is immaterial whereas the body is composed of matter and that the interaction between the two, particularly in the area of consciousness, needs to be reconciled. There are a number of approaches to this, including the rejection of the problem largely in the light of modern science.

Minor premise—The premise of a syllogism usually containing the middle term as the object or predicate.

Modal verbs—A verb attached to the main verb of an utterance that modifies it, such as, "You *may* leave the table." Such verbs cannot take an object on their own and do not change their form.

Modus ponens—Latin for "the mood that affirms." This is the principle that whenever a conditional statement and its antecedent are given to be true, its consequent may be validly inferred, as in, "If it's raining, we will get wet. It's raining. We will get wet."

Modus tollens—Latin for "the mood that denies." The principle that whenever a conditional statement and the negation of its consequent are given to be true, the negation of its antecedent may be validly inferred, as in, "If it's five, its tea time. It isn't five. So it isn't tea time."

Monist (ism)—The idea that there is only one kind of "stuff" in the universe. In religion, this usually manifests itself as pantheism.

Movement of faith—In Kierkegaard's religious stage, the way an individual becomes a knight of resignation, giving everything back, and a knight of faith, getting it back—the double movement.

Negative particular—Propositions of some/not form such as, "Some birds do not fly."

Nehemiah—Cup bearer to the king of Persia in the fifth century BC given permission to rebuild the walls of Jerusalem, which he did despite a great deal of opposition and abuse from surrounding people.

Neuroscience—The study of the nervous system now covered by many fields of knowledge.

Nödynamics—The neurosis therapy devised by Frankl that relied on holding what experiences and achievements the patient has already had in life in tension with what they could achieve in the future.

Nögenic—Having its origins in the soul and spirit.

Noumena—In the philosophy of Kant, those things that exist but that we will never be able to experience directly.

Objective—In philosophy, facts and conclusions that are true or operative independently of anyone as opposed to subjective truths that matter primarily to the individual.

Object—In logic, the part of a proposition taking the accusative case; the noun phrase of a proposition having something done *to* it by the subject through the transitive verb.

Operands—In math and logic, something that the math or logic is being applied to; in logic, usually a proposition, and in math, usually a number.

Ordeal—The experience of being tested by God. Because of the constant anxiety, the constant possibility of retreating into the ethical, the experience becomes an ordeal that must be borne patiently.

Ordinary reflexes—Involuntary reflexes such as the movement of a leg when the knee is struck by a doctor's mallet.

Panentheism—The idea that an eternal, cosmic, animating force or spirit interpenetrates every part of nature and timelessly extends beyond it; so, God is not above his creation or transcendent; he is totally immanent.

Pantheism—The idea that God and the universe are ultimately one in the same inseparable thing, In a nutshell, pantheism states, "Everything is God," whereas panentheism states, "God is in everything."

Paradoxical Intention—In the psychotherapy of Viktor Frankl, the deliberate practice of a neurotic habit undertaken to remove it.

Paradoxical religiousness—To Kierkegaard, this represents the essence of Christianity. It posits a radical divide between immanence and transcendence, recognizing the great gulf between humanity and God but claiming the eternal came into existence in time. This is a paradox and can be believed only "by virtue of the absurd."

Paradox—The paradox in *Fear and Trembling* deals essentially with the contradiction inherent in the religious. The religious states that the individual is higher than the universal, that the finite is higher than the infinite, that one must make the leap of faith by virtue of the absurd. On the ethical level, on the level that we can all understand and talk about, Abraham was a murderer who almost killed his only beloved son. The paradox then lies in explaining why this murderer should be praised as the father of faith. Abraham's faith cannot be explained or understood;, it must simply be accepted as the only solution to the paradox.

Particular—In logic, that which applies to some or part of a set but not all.

Pascal's wager—Wagering that God is rather than is not. If you win, you win all; if you lose, you lose nothing.

Passion—Used in opposition to reflection, which was characterized by Kierkegaard as the dominant mood of his day. Reflection is the disinterested intellectualization of matters, while passion throws itself in wholeheartedly. In particular, he emphasized the importance of passion to faith.

Hegel approached faith from the perspective of reflection and so failed to understand it. To make sense of faith, one has to work toward it. The fruits of reflection can be learned from someone else, but one must experience passion oneself in order to learn it.

Passive voice—In grammar, an intransitive form that has the rhetorically useful effect of hiding who or what the agent of the action is. For example, saying, "Juliette was kissed" does not reveal who kissed her.

Phenomenology—In philosophy, the study of the structures of subjective experience and consciousness; this school of thought was founded in the early twentieth century by Edmund Husserl.

Philosophical logic—A branch of **epistemology** that investigates the relationship between logic and other branches of philosophy and vice versa.

Pietism—Lutheran people's movement that sought from the late seventeenth century a deeper and more personal experience of God than the state churches provided; it was characterized by personal and group prayer and Bible study in homes.

Positivism—In philosophy, a school of thought founded by Auguste Compte (1798–1857) that taught that there is valid knowledge and ultimate truth to be found only in empirical, scientific knowledge. It thus rejected any innate ideas, intuition, religion, or metaphysics. It is self-contradictory in that itself it is a metaphysical concept and as such is largely rejected.

Predicate—The noun-phrase object of a proposition. Predication is sought in all rational arguments.

Promoting the object to the subject—In grammar, the operation of changing a sentence from the active, transitive

voice to the passive, intransitive voice. In the proposition "Romeo kissed Juliette," by promoting the object "Juliette," we get "Juliette was kissed."

Propositions—Utterances that contain a subject, transitive verb, and object.

Pseudonym—A false name, one different from someone's real name used to give him or her a persona that fits with the purpose he or she wants it for. A female writer may wish to appear in print as a male, or an actor may want a better "stage" name; Horace Pratt became the sinister Boris Karloff. Kierkegaard wrote under many pseudonyms to distance himself from them and to inject the attitudes of the roles into the ideas he wanted to express.

Pseudoreflexive verbs—In grammar, an intransitive form in some languages. For example, "The cup broke" in English would be "La taza se rompio," "The cup broke itself" in Spanish.

Psychosomatic—The way that the workings of the mind from the brain affect the body and vice versa.

Qualia—Plural of Latin *quale*, "quality." The subjective qualities of conscious experience such as how a thing tastes, smells, sounds, and looks. It presents a problem for those who want to analyze these phenomena only in a materialist or mechanistic way as they are comprehensible only from the viewpoint of the conscious sentient being experiencing the *qualia*.

Rabbi—A teacher of the Jewish law. It means "my master." It is usually authorized but may not be a professional, full-time job.

Rationalism—The view that regards reason as the chief source and test of knowledge.

Recollection—According to Plato, the soul is immortal, and in previous lives, it learned about the unchanging, eternal forms that are ultimate reality. In this life, we are distracted by our senses and forget about the forms. Learning about them, then, is a matter of recollecting what we have learned in past lives. All learning, according to Plato, is recollection, and so is the process by which we bring ourselves closer to the "Good." Plato's recollection is contrasted with Hegel's mediation and Kierkegaard's repetition as one way that change can be accounted for.

Reductio ad absurdum—Taking an argument to an absurd conclusion to show its falsehood.

Referential contradiction—Things referred to as existing that have no real, present existence as is the case with extinct objects or fantasies.

Reflection—The dispassionate examination of the world that expresses itself in objectivity and propositional truths.

Regression—In psychiatry, a retreat into less-controlled, childish behavior.

Relation—In logic, the connection between the subject of a proposition and its object provided by the transitive verb.

Religion A—In Kierkegaard's religious stage, those features of religion that all religions hold in common.

Religion B—Kierkegaard's final stage, religion of paradox, which is true Christianity. It may be preceded by religiousness A.

Religious—The highest of Kierkegaard's three stages on life's way: the aesthetic, the ethical, and the religious. The religious finds the individual in an absolute relation to the absolute. That is, the individual exists in a private relationship with God above the ethical and the universal. The knight of faith who represents the religious cannot be understood, but exists in total isolation and finitude.

Repetition—The process by which the knight of faith can give up what he most values only to regain it by virtue of the absurd. By getting back what one has given up, one learns to appreciate it as though for the first time. In experiencing repetition, the knight of faith comes to learn that everything that exists does so only by the grace of God. Kierkegaard wrote *Repetition,* a book published the same day as *Fear and Trembling.* In it, repetition is contrasted with and prized over Platonic recollection and Hegelian mediation.

Resignation—The experience of giving up what one holds dearest and reconciling oneself with the pain of that loss. The movement of infinite resignation is exemplified by the tragic hero, like Agamemnon, who must resign himself to the loss of his daughter, Iphigenia. The knight of faith also experiences infinite resignation but moves beyond this point to regain what he has lost by virtue of the absurd.

Rhetorical questions—Questions that demand a yes or no answer in keeping with the rhetorical arguments of the questioner, such as, "Is it not true that Caesar wished to be king?"

Rhetoric—The art of persuasive speaking or writing.

Sadducees—The sect identified with the upper social and economic echelon of Judean society at the time of Jesus. As a whole, the sect fulfilled various political, social, and religious roles, including maintaining the temple, but in other respects held somewhat minimalist views, not believing in resurrection for example.

Sartre, Jean-Paul—(1905–1980); French philosopher whose school of existentialism has almost become synonymous with his name. He was also a playwright, novelist, screenwriter, Marxist political activist, biographer, and literary critic who influenced sociology, critical theory, postcolonial theory, and literary studies. Sartre was noted for his relationship with the prominent feminist theorist Simone de Beauvoir, who rejected his proposal for marriage on more than one occasion. He was awarded the 1964 Nobel Prize in literature but refused it, saying that he always declined official honors and that "a writer should not allow himself to be turned into an institution."

Schelling (Von), Friedrich Wilhelm Joseph—(1775 –1854), German philosopher often seen as the midpoint in the development of German idealism. He was situated between Fichte, his mentor in his early years, and Hegel, his former university roommate, early friend, and later rival. Three aspects of his work are especially relevant. The first is his natural philosophy, which does not restrict nature's significance to what can be established about it in scientific terms. The second is his anti-Cartesian account of subjectivity, showing how the thinking subject cannot be fully transparent to itself. The third is his later critique of Hegelian idealism, which influenced Kierkegaard.

Scholastic—The rational, objective medieval way of university thinking and teaching first developed by Anselm in the eleventh century. As a *disce doce* (learn, teach) method scholasticism placed strong emphasis on dialectical reasoning to extend knowledge by inference, resolving contradictions, rigorous conceptual analysis, and the careful drawing of distinctions. It usually took the form of a disputation, a topic drawn from the tradition such as the *Sentences* of Peter Lombard set as questions. Responses were given, counterproposals argued, and these were then rebutted. The attraction of its rigor led to its application to other fields of study.

Self—The individual being. In existential thought, people are separated from their true selves, which they must actuate.

Semiotics- The study of signs and sign processes.

Septuagint—LXX, the Greek version of the Old Testament canon including the apocrypha.

Sheol—Possibly from the Hebrew *shahat*, the place where those who had died were believed to be congregated as "shades" (Hebrew *rephaim*). In the nonresurrection Jewish view, sheol is like a deep pit toward the setting sun (Ezekiel 32; Isaiah 14; Job 30:23). The dead, without distinction of rank or condition, merely exist without knowledge or feeling. In many ways, it is similar to the Greek hades and is translated as such.

Shofar—The Jewish ritual ram's horn trumpet.

Single individual—A term used in opposition to the universal. Single individuals find themselves either in the aesthetic, living for themselves, or in the religious, living for God. To express themselves in the ethical, single individuals must annul their individuality and become a part of the universal, ethical consensus.

Sin—In its broadest sense in Judeo-Christianity, the refusal to follow the will of God and to be like gods, leading to alienation not only from God but from others and his creation. This rebellion started with Satan, who spread it to humanity. Particular sins are but a consequence of this broken relationship with God.

Socrates—(469–399 BC); by trade a sculptor, his avocation was posing philosophical conundrums in the marketplace of Athens. He was accused of corrupting youth and was ordered to kill himself by poison. He did not write anything himself; most of his conversations were recorded by Plato.

Solomon—King of Israel and the son of King David and Bathsheba. He was promoted to the crown by his mother and Nathan the prophet, according to the Bible. The conventional dates of Solomon's reign are ca. 970 to 931 BC, again in accordance with Bible chronology.

Sound—In logic, whether a proposition is immediately true or sensible before any logical process.

Spirit—Latin *spiritus*, "breath," but also "spirit," "soul," "courage," "vigor." It is distinguished from Latin *anima*, "soul." In Greek, this distinction exists between *pneuma*, "breath," "air," spirit" and *psyche*, "soul." However, the language meanings can all be traced to an original, arcane meaning of breath, signifying "alive" as opposed to "dead" and substances contrasted with the material body that like the air we breathe are independent of it. The word *soul* is best used now in metaphysics and religion to refer to the consciousness or personality that is understood as surviving bodily death and spirit as that energy that gives it life in a symbiotic relationship. The word may also refer to any incorporeal or immaterial beings such as demons or deities or in Christianity specifically, the Holy Spirit, the omnipotent person of activity of the triune God.

Spiritual trial—Unlike a test, a spiritual trial is the situation in which the individual overstretches his or her limits. Had Abraham tried to explain himself, he would not have been able to explain that he was being tested but only that he was experiencing a spiritual trial. By speaking, he would be descending to the universal, where his sacrifice of Isaac would have been seen only as murder. By speaking, therefore, he would have failed, and his test would become spiritual trial.

St. Augustine of Hippo—(354–430); influential church father who wrote *City of God* and developed the Western Church's doctrine of original sin. He was influenced by Platonic ideas.

Stoics—A school of Greek philosophy founded by Xeno of Citium in the early third century BC, so called because its adherents taught on a *stoa* or porch. In addition to their other encyclopedic teachings, they thought there was a single, sole, and simple good that was the only goal to strive for. "Happiness is a good flow of life," wrote Xeno against all misfortune. He believed in a universal *logos* or reason that governed things. Goodness and peace of mind were to be gained through living in harmony with nature. St. John seems to have adopted their style in his gospel if only to interest them in Christ.

Subject—In logic, the noun phrase of a proposition that takes the nominative case. Generally, the noun is the element doing something.

Sunday neurosis—A condition described by Viktor Frankl for those who could not be at peace with themselves at the end of a working week with their empty leisure time.

Syllogism—Greek *syllogismos*, "conclusion," "inference," a logical argument in which one proposition (the conclusion) is inferred from two or more others (the premises) of a specific form. They are usually set in the format outlined by Aristotle.

Symbolic logic—Logic in which words are replaced by letters and symbols for the logical relationship between them similar to algebra.

Sympathetic antipathy—The desire for what one fears. Once you know something is a sin, it increases its attraction. Antipathic sympathy is the reverse—the fear of what one desires.

Synoptic gospels—The gospels of Matthew, Mark, and Luke, which are set out in the largely narrative form of synopses or summaries of the life of Jesus; the gospel of John gives more of a philosophical commentary.

Synthesis—In Hegelian thinking, the "dialectic" product of two contrary or contradictory ideas.

System—The name given to Hegel's body of thought. Hegel organized his thought into one coherent "system" that was meant to comprehend all philosophy. Hegel represents the height of "system thinking." In our times, this kind of philosophizing has been largely rejected as overstepping the limits of human reason.

Talmud—Hebrew *talmud*, "instruction," "learning" (from the root *lmd*, "teach," "study") is a central text of rabbinic **Judaism**. It is also traditionally referred to as *shas*, a **Hebrew** abbreviation of *shisha sedarim*, the "six orders." The Talmud has two components. The first part is the *Mishnah* (AD 200), the written compendium of rabbinic Judaism's oral Torah (*torah*, Hebrew for "instruction," "teaching"). The second part is the *Gemara* (c. AD 500), an elucidation of the Mishnah and other related writings that often ventures onto other subjects and expounds broadly on the Hebrew Bible.

Taunt songs—A satirical poke dirge or mock funeral lament over an enemy, dead or alive.

Teleological suspension of the ethical—*Teleology* derives from the Greek *telos*, "end," "goal." Ethics is often considered teleological because it has some end in mind. For instance, for Hegel, all ethical actions are done with the goal of uniting with the universal. The question is whether there is some higher end or goal in favor of which we might suspend our ethical duties. Hegel would say no; Kierkegaard, Johannes, and Abraham would say yes.

Temptation—The word *temptation* is used in two different ways in *Fear and Trembling*. Earlier in the book, it is used synonymously with "test," denoting the ordeal God put Abraham through. As the book progresses, it begins to be used to denote the draw of a lower stage of life upon a higher. Abraham is thus tempted by the ethical; he knew he could choose at any moment to take the ethical rather than the religious path.

Tertullian—(c. AD 160–c. 225); maverick church father from Carthage in the Roman province of Africa. He was the first Christian author to produce an extensive corpus of Latin Christian literature. He is perhaps most famous for being the oldest extant Latin writer to use the word *Trinity* (Latin *trinitas*) and giving the oldest extant formal exposition of a Trinitarian theology. However, unlike many church fathers, he was never canonized by the Catholic Church, as several of his later teachings seemed to directly contradict the actions and teachings of the apostles. His trinity formulation was considered heresy by the church during his lifetime; however, it was later accepted as doctrine at the Council of Nicaea. His recognition of the paradoxical nature of Christianity is shown both in his view of the Christ event and his trinitarianism.

Test—In religion, a test is something God imposes upon people to test their faith. God demands a suspension of one's ethical assumptions and asks that His subjects act in complete faith and obedience to His guidance. In the story of Abraham, God tested Abraham.

The moment—A central category in Kierkegaard's understanding of Christian enlightenment of individual existence before God; it is the point in historical time and space when the individual in the religious sphere is confronted with the necessity of belief in the risen Christ. It is a category that speaks philosophically and theologically of the crucial link between the individual and Christ.

Theodicy—A problem in theology first stated by the philosopher Leibnitz in 1710; it involves reconciling the goodness and omnipotence of God with the evil in the world.

Theophany—The visible appearance of a god or God. There are a few examples in the Old Testament; Christianity tends to see these as appearances of the pre-incarnate Christ.

Thesis—In Hegelian thinking, followed by Marx, an intellectual proposition negated by a reaction to the proposition, the antithesis. There is some doubt as to the degree in which Hegel used the term.

Torah—(Hebrew "instruction"); the Jewish Law from the first five books of the Bible.

Tragic Hero—The ethical counterpart to the religious knight of faith. The tragic hero gives himself over completely to the universal and is willing to make the movement of infinite resignation, giving up what he values most for the sake of the universal. Unlike the knight of faith, the tragic hero can be understood and wept for.

Transcendence—The aspect of God's nature and power that is wholly independent of and removed from the material universe, contrasted with immanence, whereby God is fully present in the physical world and thus accessible to creatures in various ways. Thus, the immanent God may be experienced in nature but as a transcendent being is experienced by prayer and meditation.

Transitive—Verbs that "carry over" meaning from the subject of a proposition to its object.

True or **false**—Propositions that may be considered immediately reasonable or sound. As conclusions, they are usually the result of valid arguments based on sound premises, although a valid argument may give a false conclusion if one of the premises is unsound, or an invalid argument may sometimes throw up a true conclusion (right for the wrong reasons).

Turing test—A test devised by computer pioneer Alan Turing to determine whether an intelligent machine was capable of human reasoning, involving comparison to answers from human and computer interlocutors. So far, no such machine has passed the test.

Understanding—The mind's ability to comprehend something. According to Hegel, understanding is dictated by mediation. The significance of understanding in *Fear and Trembling* is Johannes's constant assertion that Abraham could not be understood. Understanding deals with language and with the universal, and the knight of faith is above all these. As a result, we cannot make sense of his behavior; we can just be awed by it.

Undistributed middle term—An invalid syllogism in which the term common to both premises is either the subject in both of them or the object in both of them, leading to an invalid conclusion. The law of the excluded middle is fundamental in Aristotelian logic;: the middle term common to both premises must be the subject in one and the object in the other to give a valid conclusion.

Universal negative—Propositions that totally deny the subject such as "No men are stones."

Universal—In the context that Kierkegaard used it, it is commonly accepted ethics or morality, behaving like everyone else in the worst case as one of the crowd or a "mass man." It should not be confused with its other meaning in metaphysics.

Valence—In grammar, the number of objects or predicates the subject is transferred to by the verb. So "My dog smells" has zero valence; "My dog smells a bone" has valence one; "My dog smells a bone and a bomb" has valence two; and so on.

Valid—An argument that has obeyed the rules of logic.

Virtue of the absurd—The action based on a concept so contrary to normal experience that it must have substance, based on the concept, "Truth is stranger than fiction."

Weltanschauung—To have a good lifestyle in step with the rest of the community.

Will to meaning—The desire to have meaning to life rather than pleasure or power.

Wisdom—In the Old Testament, the province of practical wise men or sages, a third estate along with prophets and priests or leaders. This was not the philosophy of ancient Greece, which was more abstract.

Bibliography and Further Reading

1. Bretall, Robert, ed. *A Kierkegaard Anthology*. Princeton, NJ: Princeton University Press, 1946.
2. Cox, James L. *An Introduction to the Phenomenology of Religion*. London: Continuum, 2010.
3. Spier, J. M. *Christianity and Existentialism*. Philadelphia: Presbyterian & Reformed, 1953.
4. McDowell, John and John Stewart. *Concise Guide to Today's Religions*. Amersham: Scripture Press, 1988.
5. Kaye, Sharon M. *Critical Thinking*. Oxford: One World, 2009.
6. Christiansen, E. S. *Ecclesiastes through the Centuries*. Oxford: Blackwell, 2007.
7. Kierkegaard, S. A. *Edifying Discourses in a Different Vein*. London: James Clarke, 1955.
8. Kierkegaard, S. A., trans. Alexander Hannay. *Either/Or*. London: Penguin, 1992.
9. Kierkegaard, S. A., trans. Alexander Hannay. *Fear and Trembling*. London: Penguin, 1985.
10. Strawson, P. F. *Introduction to Logical Theory*. London: Methuen, 1952.
11. Krauze, L. and Spencer, A.. *Hegel for Beginners*. Cambridge: Icon, 1996.
12. Palmer, Donald D. *Kierkegaard for Beginners*. New York: Writers and Readers, 1996.

13. Gordis, R. *Koheleth: The Man and His World*. New York: Block, 1962.
14. Lane, Tony. *Lion Book of Christian Thought*. Oxford: Lion, 1984.
15. Gordon, W. Terence. *McLuhan for Beginners*. New York: Writers and Readers, 1992.
16. Frankl, V. E. *Man's Search for Meaning and An Introduction to Logo Therapy*. London: Hodder & Stoughton, 1964.
17. Buber, Martin, Nahum Glatzer, ed. *On the Bible*. New York: Schocken, 1968.
18. Bullock, Alan, ed. *New Fontana Dictionary of Modern Thought*. London: Harper Collins, 1999.
19. Newton, Sir Isaac. *Observations on the Prophesies of Daniel and the Apocalypse*. London: Darby & Brown, 1733.
20. Neil, William. *One Volume Bible Commentary*. London: Hodder & Stoughton, 1962.
21. Strawson, P. F. *Philosophical Logic*. Oxford: Oxford University Press, 1967.
22. Osborne, Richard. *Philosophy for Beginners*. New York: Writers and Readers, 1992.
23. Rohmann, Chris. *The Dictionary of Important Ideas and Thinkers*. London: Hutchinson, 2001.
24. Kierkegaard, S. A., Alexander Dru, trans. *The Journals*. London: Fontana, 1958.
25. Brown, J.A.C. *The Medical Encyclopedia,* London: Pelham Books, 1962.
26. Douglas J., F. F. Bruce, J. Packer, and D. Wiseman, eds. *The New Bible Dictionary*. London: I.V.P., 1962.
27. Honderich, Ted, ed. *The Oxford Companion to Philosophy*. Oxford: Oxford University Press, 1995.
28. Goulder, G. M. *The Song of Fourteen Songs*. Sheffield: J.S.O.T Press, 1986.

29. Murphy, R. E. *The Tree of Life: An Exploration of Biblical Wisdom Literature.* Grand Rapids, MI: W. B. Eerdmans, 2002.
30. Martin, H. V. *The Wings of Faith.* London: Lutterworth, 1950.
31. Allport, G. *The Person in Psychology.* Boston:Beacon Press 1968

Index

Holy Spirit 32, 47, 56, 58, 124, 140,
    141, 142, 172, 173, 174, 178,
    220, 221, 265
honesty 27
hormones 161
Hosea 14
humanism 84
humble 18
Hume 172
humor 36, 62, 85, 86, 99, 100,
    131, 198
Husserl 146, 152, 154, 251, 252, 259
hypnotic 150
hypocrisy 110
hypocrites 120
Hypostasis 251
hypothalamus 160, 163
hypothetical 66, 184, 192,
    238, 242
Hypothetical 184, 251

I

Icelandic 204
Idealist 251
Immanence 221, 251
Immediately 252
Implication 252
Indicative mood 252
Inductive Method 252
Innatism 252
Intentionality 252
Intersubjectivity 252
Invalid 252
ironical xiv, 36, 37, 56, 62, 99,
    113, 130
Irony 62, 81, 99, 100

J

Jamina 4, 36, 253
Jaspers viii, 211, 213, 244, 245, 253
Jeremiah xiii, 241
Jesus xiv, 2, 3, 5, 6, 20, 31, 45, 46,
    47, 50, 54, 56, 57, 62, 72, 95,
    96, 112, 118, 120, 121, 138,
    142, 143, 151, 153, 164, 166,
    167, 168, 169, 170, 190, 191,
    194, 199, 205, 215, 216, 230,
    241, 246, 250, 255, 262, 266
John 5, 29, 34, 54, 57, 87, 97, 112,
    118, 133, 134, 136, 148, 169,
    175, 212, 217, 228, 230, 266
joke 90, 91, 197, 198, 199
Joshua 177
Journal 67, 74, 75, 81
joy 36, 39, 42, 92, 126, 141, 174,
    178, 228, 231, 235
judgment xvii, xviii, 33, 49, 51,
    52, 66, 126, 147, 171, 221,
    231, 241
justice xviii, 34, 45, 51, 52
Jutland 79, 81

K

Kalmar 83
Kant 65, 66, 67, 71, 72, 77, 100,
    122, 164, 169, 196, 242, 248,
    253, 257
Kaufering 224
key board 158
king xvii, 4, 6, 15, 23, 24, 33, 37,
    38, 41, 83, 87, 106, 241, 250,
    256, 262

work xi, xiv, xv, 10, 38, 42, 44, 63,
64, 71, 72, 76, 81, 82, 83, 84,
86, 87, 88, 89, 90, 91, 92, 93,
101, 104, 105, 106, 108, 113,
120, 131, 148, 157, 172, 174,
188, 195, 199, 204, 211, 217,
221, 227, 229, 230, 232, 234,
235, 246, 259, 263
worm 177

Y

youth xvi, xviii, 4, 42, 71, 80, 264

Z

Zeno's 88
zero 196, 206, 270
Zion 31, 32, 55

About the Author

R. I. Johnston's interest in philosophy, biblical studies, and theology comes from his technical, pedagogic, and linguistics training. The core of his work, teaching English as a Foreign Language in the Middle East and Scandinavia, has given him insight into the Semitic and Nordic mindsets. He lives with his wife in Bristol.